THE DICTIONARY OF THE
GLOBAL ECONOMY

CONSULTING EDITOR
Peter Bell, Ph.D.
New York Council on Economic Education
SUNY Purchase

AUTHORS
Steve Bookbinder
Lynne Einleger

THE DICTIONARY OF THE
GLOBAL ECONOMY

CONSULTING EDITOR
Peter Bell, Ph.D.
New York Council on Economic Education
SUNY Purchase

AUTHORS
Steve Bookbinder
Lynne Einleger

Franklin Watts
A Division of Scholastic Inc.
New York Toronto London Auckland Sydney
Mexico City New Delhi Hong Kong
Danbury, CT

ACKNOWLEDGEMENTS

Photographs ©: Corbis Images: 15, 18, 20, 28, 31, 44, 45, 50, 54, 56, 62, 67, 68, 79, 82, 86, 94, 97, 100, 104, 105, 106, 113, 115, 122, 135, 137 **Library of Congress:** 22, 23, 25, 35, 39 (top and bottom), 41, 71, 93, 116, 120, 121, 128, 140, 143, 145, 146, 148 **Newscom: UPI News:** 9, 10, 69, 73, 84, 90, 95, 138 **Blaug, Mark.** *Great Economists Before Keynes: An Introduction to the Lives and Works of One Hundred of the Great Economists of the Past.* Brighton, Sussex: Wheatsheaf Books, 1986: 43, 81, 88, 136 **Blaug, Mark.** *Great Economists Before Keynes: An Introduction to the Lives and Works of One Hundred Modern Economists.* Totowa, NJ: Barnes & Noble, 1985: 40, 87, 92 **United Nations:** 57, 75, 118, 132 **Photos by Brent Hoff:** 26, 52, 101 **National Archives:** 16, 117 **Board of Governors of the Federal Reserve System:** 51 *Dictionary of American Portraits.* New York: Dover Publications, Inc., 1967: 29 **Ford Motor Company:** 83 **The Hoover Institute, photo by Steven N. S. Cheung:** 85 **The International Joseph A. Schumpeter Society:** 19 **National Park Service:** 141 **New York Convention and Visitation Center:** 108 **New York Public Library:** 14 **Remington Arms Co.:** 65 **U.S. Department of Treasury:** 130 **White House:** 125 **Cover:** Art direction and design by Oxygen Design. Train photo: Peter Dolan. Illustrations by Aaron Murray.

Every endeavor has been made to obtain permission to use copyrighted material. The publishers would appreciate errors or omissions being brought to their attention.

CREATED IN ASSOCIATION WITH MEDIA PROJECTS INCORPORATED
C. Carter Smith, *Executive Editor*
Carter Smith III, *Managing Editor*
Karen Covington, *Project Editor*
Aaron Murray, *Production Editor*
Athena Angelos, *Picture Researcher*

FRANKLIN WATTS STAFF
John Selfridge, *Publishing Director*
Andrew Hudak, *Editor*
Marie O'Neill, *Art Director*

Library of Congress Cataloging-in-Publication Data
Bookbinder, Steve.
      The dictionary of the global economy/Peter Bell, consultant; Steve Bookbinder and Lynne Einleger, writers
        p. cm.
      "A Watts reference book".
      Includes bibliographical references and index.
      ISBN 0-531-11975-0
       1. International business enterprises—Dictionaries. [1. Economics—Dictionaries.]
      I. Bookbinder, Steve. II. Einleger, Lynne. III. Title.

HD2755.5 .B66 22001
330'.03—dc21   00-065425

Contents

Preface

The English writer and artist William Norris once observed: "Settle the economic question and you settle all the other questions. It is the Aaron's rod which swallows up the rest."

"Aaron's rod," the Bible tells us, was the rod used to perform miracles in Egypt on behalf of the captive Hebrew people at the time of Moses. Taking a cue from Norris, one might argue that the study of economics in the modern era is, in essence, the study of the architecture of social "miracles" on the local, national, and global levels.

Although he died in 1896, it is hard to imagine that Norris would have found reason to revise his opinion if he lived in today's fast-paced era of globally interdependent economies, on-line investors, and pan-European currencies. Global economic issues are relevant to just about everyone, even though not everyone realizes that. Ours is, after all, a world in which economic changes in Indonesia or Japan can—and do—have instant, impossible-to-ignore effects on intrepid Internet purchasers of mutual fund shares who live in the suburbs of Massachusetts.

Why study economics? Because miracles matter—and because people tend to notice their absence. Consider, for instance, that seven decades ago, the United States was running low on economic miracles: a third of the workforce was unemployed. The gross national product had dropped to a little over $55 billion in 1933. Compare that to the robust $103 billion figure of four years earlier, and you will get some sense of the effects of the stock market crash that commenced in the fall of 1929. The shockwaves from America's economic collapse were felt around the world, and especially in Europe. In Germany an economic crisis marked by massive price inflation and a truly frightening period of social chaos proved a perfect setting for the disastrous career of an ambitious and opportunistic politician by the name of Adolf Hitler. At the beginning of 1933, the world's supply of economic "miracles" appeared to have been exhausted.

Thirty years later, the economy of the United States was an unparalleled engine of prosperity, and Western Europe had recovered from economic chaos—and, of course, from World War II, a conflict that, like most wars, had causes that could be traced to economic issues. A fair number of economic "miracles" appear to have taken place. But why? How?

What, precisely, caused the Great Depression in the United States? Why did that crisis affect other countries so dramatically? Why did some countries prosper after the war, while others stagnated? Could such a tragic global crisis have been averted? Could it all happen again? If so, what steps can today's decision makers take to avoid it?

People who pose such questions—and search earnestly for their answers—might be called analyzers of miracles. They are more commonly called *economists*, and the fact that they don't always agree is not as important as what they have learned, and continue to learn, about what supports or obstructs the growth and development of nations across the globe. Nations are composed of communities. Communities are composed of people. And economic decisions, by their nature, determine the kinds of lives people find themselves living.

This book is intended to help you take the first crucial steps toward becoming an analyzer of miracles, rather than a passive observer of them. It is meant as an introduction to the key concepts and questions associated with the study of economics. Use it as a tool for asking important questions about what people actually do, how they are compensated for doing it, and how they can work together to do things better, more efficiently, and with greater rewards.

—Steve Bookbinder
 Lynne Einleger

ACKNOWLEDGMENTS

Our grateful thanks go to the following people, all of whom made essential contributions of various kinds to this work: Suzanne Lieurance, Erin Flynn, Carter Smith III, Karen Covington, Nancy Bellard, Tina Bradshaw, Alexander Cicogna, Andrew Daino, Charles Fox, Michael Hellerman, Alan Koval, Virginia Kulesa, Brad Norton, Judith Burros, Elin Woodger, Mary Toropov, Leslie Hamilton, Robert Tragert, Cassandra Burros, George Richardson, Greg Riebe, Gino Sette, and Brandon Toropov. Special thanks go out to the President of D.E.I. Management Group, without whose guidance, support, and inspiration this book would not have come about.

HOW TO USE THIS BOOK

The Dictionary of the Global Economy includes more than 400 entries, arranged in an A-to-Z format, and 130 photographs, graphs, maps, and charts illustrating fundamental concepts in the study of the global economy. Throughout the A-to-Z section of the book, you will notice that various terms are emphasized in boldface type. This indicates to the reader that these words also appear in the book as an entry. The bolded word, in other words, implies a cross reference. Cross references are sometimes found at the end of a definition as well.

The yellow key point boxes scattered throughout the book highlight an interesting concept or important idea of a particular definition. Also featured in *The Dictionary of the Global Economy* are brief biographical profiles of influential historical and current economists.

After the A-to-Z section, the reader will find a chronology of the global economy, which highlights important events in the history of economics beginning in 9000 B.C. through today. Also included is a list of helpful resources for further research in a particular area of global economics. The resource guide lists the contact information for various agencies and organizations and also includes a list of websites. The dictionary concludes with a selected bibliography of other books and websites used in creating it.

A

ABSOLUTE ADVANTAGE

Absolute advantage is the ability of one person or nation to produce a good or service using fewer **resources** (See **economic goods and services**.) One nation can have an absolute advantage over another in the **production** of a particular good or service if it has a more advanced level of technology or better resources . Similarly, one person can have absolute advantage over another in some area because of natural abilities or a higher level of training or experience. For example, Saudi Arabia has absolute advantage over Japan in oil production (thanks to its natural resources), while Japan has an absolute advantage in car production (thanks to its **investment** in technology and **capital** goods. (See **comparative advantage.**)

ADVERSE SELECTION

Adverse selection may occur in a transaction when one party has more information than the other prior to the transaction. The less desirable transactions from the uninformed person's point of view are the most likely to occur. For example, people who know that their car is not a good one are likely to sell in the used car **market**. Also, people who privately know their health is bad are likely to buy health insurance. Thus an "adverse" or bad selection of transactions is offered.

AGGREGATE DEMAND CURVE

Aggregate demand is the total of all demand in the economy including consumption, investment, and government spending. The aggregate demand curve is a graph that plots the total **demand** for goods and services in the country against the overall **price** level. Aggregate demand is determined by adding up:

1) All personal spending within the **economy**
2) All planned business investments
3) Net **exports** (the amount of exports minus the amount of **imports**)
4) All government spending

As the price level for goods and services increases, the aggregate demand decreases.

AGGREGATE SUPPLY CURVE

Aggregate supply is the total amount of all goods and services produced by a nation's businesses and government, including **consumer** goods and **capital** goods. (See also **gross domestic product.**) The aggregate supply curve shows the total supply of a country's total economic **output** in relation to the price for the goods and services the **economy** produces. As the price for goods and services goes up, the aggregate supply goes up. As the price for goods and services goes down, aggregate supply goes down.

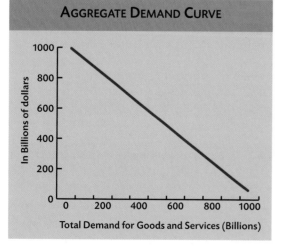

AGGREGATE DEMAND CURVE

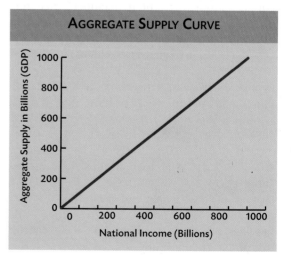

AGGREGATE SUPPLY CURVE

Traders and tabulators at work on the floor of the American Stock Exchange on February 14, 2000.

AGRICULTURAL COOPERATIVES

A cooperative is an organization that is owned and controlled by the people who use its products, supplies or services. Although cooperatives vary in type and membership size, all are formed to meet the specific objectives of members and are structured to adapt to member's changing needs.

Agricultural cooperatives help producers assure markets and supplies, achieve **economies of scale**, and gain market power through marketing, bargaining, processing, and purchasing supplies and services together as an organization.

There are nearly 4,000 U.S. agricultural cooperatives operating today, through which farmers and ranchers purchase needed supplies or services or market their products. In general, agricultural cooperatives range in size from small country grain elevators and cotton gins to huge industry food companies like Sunkist and Land O'Lakes. Agricultural cooperatives are also used frequently in developing countries.

AMERICAN STOCK EXCHANGE

The American Stock Exchange (or AMEX) is one of the largest **stock** exchanges in the United States. The other two largest are the National Association of Securities Dealers Automated Quotations **(NASDAQ)** and the **New York Stock Exchange** (NYSE).

Located on **Wall Street** in Manhattan, the AMEX began in the 1800s with traders who could not afford a place on the NYSE and had to buy and sell stocks in the street. The AMEX moved indoors in 1921, but its nickname ("The Curb") is a reminder of its early days. In 1998 NASDAQ merged with the American Stock Exchange.

ANTITRUST LAWS

Sometimes large **businesses** are able to control the market for the types of products or services they sell by gaining a **monopoly**. In order to prevent unfair control of the market by a single company or by arrangements of companies, and

Microsoft founder and CEO Bill Gates speaks before the Senate Joint Economic Committee.

to promote competition, the United States government passed a series of antitrust laws. The Sherman Antitrust Act, passed in 1890, became the first such law that made it illegal to establish "agreements in restraint of trade" or to make "attempts to monopolize" industry. In 1914 two other acts, the Clayton Act and the Federal Trade Commission Act, were passed, further strengthening the government's hand in preventing a monopoly. The Robinson-Patman Act (1936) and the Celler-Kefauver Act (1950) have since been passed.

Antitrust laws prohibit monopolies and abuse of **market power.** If large businesses begin to monopolize a market, antitrust laws give the Justice Department or the Federal Trade Commission the authority to take legal action against a situation that discourages **competition** and encourages monopolies. Among the many huge companies that have been affected by antitrust laws was the Standard Oil Trust in 1911. The companies we know today as Exxon, Mobil, Chevron, British Petroleum, and Amoco were all once part of the Standard Oil Trust. In recent years, the justice department has taken antitrust action against large companies like AT&T and Microsoft.

APPRECIATION

Appreciation is an increase in the value of an **asset**. Assets such as **stocks** or **bond**s, a piece of real estate, or a work of art, for instance, might increase in value over time. The rise in value of these items might be due to circumstances such as new market conditions, changes in replacement costs, the ability of the asset to generate cash income for the owner, and so on. Appreciation also describes an increase in the value of a **currency** under a **flexible exchange rate system**. When the U.S. dollar is worth more in terms of the Euro or other currency (see **European Community**), it is said to "appreciate." Appreciation is contrasted with **depreciation,** which means a decrease in the value of an asset.

ARBITRAGE

Arbitrage means buying something in one **market** and selling it again, as soon as possible, at a higher price in another market. If an investor purchased $5 million in French francs, and immediately sold the francs for more than $5 million in another market, this would be an example of arbitrage. Arbitrage helps stabilize prices between markets for the same goods.

When someone buys a large quantity of something, that causes the price of that item to go up. The act of selling a large amount of the same item causes the price to go down. If arbitrageurs buy francs for a low price in one market and sell for a higher price in another market, this would help eliminate the price differences for French francs between these two markets.

Arbitrageurs, or "arbs," are market speculators, meaning that when they buy in one market they speculate that if they sell in another market they will get a higher price and make money.

ASIAN DEVELOPMENT BANK

The Asian Development Bank (ADB) was founded in 1966. It is a financial institution that today is owned by 59 member countries, mostly from Asia and the South Pacific.

ADB's main goal is to make loans and provide technical assistance which it gives to governments for specific projects and programs. Their work also helps to reduce poverty, foster **economic growth**, support **human development**, improve the status of women, and protect the environment. The ADB lent $5 billion in 1999 and offered technical assistance grants that amounted to $173 million.

ASIAN ECONOMIC CRISIS

The Asian Economic Crisis is a financial crisis that emerged in 1997. It began in Thailand and spread rapidly to other countries in Asia, among them Indonesia, Malaysia, and South Korea. The effects of the crisis were felt as far away as Brazil and Russia.

The Asian Economic Crisis was characterized by a rapid withdrawal of **money** that had been invested in local **currencies**, **stock markets**, and real estate. This withdrawal led to a sharp downturn in most Asian economies.

ASSET

An asset is something that an individual owns that holds monetary value. For an individual, assets can be financial, like **money**, **stocks**, **mutual funds**, checking accounts, and government securities; or they can be physical things, like houses, clothes, cars, boats, and land. For a firm, assets are all that a company owns, listed on a balance sheet, against **liabilities**. In a developed economy, the most important assets are the **output** produced and the physical **resources**, **capital**, and natural resources used to create that output.

AUDIT

An audit is the legal requirement of a **corporation** to turn over all financial statements and accounting records to a qualified auditor to determine whether its financial statements accurately reflect the company's financial situation. An individual can also be audited by the **Internal Revenue Service**.

AUTOMATIC STABILIZERS

Automatic stabilizers are taxes and government expenditures that automatically increase or decrease in a stabilizing manner depending on the state of the **economy**. Examples in the United States include unemployment insurance, **welfare**, and **income taxes**.

For example, if the economy is sluggish, and many people are without jobs, more people receive unemployment insurance and welfare. Therefore people can afford to buy more than they could without this financial assistance. They are also paying less to the government in taxes than they would in a strong economic climate, since they are earning less. These factors increase spending at a time when spending is otherwise slow, thus "stabilizing" the economy.

When the economy is booming, however, and more people have jobs, fewer people receive unemployment compensation and other government money and **subsidies**. Tax payments increase, since workers are earning more. These factors decrease spending at a time when spending is high and again "stabilize" the economy. Notice that more often the changes require no government action by Congress or the President and are thus automatic.

> ### KEY POINT TODAY
> A decrease in national income and **output** reduces government revenue from taxes and increases unemployment and welfare payments. Lower tax revenues and a higher rate of payments means an increase in the government's **budget deficit** and restoration of some of the government's lost income.

AUTONOMOUS CONSUMPTION

Autonomous consumption is the portion of **consumption** expenditure (**household** purchases) that does not depend on **income**. Even

A

Disposable Income	Consumption Expenditures	Average Propensity to Consume (APC)		AVERAGE PROPENSITY TO SAVE	
			Disposable Income	Net Saving (Disposable Income Minus Consumption Expenditures)	Average Propensity to Save (APS)
$ 5,000	$ 6,000	120%	$ 5,000	$ -1000	-12%
10,000	10,000	100%	10,000	0	0%
15,000	13,500	90%	15,000	1,500	+10%
20,000	17,000	85%	20,000	3,000	+15%
25,000	20,000	80%	25,000	5,000	+20%
30,000	22,500	75%	30,000	7,500	+25%
35,000	24,500	70%	35,000	10,500	+30%

if the head of the household loses his or her job, and there is no income for 30 days, the family still has to eat. The money for trips to the grocery store might come from savings or by borrowing it, but the family will spend some money on food, clothing, and other basic needs for survival over that 30-day period, regardless of the family's income (or lack of income). Such money that must be spent is autonomous consumption. This is in contrast to **induced consumption**)

AVERAGE

An average is a mathematical mean of a group of **stocks** designed to represent the overall **market** or some part of it, differing from an index in that it is not weighted. The **Dow Jones Industrial Average** is the most common stock market average used by analysts and the public.

AVERAGE PROPENSITY TO CONSUME/SAVE

A propensity is a person or group's natural inclination or tendency to do something. The "average propensity to consume" (APC) refers to the share of personal **income** that an individual or group tends to spend or consume. This is stated as a fraction found by dividing the amount of money spent (**consumption**) by income.

For example, if a country's total personal income is $500 billion, and the country's total personal expenditures equal $400 billion, then the average propensity to consume is four-fifths, or 80 percent. This means that citizens in that country would tend to spend, or have a propensity to consume, four-fifths of their income.

The "average propensity to save" (APS) is the opposite of the average propensity to consume. Using the same example, if the residents of a country save $100 billion of their $500-billion income, then the average propensity to save is one-fifth of total income. The average propensity to consume, when combined with the average propensity to save, should equal one. In this example, as seen in the equation below, it does because 4/5 + 1/5 = 1.

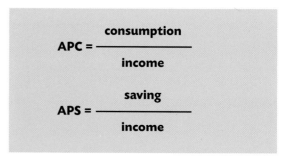

$$APC = \frac{\text{consumption}}{\text{income}}$$

$$APS = \frac{\text{saving}}{\text{income}}$$

BAD

(See **economic bad.**)

BALANCED BUDGET

A balanced budget occurs when revenues (**money earned**) equal expenditures (amount of money spent). Government revenues come from various taxes such as **income tax**, sales tax, property tax, and licensing fees, etc. Expenditures include administrative expenses, public works (money for roads, bridges, etc.), and federally funded programs such as **Social Security** and **welfare** payments. If expenditures exceed revenue to achieve a balanced budget, it is necessary to increase revenue spending.

U.S. BALANCE OF PAYMENTS—2ND QUARTER 2000 (BILLIONS OF DOLLARS)		
	Exports	**Imports**
Current Account		
Goods	+192	−302
Services	+73	−52
Investment		
Income/Payments	+87	−92
Transfers		−12
(Goods + services + investment + transfers)	+352	−458
Balance on Current Account		−106
Capital Account		
Capital flows	+223	−74
Balance on Capital Account	+149	

Source: U.S. Department of Commerce, Bureau of Economic Analysis

 **KEY POINT TODAY**

The J-curve effect illustrates the tendency for a nation's balance of payments **deficit** to initially increase when its **currency** experiences a devaluation before it moves into a **surplus**. At first, export **prices** fall and import prices rise, so exports earn less foreign exchange while imports absorb more foreign exchange. This increases the size of the deficit. Over time, however, lower export prices create a higher demand overseas and the export income eventually rises. Meanwhile the high import prices lower the domestic demand for imports, which ultimately improves the balance of payments.

BALANCE OF PAYMENTS

Balance of payments describes the relationship between the amount of **money** a nation spends overseas and the income it receives from other nations. The balance of payments is officially known as the Statement of International Transactions. It includes two main accounts. The first is called the "**current account;**" it tracks activity in merchandise trade (**exporting** and **importing**), income earned from **investments** overseas, money paid to foreign investors, and transactions on which the government expects no returns. The second account is called the "**capital account.**" This account tracks both changes in U.S. **assets** held abroad and changes in foreign assets held in the United States.

BALANCE OF TRADE

Balance of trade is the difference between the value of a nation's **imports (economic goods and services** being sold to that nation) and **exports** (goods and services sold by that nation to another nation) over a given period of time.

When the value of exports for a nation is greater than the value of its imports, its trade balance is "favorable," and the nation has a balance

of trade surplus. However, if the value of imports is greater than the value of exports for a nation, then its trade balance is "unfavorable," and the nation has a balance of trade **deficit**.

BALANCE SHEET

A balance sheet is an accounting statement that reflects a company's **assets** and **liabilities** on the last day of an accounting period (a month, year, etc.). Assets include fixed assets, such as buildings and machinery, and **current assets**, such as inventories and cash. The liabilities include **loans** from **banks** and **money** owed to suppliers of raw materials. The assets are listed against the liabilities, and the difference between the two is known as the net worth of the company.

BANK

A bank is a financial entity that accepts deposits and makes **loans**. Banks raise funds mostly by accepting checking deposits, **time deposits**, and **savings deposits**. They use funds to make business loans, consumer loans, **mortgage** loans, and to buy government and municipal **bonds**. Banks **profit** in part by lending at a higher rate than they pay for deposits. Financial entities such as **credit unions** and **savings and loan institutions** are also depository institutions, but they have different structures than banks.

BARRIERS TO ENTRY

Barriers to entry are conditions that make it difficult for a firm—say, Company A—to enter a **market** or an **industry** in which one or more established companies are already selling the good or service that Company A wishes to sell. (See **economic goods and services**.) A classic barrier to entry is a patent. If one company has a patent on a product—that is, the exclusive right to make, use, or sell that product—this would be a barrier to entry for other companies wishing to sell it. Other barriers to entry might be the lack of access to **resources** needed to make a product, high start-up costs, or difficulty in finding qualified workers.

When government formally grants a **monopoly** to a firm, this creates what might be called the "ultimate barrier of entry" for other companies wishing to provide the products or services the company with the monopoly provides. Sometimes the motivation for this is that an industry is a natural monopoly.

BARTER

Barter is the act of trading economic goods and services without the use of money. There are some inherent problems with this method of trade, however. For one thing, each trader has to have something that the other trader wants. For

The Bank of the United States on 3rd Street, Pennsylvania in 1799.

another, both goods or services must be considered to be of equal value so that a fair trade can take place. Establishing an appropriate rate of exchange for both goods can often be difficult and hard to standardize. **Money** is a **medium of exchange** that evolved to make trading easier and faster than bartering.

BASE YEAR

The base year is set up as a beginning year or "reference" year when constructing any economic index. For example, the base year is the year used for **price** level comparisons. Direct comparisons of dollar values from different years are meaningless, since the value of a dollar always changes. Thus to compare, for example, **output** in 1984 with the output in 1994, one has to choose one year's dollar value and convert the other year's output to its value in that year's dollar. The year chosen is the base year.

BEAR MARKET

When prices in a given **market** (particularly the **stock market**) are declining and are expected to continue to decline, investors refer to this situation as a bear market. A bear market may be caused by investors who do not expect the **economy** to grow. They purchase cautiously or not at all, and prices in the market remain low. (See **Bull Market**.)

BLACK MARKET

A black market is an illegal **free market**. This kind of market occurs when (for instance) a government places **price** restrictions on a product, so that the legal price cannot reflect the true **demand** and **supply** conditions for that product. Such price restrictions are sometimes put on items in short supply in an effort to make these items more affordable to a greater number of people. However, when coveted products are in such short supply, many people will risk obtaining them so they can sell them illegally for an abnormally high price. Then a black market comes into existence. An example of something that is sold on the black market might be items that are rationed during wartime such as meat or sugar. A black market often emerges for items that are not legally sold at any price. For example, the alcohol that was sold during Prohibition or the market for all illegal drugs is considered a black market.

Two men in Italy make a deal for white truffles on the black market.

BLUE CHIP

A blue chip company is a successful firm widely known for its ability to make money and pay **dividend**s on a consistent basis. The **stock** of a company that is considered blue chip is referred to as blue chip stock. Examples of blue chip stock include IBM, General Motors, General Electric, and Proctor and Gamble. The name is derived from the highest paying poker chip.

BOND

A bond is a fixed interest security in which a borrower agrees to make scheduled payments over a specific period of time. **Corporations** and federal, state, and local governments issue bonds to raise funds. Most bonds are negotiable. This means they can be traded before they reach their maturity date.

A bond's selling price depends on the amount borrowed, the **interest rate** the bond pays on the face value, and relevant interest rates and

A World War I poster advertises government bonds.

returns on other investments in the **economy**. For example, a $50,000 bond with a fixed 10 percent interest rate will sell for $50,000 if comparable interest rates are 10 percent. If comparable interest rates are less than 10 percent, the bond will sell for more than $50,000. If comparable interest rates are more than 10 percent the bond will sell for less than $50,000. Bond prices move in a direction opposite from interest rates. When bond prices are up, interest rates are down.

There are many different kinds of bonds. A corporate bond is issued by a **corporation** to raise funds for **capital investment**. Corporate bonds usually have a maturity date of five years or more, but 30 years is also common. Most corporate bonds can be traded before their maturity date.

Government bonds are used to designate debt obligations of the U.S. government. They consist of **Treasury bills**, notes, and bonds. They carry the highest **credit** rating possible. Government bonds are also referred to as government securities.

Municipal bonds are bonds issued by any of the 50 states, the territories and their subdivisions, counties, cities, towns, villages, and school districts, agencies, etc. There were approximately $1.3 trillion municipal bonds outstanding in the year 2000. These bonds generate about $50 billion tax-free interest income each year. (See **Federal Reserve System** and **open-market operations.**)

> **KEY POINT TODAY**
>
> **Money** authorities sometimes use government bonds to regulate the **money supply**. For example, if they wish to reduce the money supply, they sell bonds to the general public. This strategy reduces **bank** reserves as customers withdraw money to pay for these bonds.

BOTTOM LINE

Bottom line is a term used in accounting to signify the total profit from a company after all costs have been paid. In accounting, **profit** means the total sales revenue (money made) after the costs of production, marketing, finance, taxes, etc.

FEDERAL GOVERNMENT BUDGET Deficit/Surplus (Billions of Dollars)	1996	1997
Receipts	1,584.7	1,719.9
Personal tax and non tax receipts	687.0	769.1
Corporate profits tax accruals	193.0	210.0
Indirect business tax and nontax accruals	94.5	93.8
Contributions for social insurance	610.2	647.0
Expenditures	1,695	1,741
National defense	304.1	306.3
Transfer payments		
To persons	748.0	779.2
To foreigners	16.2	12.7
Grants-in-aid to State and local governments	218.9	225.0
Net interest paid	228.4	231.2
Subsidies less current surplus of government enterprises	32.7	32.5
Current surplus or deficit (-) (NIPA)	-110.3	-21.1

Source: U.S. Department of Commerce, Bureau of Economic Analysis

BUDGET

A budget is estimated income and expenditures during a certain time period (usually one year). Every year the United States government makes out a budget. It is a statement of the estimated **income** and expenses for the U.S. government for the following year. The main sources of income for the federal government are **taxation**, primarily income and expenditure taxes, and **social security** taxes, and main types of expenditure are transfer payments.

BUDGET DEFICIT/SURPLUS

When there is more revenue than expenditures (that is, when more money comes in than goes out), a budget surplus exists. Individuals operate a budget surplus when they put part of their income in savings.

A budget deficit is the opposite of a budget surplus. In such a case, there are more expenses than there is revenue—bills to be paid exceed **money** to pay them. A budget deficit is quite common for both governments and individuals, because it is often difficult to tell in advance exactly how much revenue will be received. Sometimes a government receives less tax revenue than expected; sometimes individuals make less money than anticipated, or must pay out more money (for instance in taxes) than they had forecast.

When a budget deficit occurs, both governments and individuals sometimes borrow to meet expenses. To do this, the federal government usually issues government securities (which is a way of borrowing money from the private individuals, or whoever buys the securities). Individuals usually get a loan from a **bank**, use a **credit** card, or deplete their own savings in order to pay their bills.

BULL MARKET

When **prices** on the **stock market** are rising, and are expected to continue to do so, investors refer to this situation as a bull market, because the market is charging ahead like a bull. The term was originally coined in 1761 when bull

A sculpture of a bull stands in the financial district in New York City.

and bear baiting was still considered a popular sport. Once "bear" became a common reference to a falling **market**, bull soon took on the opposite meaning. A bull market may occur because investors are optimistic, expecting a healthy, profitable **economy** in the near future. (See **bear market**.)

BURDEN OF DEBT

A burden of debt refers to the **interest rates** that are charged on a **debt** borrowed by people, companies, and the government.

When the government pays interest charges on the **national debt** it uses revenue earned from taxes. If the interest payments on debt rise faster than the national **output** of **economic goods and services**, then government borrowing and taxation can lead to an **inflation rate**.

BUSINESS

A business is a supplier of **economic goods and services**. In **economics**, businesses have two important functions. First, they play the part of

producers, because their products are bought by **households**. Second, they use **labor** and sometimes **capital** and land that is supplied, in part, by these households in order to produce their goods and services.

The term "business" is used most often in **macroeconomics**, while "firm" or "company" is used primarily in **microeconomics**.

BUSINESS CYCLE

A business cycle is the cycle of growth and decline a nation's **economy** goes through over a period of several years. A complete business cycle typically includes four stages—**contraction** (or **recession**), trough, **expansion**, and peak.

A contraction occurs when the production of **economic goods and services** is high, but the **demand** for them is low. The economy drops into a contraction, then a recession, typically marked by an increase in unemployment. A recession usually lasts from several months to two years before recovery, or growth, starts and moves toward a full expansion.

JOSEPH SCHUMPETER

Joseph Alois Schumpeter was an Austrian-American economist and social theorist who wrote extensively on business cycles and other important economic topics. He was born in 1883 in Triesch, Moravia and  was educated at Vienna University. He practiced law in Vienna in 1907, but later taught economics for various periods at the universities of Vienna, Gernowitz, Graz, and Bonn.

Schumpeter visited the United States as an exchange professor at Columbia University in 1913 and at Harvard University in 1927 and 1931. In 1932 he received a permanent position at Harvard and remained there for the rest of his career.

Schumpeter was noted for his theories about the importance of the **entrepreneur** in business. These theories emphasized the entrepreneur's role in stimulating **investment** and innovation, thereby causing "creative destruction" (the result when innovation makes old ideas and technologies obsolete).

His best-known books are *The Theory of Economic Development*; *Business Cycles*; *Capitalism, Socialism, and Democracy*; and *The History of Economic Analysis*. Schumpeter died in 1950.

Expansion is the result of the steady growth of **real gross domestic product** and is marked by lower levels of unemployment. Expansion typically lasts from two to three years. If the demand for goods and services expands faster than the production of these goods and services, however, **inflation** occurs.

The extremes of a business cycle occur at the upper turning point of expansion and the bottom of a recession. When economic growth reaches its height before it begins to decline, it is called a peak. The end of a recession, which leads to new expansion, is called a trough. The federal government tries to moderate these business cycles to avoid destabilizing episodes of inflation and unemployment.

KEY POINT TODAY
Monetarist economists believe that change in the **money supply** is the main cause for fluctuations in the business cycle. They advise that money supply changes should regularly be the same, or an amount equal to the average rate of increase of the **gross national product (GNP).** This theory is called the Friedman Rule. (See **Milton Friedman,** page 85.)

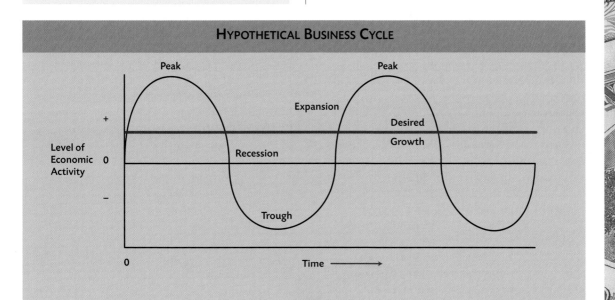

HYPOTHETICAL BUSINESS CYCLE

C

CAPITAL

In economics, capital is one of the four **resources** used in **production**. (The other three are entrepreneurship, **labor**, and land.) Capital consists of man-made resources such as machinery, products, factories, and other physical equipment used in the production of **economic goods and services**. Confusion sometimes arises because in finance, the term *capital* refers to financial assets such as corporate **equity**, **debt** securities, and cash. (See **human capital**.)

CAPITAL ACCOUNT

A nation's **balance of payments** has two elements: the **current account** and the capital account. The capital account records a country's purchases of financial **assets** with the rest of the world for a given period of time (usually one year). The capital account has a **surplus** if a nation's investments abroad are less than foreign investments at home.

For example, if the United States were to purchase less assets from foreign countries than foreign investors were spending on United States assets, then the U.S. capital account would have a surplus. If the reverse were true—if foreign countries were buying less U.S. assets than American investors were spending abroad—then the capital account would have a **deficit**. (See **balance of payments**.)

CAPITAL GAIN

Capital gain is the difference between the sale and purchase **price** of an **asset**. In other words, capital gain is part of **profit**. For example, if Sally buys a house for $100,000 and then sells it a year later for $150,000, she has made a capital gain of $50,000. Capital gains are normally taxed.

CAPITALISM

Capitalism is a system of economic organization in which all or most of the means of **production** and distribution (land, factories, railroads, computer networks, etc.) are privately owned and operated for a **profit**. **Capitalism** usually involves intense **competition** for **markets** and often results in the growth of large **corporations** as economies develop. (See **capital**.)

> **KEY POINT TODAY**
> Capitalism is based on the principle that capital goods are under private, not government, ownership.

CARTEL

Sometimes **businesses** in the same industry make a formal agreement, often across national lines, to gain control of their market through control of **price** and/or **output**. Such agreements usually involve a series of joint decisions to set the **market** price, and to operate in much the same way a **monopoly** would. When businesses gather together to make such an agreement, they form a cartel. Cartels are illegal in the United States.

The 11 heads of OPEC open a summit of the oil-producing cartel in Caracas, Venezuela.

The **Organization of Petroleum Exporting Countries (OPEC)** is probably the best-known international cartel. OPEC often tries to exert control over the world oil market. Other cartels exist to control products and services such as uranium and diamonds.

Cartels are often unstable because they set such high prices that each member of the cartel is tempted to "cheat" and sell at a lower price, thereby eroding the customer base of other members of the cartel.

CENTRAL BANK

The central **bank** is the main banking authority of a nation. The central bank issues **currency**, regulates the supply of **money** and **credit**, and acts as a **lender of last resort** in the country's **economy**. It is usually authorized by the government in support of **full employment**, low **inflation rates**, and **economic growth**. The central bank for the United States is the **Federal Reserve System**.

CERTIFICATE OF DEPOSIT

A **bank** deposit that is made for a certain amount of **money**, for a set period of time, with a set **interest rate** is called a certificate of deposit (CD). Most Ds can not be withdrawn or sold before a set maturity date without paying an early withdrawal fee. However, large certificates of deposit of $100,000 or more are often offered in a negotiable form. This means that they can be sold or transferred before they reach their maturity date

CETERIS PARIBUS

Ceteris paribus is a Latin phrase that means "other things being equal." In **economics** it is an assumption used to indicate that something would be the case if everything else under consideration remains the same. For example, if the price of toothpaste goes down by 10 percent, *ceteris paribus* people will buy more toothpaste. This assumption is used by economists to isolate the effect one economic factor has on another.

CHECKABLE DEPOSITS

Checking account deposits at **banks**, **savings and loan institutions**, **credit unions**, and similar institutions. With a checkable deposit the account holder can easily and quickly transfer money to another person by writing a check.

CHINESE ECONOMY

China has the world's largest population. It is in the process of privatizing many industries, although there is still a huge amount that is publicly owned. China is the largest economy to make the transition from a communist economy to a **free market economy**. It is one of the United States' largest trading partners. Economists interested in the global economy are studying China's major transformation. (See **communism**.)

CIRCULAR FLOW DIAGRAM

A circular flow diagram is a diagram that charts the continuous movement of **production**, **income**, and **resources** between producers and consumers. For example, the information in the

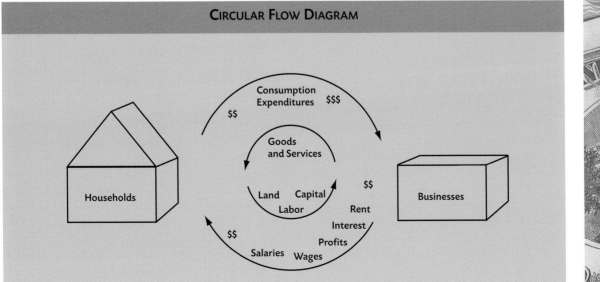

CIRCULAR FLOW DIAGRAM

chart on page 21 tracks the circular flow of economic activity between **households** and **businesses**.

First on the chart is the **gross domestic product**, followed by payment for these products. Businesses have to pay their suppliers, so the chart next lists these payments. These payments make up the **income** of the work force. This income is then used to purchase **economic goods and services**, which is actually the gross domestic product once again.

CLASSICAL ECONOMICS

Classical economics is a theory of **economics** based on the writings of Adam Smith, David Ricardo, Thomas Malthus, John Mill, and others who examined the causes of increase in national wealth and how the income was divided among a nation's population. They supported **laissez-faire** and free trade among nations, feeling that decisions made by laborers and capitalists could balance one another through the market system to create **economic growth**. They did not believe that unemployment could be caused in

any way by a decrease in **aggregate demand,** because market forces would work to keep aggregate demand and potential **gross national product** in balance.

CLOSED ECONOMY

An **economy** featuring little or no **foreign trade**. In theory, a country with a closed economy provides for the needs of its citizens without trade relations with other nations. In practice, it is difficult if not impossible to find any country with a completely closed economy in the modern world. Virtually every nation trades with at least one other country in order to obtain the goods and services it needs. However, economists sometimes use the simplifying assumption that an economy is closed when modeling the economy.

COLLECTIVE BARGAINING

If unionized workers are not satisfied with working conditions, **wages**, fringe benefits, work hours, promotion criteria, grievance procedures, and other aspects of their employment, they may negotiate with the employer for new terms through their **union**. The process of negotiating between the union and a company's management is called collective bargaining.

When a union and company management arrive at an agreement concerning employment-related issues, they make a formal contract called a collective bargaining agreement. Sometimes, however, the negotiation process breaks down before an agreement can be reached, leading to a **strike**, a lockout (a temporary closing of a plant or factory in the hopes that this will give the owners a negotiating advantage over the employee's union), or mediation by a third party.

COLONIALISM

Colonialism typically refers to a political-economic event whereby various European nations—primarily Portugal, Spain, France, England, and the Dutch Republic—explored, conquered, settled, and exploited areas around the world. Modern colonialism began about 1500, after the European discoveries of a sea route around Africa's southern coast (1488) and of the Americas (1492). By discovery, conquest, and settlement, these European countries expanded and colonized throughout the world, spreading European control and culture to the Americas, Asia, and Africa.

ADAM SMITH

Adam Smith is considered to be the founder of classical **economic theory**. He was born in the 1723 in the Scottish fishing village of Kirkcaldy and later studied at Glasgow and Oxford Universities.

Smith was both a philosopher and a political economist. He developed much of the theory about markets that is considered standard theory today and the basis of the **free market economy.** According to Smith's theory, in a free market economy the market **price** for any given product or service will, in the long run, adjust to the cost price.

In 1776 Smith published *An Inquiry into the Nature and Causes of the Wealth of Nations*, the first book of modern **economics** and a cornerstone of modern **capitalism**. Smith died in 1790.

From the standpoint of the global **economy**, colonialism established two things. The first was the development of the slave trade. Because the colonists often killed off the indigenous people they colonized (either by warfare or the introduction of foreign diseases), they needed a replacement labor force, which they found in slaves from Africa. The second development brought about by colonization was the specialization of raw materials produced to service European countries. The colonists were concerned with the gold, silver, and other valuable raw materials they discovered in the colonies. They turned these economies into producers of their raw materials. Many previously colonized countries still produce their raw materials to service industrialized nations. (See **imperialism.**)

COMMODITY MONEY

A commodity is any item that is bought and sold. Commodity money is a form of **currency** that has another value besides its use as currency. For example, food and clothing were among the first types of commodity money. Both of these items could be used or consumed if they were not used for currency (that is, traded for something else). Since everyone needs food and clothing, even people who did not need these items immediately were willing to accept them as payment for other items, because they knew they could be used to obtain other goods and services. Gold has been the most common commodity money through history. Precious stones and metal have also been used as commodity money. (See **fiat money; money**)

COMMON STOCK

The word "**stock**" refers to the ownership shares in a **corporation**; stockholders have legal claim to the corporation's **assets**. Common stock is the most frequently issued class of stock. It usually provides a voting right, and shareholders may receive **dividends**, but it is seen as secondary in rank to **preferred stock** for a variety of reasons, including income-producing potential. If a corporation has no preferred stock, however, the common stock has exclusive claim.

Usually, the holders of common stock are able to elect the company's board of directors. Most stocks are negotiable and are traded on a **stock market**. (See **equity** and **initial public offering.**)

COMMUNISM

In theory, communism is a form of economic organization that is based on a classless society where all citizens work equally for the common good of all, there is no privately owned property, personal **income** is based entirely on need rather than on performance, and there is no per-

Beads, jewels, and precious metals were all commonly used as commodity money.

C

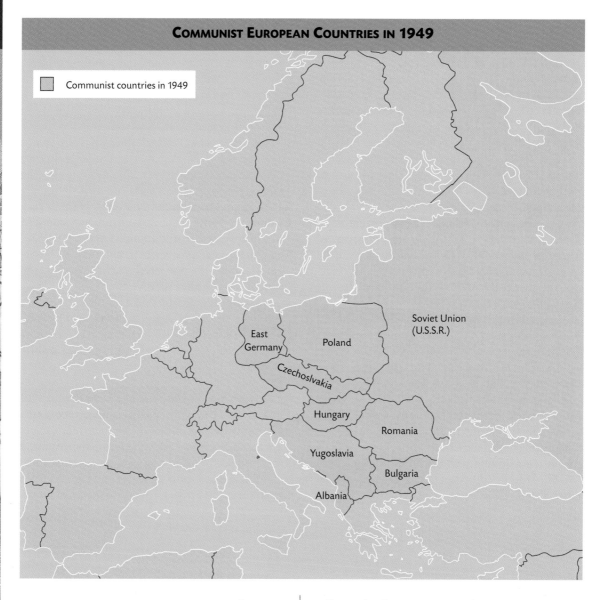

COMMUNIST EUROPEAN COUNTRIES IN 1949

Communist countries in 1949

East Germany
Poland
Czechoslovakia
Hungary
Yugoslavia
Romania
Bulgaria
Albania
Soviet Union (U.S.S.R.)

manent government or state structure (because the government is in the process of "withering away" and will eventually disappear).

One of the most important economists to influence the spread of communism was Karl Marx. He and Friedrich Engels published *The Communist Manifesto* in 1848. Although at first it had little or no impact on the widespread and varied revolutionary movements of mid-19th century Europe, *The Communist Manifesto* was to become one of the most widely read and discussed documents of the 20th century. Marx sought to differentiate his brand of socialism from others by insisting that it was scientifically based in the objective study of history, which he saw as being a continuous process of change and transformation. Just as feudalism had natu-

rally evolved into **mercantilism** and then **capitalism**, so capitalism would inevitably give way to its logical successor, **socialism** (a term which in Marx's usage includes its most advanced form, communism) as the necessary result of class struggle.

In a utopian sense, communism is meant to be the highest level in the development of government. In practice, however, communism is a usually an authoritarian political system, featuring a reliance on centralized economic planning. Communism was practiced in Eastern Europe; in the Soviet Union from 1917 until the 1990s, when the Soviet Union broke apart; and in China, Poland, Czechoslovakia, and many other countries, all of which are in transition to **market**-based economies. As an **economic system**,

KARL MARX

Karl Heinrich Marx, the political and economic theorist on whose works communism is based, was born into a comfortable middle-class family in Germany on May 5, 1818. He was educated as a philosopher but later became a journalist; in 1842 he was made editor of a liberal newspaper backed by industrialists. When the Prussian government forced the newspaper to close, Marx moved to France, where he developed a lifelong friendship with Friedrich Engels (1820-1895). Together Marx and Engels wrote *The Communist Manifesto* and founded the International Workingmen's Association.

Marx saw human history as the "history of the class struggle" and argued that workers should take action to hasten the eventual (and, as he saw it, inevitable) collapse of the capitalist system. He foresaw a final triumph of the proletariat (working class) over the bourgeoisie (or property-value-obsessed class) that would be followed by a classless society and the disappearance of state authority, as well as the evaporation of such institutions as church and family.

communism in practice tends to provide individuals with virtually no incentive to contribute at higher levels, very little personal freedom, and extremely narrow political and lifestyle options. Communist governments remain in place in some countries—for example, North Korea and Cuba—although in recent years many of these governments have begun to accommodate private, entrepreneurially driven **economic development** in ways that would have been condemned by the Communist theorists and politicians of the cold war era and earlier.

As seen in the map (above left), after World War II the majority of Eastern European nations fell under a communist regime. Beginning in the late 1980s, this changed when the Soviet Union split apart and the Berlin Wall was taken down.

KEY POINT TODAY

Although the 20th century did not bear out Marx's predictions, he was nevertheless one of the most influential thinkers of the 19th century. His social, political, and economic ideas became highly accepted by the socialist movement after his death in 1883.

COMPARATIVE ADVANTAGE

Comparative advantage is the ability to produce a product at a lower **opportunity cost** than anyone else's opportunity cost for producing that same product. (The opportunity cost of any good or service is the value of the other goods or services that must be given up in order to produce it.) For example, assume that two factories each manufacture combs and brushes. The first factory can produce each comb for a lower opportunity cost than the second factory, and the second factory can produce each brush for a lower opportunity cost than the first factory, Each factory has a comparative advantage over the other with regard to one product. This suggests that the first factory would be wise to produce more combs than brushes, while the second factory would make more money if it produced more brushes than combs.

Comparative advantage also motivates trade. For example, in one hour person A can produce one pound of potatoes or one pound of corn. Person B can produce two pounds of potatoes or three pounds of corn. Person B has an absolute advantage in both cases of potatoes and corn. If person A gives up one pound of corn for one pound of potatoes, and person B gives up three pounds of corn for two pounds of potatoes, or 1.5 pounds of corn for one potato, then person A has a higher opportunity cost, so he should not produce potatoes. Instead, he should produce corn, because this trade is possible even when one has **absolute advantage** in each.

COMPENSATING DIFFERENTIAL

Sometimes **wages** for some jobs are higher than wages for very similar jobs. For example, a welder on a high-rise building may receive a higher salary than a welder who works in a ground floor factory. In other words, the worker who takes the greater risk is likely to be paid more to compensate for the difference in the

probability of being injured on the job. This difference in pay is known as a compensating differential.

Sometimes differentials occur for other reasons—for example, as the result of the workers' personal preferences. A lower-wage job could have some benefit that has nothing to do with salary, such as more leisure time. This is also an example of compensating differentials.

COMPETITION

Competition occurs when two or more businesses compete or strive for the same customers in the same **markets**. Rival companies will use **price** variations in order to attract customers. Competition is one of the most important concepts in **economics** because it helps ensure that the maximum number of goods are produced at the lowest possible prices. For example, customers usually like to buy an item at the lowest possible cost, and they will shop around (read ads for many different stores or actually visit different stores) to see who has the best prices. For this reason, stores usually try to offer the most competitive prices. (See **perfect competition.**)

COMPETITIVE MARKET

A competitive market is one in which there is such a large number of buyers and sellers that no single buyer or seller is able to influence price or

This supermarket window displays advertisements for competing prices to lure shoppers.

any other aspect of the **market**. Within a competitive market there is competition among buyers and among sellers. Competition among sellers forces companies to sell products at a price that allows only a **normal profit**. This occurs in other markets too. (See **perfect competition.**)

COMPLEMENTS

Complements are two goods that "go together," or complement each other, and therefore have a complementary relationship. In other words, an increase in the **price** of the first good will cause less **demand** for the second good at any available price, and a decrease in the price of the first good will result in an increase in demand for the second good at any given available price. Usually two goods are complements when they tend to be consumed or used together at least some of the time.

An example of two complementary **consumer goods** would be hot dogs and hot dog buns. If a grocery store has a "special" on hot dogs, then consumers will probably buy more hot dog buns as well (even if the buns are not on sale), since hot dogs are usually eaten on buns. However, the overall price for eating a hot dog on a bun is still lower, because the hot dogs were on sale.

CONCENTRATION RATIO

A concentration ratio signifies a number indicating what percentage of the total **output** of an **industry** is produced by the few largest firms in that industry.

The two most common concentration ratios are for the four largest and eight largest firms. (The four-firm concentration ratio is the proportion of total output produced by the four largest firms in the industry; the eight-firm concentration ratio is the proportion of total output produced by the eight largest firms in the industry.) A four-firm concentration ratio over 80 (meaning 80 percent of industry output is produced by the four largest firms) indicates that four firms have significant market control. (See **oligopoly.**) A four-firm concentration ratio over 20 (meaning 20 percent of industry output is produced by the four largest firms) indicates that these four firms have only limited market control.

As seen in the table on page 27, the primary copper industry is almost entirely, or 98 percent, controlled by four major companies. The concentration ratio for the industrial machinery

FOUR-FIRM CONCENTRATION RATIOS, SELECTED INDUSTRIES

Product	Concentration Ratio
Primary copper	98
Household laundry equipment	94
Cereal breakfast foods	85
Camera and photo supply stores	25
Sporting goods stores and bicycle shops	13
Commercial printing	6
Plastic products	5
Industrial machinery	1

market, however, shows us that there are many companies with limited market control involved in the production of industrial machinery.

CONSERVATISM

Conservatism is a political school of thought whose followers tend to protect and promote established customs, ideals, and beliefs. Economic conservatives in the United States typically favor a limited government, a **free market economy,** and a strong national defense. In the United States, conservatism is more associated with the Republican Party.

CONSUMER GOODS

Consumer goods are goods that are purchased, leased, or rented primarily for personal, family, or **household** purposes, as opposed to those used to create other goods or for business or government. (See **economic goods and services; producer goods.**)

CONSUMER PRICE INDEX (CPI)

An index is a tool that simplifies the measurement of movements in a numerical series. The Consumer Price Index (CPI) is an index of **prices** of **economic goods and services** typically purchased by people in cities. This index is compiled

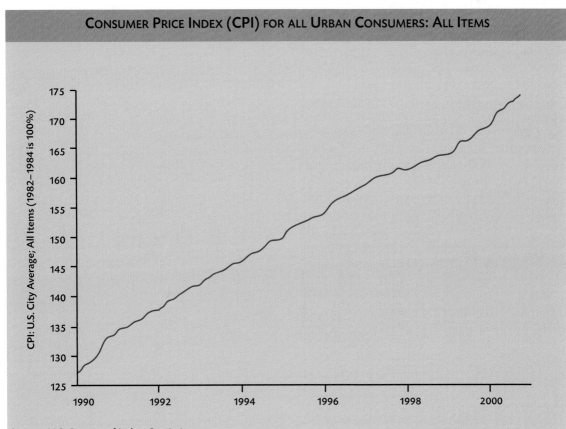

CONSUMER PRICE INDEX (CPI) FOR ALL URBAN CONSUMERS: ALL ITEMS

CPI: U.S. City Average; All Items (1982–1984 is 100%)

Source: U.S. Bureau of Labor Statistics

and published each month by the Bureau of Labor Statistics (BLS). The BLS obtains the data for this index from a survey of 25,000 retail outlets and the quantity data generated by the Consumer Expenditures Survey. The CPI is used as an **indicator** of the current price level and can be used to calculate the **inflation rate**. It is also used to adjust wage and income payments, such as Social Security, for inflation.

Most CPI indexes have a 1982–1984 reference base. That is, BLS sets the average index level (representing the average price level)—for the 36-month period covering the years 1982, 1983, and 1984—equal to 100. The Bureau then measures changes in relation to that figure. An index of 125, for example, means there has been a 25-percent increase in price since the reference period. Similarly, an index of 90 means a 10-percent decrease. Index movements from one date to another can be expressed as changes in index points (simply, the difference between index levels), but it is more useful to express them as percent changes. (See **price index.**)

CONSUMER SOVEREIGNTY

Sovereignty means "rule," so consumer sovereignty is the notion that consumers (buyers) rule the **economy** because they are the ones who will ultimately determine what goods are produced and how **resources** are used.

Of course, businesses can produce whatever products they choose, but consumers will not buy them unless they want them. If consumers do not buy the products a **business** makes, then that business will most likely shut down, and resources will be used by other businesses who make products that consumers actually do want to buy. (See **producer sovereignty.**)

CONSUMER SURPLUS

Consumer surplus deals with a product's **price** as it relates to customer satisfaction. When consumers are satisfied with a good over and above the price they paid, this is considered a consumer surplus. Consumer surplus is also the difference between the maximum **demand** price consumers are willing to pay and the price they actually do pay.

CONSUMPTION

Consumption is the process of using **economic goods and services** to satisfy **wants** and needs. It is the opposite of **production.** Consumption

usually refers to personal or **household** activities rather than business activities. When a person or household uses a good or service to satisfy a need or want, that good is usually "used up." For example, food or fuel are used up or consumed as we eat or drive our car. But other goods do not

KEY POINT TODAY
The Veblen effect is a theory of **consumption** that suggests that consumption may have an upward sloping **demand curve** rather than the usual downward sloping demand curve due to conspicuous consumption. Usually when a demand curve slopes downward it implies that when the **price** increases, the quantity demanded decreases. The Veblen effect suggests the opposite. As the price increases, so does the quantity demanded.

Two consumers check their shopping bags on a sidewalk during the holiday shopping season.

THORSTEIN BUNDE VEBLEN

Thorstein Bunde Veblen (1857–1929), was an American economist and social scientist. Born in Cato, Wisconsin, he graduated from Carleton College in Northfield, Minnesota, and went on to attend John Hopkins, Yale, and Cornell universities.

Veblen taught **economics** at Stanford University from 1906 to 1909 and at the University of Missouri from 1911 to 1918. Veblen became a staff member at the New School for Social Research in New York City in 1919. He remained there until his retirement in 1926.

Veblen's most famous work, *The Theory of the Leisure Class* (1899), describes society as two separate classes: a leisure class (or predator class), which owns business enterprises; and an industrious class, which produces the goods. According to Veblen, this leisure class is harmful to the **economy** because of its parasitic behavior. Veblen developed the phrase "conspicuous consumption," which he later used to describe the way Americans compete for social status. His writings and theory reflected his strong, non-Marxist criticism of the American capitalist system.

Veblen's many other writings include *The Theory of Business Enterprise* (1904), *The Instinct of Workmanship* (1914), *The Place of Science in Modern Civilization* (1919), and *The Engineers and the Price System* (1921). His ideas led toward more social control or governmental involvement in the economy. Veblen died in 1929.

have to be used up or destroyed in the process of using them. We can read a book, thereby using it, but the book is not "used up" or destroyed; it is still available for another person to read.

CONTESTABLE MARKET

A contestable market is a **market** in which **businesses** can enter and then, if they choose, exit without large losses. The freedom of entry and exit are the key characteristics of a contestable market. The theory of contestable markets argues that low cost of entry to, and exit from, markets leads to **efficiency**. This is true even if there are only a few businesses in the **industry**, since the constant threat of new competitors keeps businesses from charging too much for their products (so prices stay competitive).

A market would be contestable, or easy to enter, if it was one with low start-up costs and had no **barriers to entry** (such as taxes, restrictive laws, or low expectation of **profit**). The theory of contestable markets was formulated by William J. Baumol, an economist, in 1982.

CONTRACTION

A contraction is one of the four phases of the **business cycle**. It is the **recession** phase of the business cycle when **production** or the **gross domestic product** of a country decreases. A contraction occurs when the **production** of economic goods and services is high, but the **demand** for them is low. In this case, businesses will experience intentional inventory increases and so will consequently reduce production. The economy drops into a contraction (recession), which causes an increase in unemployment. The period at the end of the contraction leading to the next **expansion**, or growth in the economy, is called a trough. The end of the expansion, which leads to the next downturn or contraction, is called the peak of the business cycle. A full expansion results from steady growth of real gross domestic product and less unemployment. This recurring cycle of change in economic activity can take several years.

CORPORATION

A corporation is one of the three basic forms of business organization. A **business** can be organized as a corporation, a proprietorship, or a **partnership**. A business is a corporation when it establishes ownership through shares called corporate **stock**.

One of the advantages of organizing a business as a corporation is that owners cannot be held personally responsible for corporate **debt**s. In legal terms, this is referred to as "limited **liability**." The business is seen as having a separate legal existence from its owners. This is not the case with a proprietorship or a partnership. Owners of these types of businesses can be held personally responsible for corporate debts.

C

COST-BENEFIT ANALYSIS

Before the decision makers in businesses invest in the full-scale manufacture of products or the delivery of services, they generally analyze the cost to produce a certain product or service and compare this cost to the benefit, or **profit**, they are likely to receive in return. The benefit divided by the cost is called a cost-benefit ratio.

For example, if a pencil that sells for 50 cents costs 25 cents to make, the benefit-cost ratio would be 50 over 25, or two. In this case, it would be profitable to make pencils. Consider, however, a pencil that sells for 50 cents and costs 49 cents to make. Here, the benefit-cost ratio would be so low that the business would be very likely to consider dropping the product.

Thus, a cost-benefit analysis is an economic tool that assesses and compares benefits and costs. This analysis is used to determine the net change resulting from an initiative.

COST-PUSH INFLATION

Cost-push inflation refers to a general increase in the prices for products due to an increase in **production costs** for these same items. Production costs are influenced by a variety of factors. They may rise because **wage** rates have gone up at a faster rate than **productivity**. Sometimes production costs go up because the price of raw materials and energy costs have risen due to to a global **shortage** or perhaps, such as in the case of oil, because of a **cartel** operation. When faced with increased production costs, businesses must pay more to manufacture goods, so they must raise the **price** of these goods to continue making a **profit**. The higher production cost therefore "pushes" up the price level.

COUNCIL OF ECONOMIC ADVISORS

The Council of Economic Advisors is a three-member board that advises the President of the United States about **economic policy**. The council helps the president prepare an annual economic report, among other duties. Members of this council are usually economists who keep the president up-to-date on current economic statistics and help formulate federal economic policies. The chairman of this council is often considered one of the two most important and influential non-elected economic advisors in the United States. The other is the Chairman of the Board of Governors of the **Federal Reserve System**.

CREDIT

Loans and other deferred payment plans offered to individuals and companies are called credit. Bank loans and credit cards, for example, allow consumers and businesses to buy **economic goods and services** or raw materials that they may not otherwise afford to purchase.

CREDITOR NATION/DEBTOR NATION

A creditor nation is one that owes less to foreign governments, businesses, and consumers than foreigners owe to its domestic government, businesses, and consumers. A creditor nation is usually in the position to lend money to other nations. A debtor nation is just the opposite, since it owes more to foreign governments, businesses, and consumers than foreigners owe to its domestic government, businesses, and consumers. Although the United States was a creditor nation for many decades, it is now a debtor nation.

CREDIT UNION

A credit union operates much the same as a **bank**. The main difference is that a credit union is a nonprofit institution created for the benefit of a specific group of people who are all employed by a certain **business** or company, are members of a union, or have some other commonality, while a bank is out to make a **profit** and provides services for anyone. Teachers, the military, and government workers all have their own credit unions. Credit unions provide these individuals with low-cost banking services that include savings accounts, checking accounts, and **loans**.

CROWDING OUT

Crowding out is the claim that an increase in government borrowing or spending leads to higher **interest rates** and to a reduction in private investment. When interest rates increase, private investors borrow less to create new companies. Therefore, the private investment is "crowded out" by the government spending. Personal **consumption** may also be crowded out by government spending.

CURRENCY

Currency is paper money and coins. It is usually issued by a national government. In the United States, currency is issued by the Federal Reserve System (paper) and the **U.S. Treasury**

A collage of different currencies from around the world.

(coins). Most currency is only good for what it can buy (you can't eat money or wear it, for example; you can only spend it or save it). It has no value or purpose by itself. For that reason it is called **fiat money** which means it is money "by degree," that is because it is declared **legal tender** by the government. Currency, or cash as it is often called, makes up a part of a country's **money supply.** (See **Commodity Money** and **Fiat Money**)

CURRENCY APPRECIATION

(See **appreciation.**)

CURRENCY DEPRECIATION

(See **depreciation.**)

CURRENT ACCOUNT

A nation has two parts to its **balance of payments**. They are called the **capital account** and the current account. The capital account is the part of the balance of payments that records all trade, **exports**, and **imports** between a nation and the rest of the world. The current account also includes **transfer payments**.

If the money coming into a nation for exports and transfers is greater than the money going out, then the current account has a **surplus.** A **deficit** occurs if the opposite exists.

CURRENT ASSETS

Current assets are **assets**, such as **stocks**, **money** owed by debtors, and cash, that are held for a short time by a company. The cash made from these assets are used to pay for raw materials that are bought and made into **final products** to be sold.

CURRENT LIABILITIES

In economics, a current **liability** includes all money that needs to be paid out in the near future. Current liabilities typically include the amounts a **business** owes to its creditors and its **bank loans.**

CYCLICAL SURPLUS OR DEFICIT

A nation's government can have a **surplus** or a **deficit**. A surplus means that it has more revenue (**income**) than expenses for a given period of time. A deficit, on the other hand, means it has

C

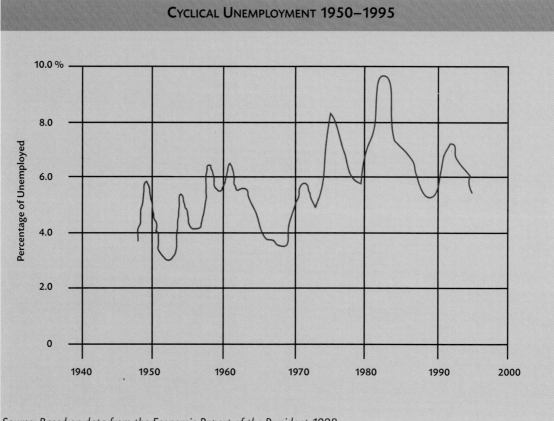

CYCLICAL UNEMPLOYMENT 1950–1995

Source: Based on data from the Economic Report of the President 1998

more expenses than revenue for a given period of time. Cyclical surpluses and deficits, however, are not the result of **fiscal policy**. Instead, they occur according to the cyclical phases in a **business cycle**.

A cyclical surplus occurs during periods of high employment, which typically exist during the growth or **expansion** phase of the **business cycle**. A cyclical deficit, on the other hand, occurs during periods of high unemployment or during the **contraction** or **recession** phase of the business cycle. Usually these cyclical deficits and surpluses cancel each other out during a complete business cycle.

CYCLICAL UNEMPLOYMENT

Unemployment means many people are without jobs. There are various types of unemployment—seasonal unemployment, **frictional unemployment**, **structural unemployment**, and cyclical unemployment.

Cyclical unemployment happens during a contraction (recession) phase of a nation's business cycle. **Demand** for products and services is less, so **production** is reduced. Fewer workers and **resources** are needed, and this results in many companies laying off their employees. People have difficulty finding new jobs as companies cut back on their production.

As a nation moves out of the contraction phase and into the growth phase of its business cycle, this cyclical unemployment decreases. Companies are able to 1increase their production and many people return to work, or find new employment.

The graph above depicts unemployment rates in the United States from the late 1940s through the mid 1990s. Notice the cyclical pattern as the unemployment rate continuously rises and falls over the years. The United States hit its peak of unemployment in the early 1980s with an unemployment rate of over 9.5 percent. Its low was in the early 1950s, when the unemployment rate was approximately 3 percent.

D

DEADWEIGHT LOSS

Consumer surplus is the satisfaction that consumers obtain from a good over and above the **price** they paid for it. This is the difference between the maximum **demand** price they would be willing to pay and the price they actually pay. With a deadweight loss, the consumer surplus is less because consumers are paying a price closer to the maximum demand price for the product. This is due to **taxes**, **market** inefficiency (something is just overpriced), or other factors. A deadweight loss is the amount of consumer surplus that is eaten away by these various taxes and other costs.

DEBT

Debt is a financial obligation resulting from borrowing money or purchasing goods and services without actual cash. The person who owes the **money**, or incurs the debt, is called the debtor. The person or company the money is owed to is called the creditor, lender, or debtee. When money is borrowed, and therefore a debt is incurred, both the debtor and the creditor usually sign a contract. According to the terms of this contract, the debtor must repay both **principal** and **interest** on monies he or she has borrowed. (See **credit**.)

DEBT-SERVICE RATIO

The payments countries make to repay loans are called debt service. If too much money is going out of a country and too little is coming in, there is a deficit on the **balance of payments**. For some countries the deficit increases because the money going out is simply to pay back loans or pay interest on already existing loans. One way of looking at the loan burden on countries is to look at what percent of earnings from exports is paid out in servicing the countries' debts. This is called the debt-service ratio. The debt-service ratios for many poorer parts of the world are very high and continues to go up. (See **burden of debt**)

DEFICIT

A deficit is a **shortage**. It usually means the amount by which a sum of money is less than what is due, expected, or needed. Over a given period of time, when anyone (a person, a **business**, or a government) is spending more money than they are making (**income**), this is called a deficit. When a person wishes to eliminate a deficit, it usually means it is time to either cut back on expenses or get a higher-paying job. When a business wishes to eliminate a deficit, it usually raises **prices** for its products or tries to cut back on **production costs**. When a government has a deficit, it may raise taxes or cut spending. Deficits are often used to regulate the level of a nation's economic activity. (See **Keynesian economics**.)

DEFLATION

Inflation is an overall increase in **prices** (over an extended period of time) for **economic goods and services**. Deflation is the opposite—an overall decrease in prices (over an extended period of time) for goods and services. Deflation is sometimes brought on by the banking authorities in order to reduce inflation and improve the **balance of payments** by cutting back on **demand for imports**.

DEFLATIONARY GAP

The difference between actual spending on **gross domestic product (GDP)** and what spending would be at **full employment** is called the deflationary gap. Due to a lower amount of spending, some of the nation's **resources** lie idle, and GDP is below its potential. In order to counteract this deficiency in spending, the authorities may use **fiscal policy** to expand **aggregate demand**.

DEINDUSTRIALIZATION

Deindustrialization occurs when there is a consistent decrease in the industrial and manufacturing sectors of the **economy**. This usually goes hand in hand with a decline in the number of people who work in industry.

There is a trend in many developed countries, like the United States, for the industrial sector to grow more slowly than the **service sector**. In the United States, the percentage of **industry** in the gross domestic product (GDP) fell from 38 percent in 1960 to 32 percent in 1984, while services increased from 58 percent to 66 percent.

DEMAND

A nation's **economy** depends on both **supply** and demand. Demand is the willingness and ability to buy a variety of goods and services at a range of prices during a given period of time. At first look, demand might seem like it means the same as "**want**." If many people want a product, that product is in demand. However, enough people must actually be willing and able to pay a certain **price** for a certain product—not merely want it—in order for that product to be in demand. For example, many people would like a Mercedes, but only a limited amount of people are able to actually afford to purchase this type of car. If the price of Mercedes suddenly went up, then the quantity demanded for them would go down, because even fewer people would be able to afford them. Total consumer demand for a product is reflected in the **demand curve**.

DEMAND CURVE

A demand curve shows the relationship between the price of a product and the quantity demanded for a particular good or service. The price is

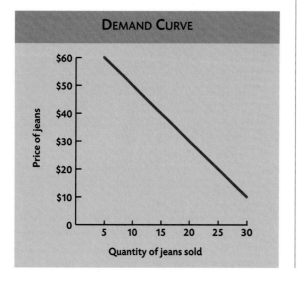

DEMAND CURVE

shown on the vertical axis and the quantity is shown on the horizontal axis of the graph. The demand curve shows an inverse relationship. As the graph illustrates, when the price of blue jeans increases the quantity of jeans sold decreases. However, when the price of jeans goes down, the **demand** for jeans increases.

DEMAND DEPOSIT

A demand deposit is a **bank** deposit that can be withdrawn "on demand"—that is, whenever the customer wants to take it out. In contrast to demand deposits, **time deposits** are savings deposits that often cannot be accessed for a predetermined period of time.

DEMAND-PULL INFLATION

Demand-pull inflation is a general increase in prices due to an increase in **demand** in relation to the existing **supply**. In other words, **businesses** are no longer willing to produce increased quantities of a product at the same price if it is in high demand. People, on the other hand, are willing to pay a higher price for items that are in scarce supply rather than not have these items at all. As a result, the increase in demand will pull the price up.

DEMAND SCHEDULE

A demand schedule is a table that shows various prices of a product and the quantities demanded at each of these prices. The information found in a demand schedule can be used to create a **demand curve** illustrating the relationship between price and quantity demanded in a graph.

DEPENDENCY THEORIES

Dependency theories are based on the belief that the dependence of less developed countries on industrialized countries is the cause of underdevelopment. Dependency theories focus on the unequal economic and political exchange that takes place between developed and developing nations and between groups and classes within nations. It is believed that in adopting development strategies defined and dominated by developed countries, less developed countries are confronted with various problems that place them at a disadvantage in relation to the developed countries. Dependency theories became popular among Latin American economists in the 1960s.

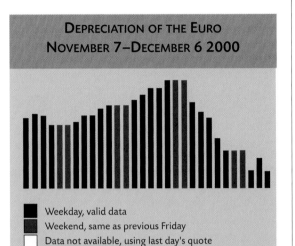

DEPRECIATION

Depreciation is a decrease in value of an **asset** such as **capital**, real estate, corporate **stock**, or **money**. The decrease in value of these items can be due to several factors. Capital goods (such as tools, machinery, etc.) depreciate because they simply wear out with time. Depreciation also refers to a decrease in the value of a **currency.** When the Euro, for example, is worth less in terms of the U.S. dollar or other currency, it depreciates. Depreciation is contrasted with **appreciation**.

The graph to the left shows the value of the Euro increasing and decreasing over a 30 day period. Although the value rises and falls, it depreciates significantly in the last ten days of the cycle.

DEPRESSION

A depression is best understood as an extreme **recession**. It is an extended period of restructuring and institutional change in an **economy**

During the Great Depression, a great number of people lost their homes. Many built temporary villages, which became known as "Hoovervilles," after President Herbert Hoover. The children above lived in one.

that is often marked by declining or stagnant growth. During this period, **unemployment** tends to be higher and **inflation** lower than a regular, run-of-the-mill recession. A depression usually lasts in the range of ten years, often encompassing two or three separate shorter-run business cycles. The most noted depression in the U.S. economy was the **Great Depression** of the 1930s. However, others occurred in the 1840s and 1870s. On the plus side, the more severe a depression is and the more actual restructuring that is accomplished, the greater the chance there is for prosperity over the next few decades. (See **business cycle**.)

DEVELOPED COUNTRY

Developed countries are countries that have relatively high standards of living as measured by the **gross domestic product** (**GDP**) per capita. They are the industrialized countries of the world where machines do much of the manufacturing. These countries have already "developed" modern economies. The United States, Canada, Great Britain, France, and Japan are examples of developed countries. Countries that are in the process of working toward industrialization are called developing countries. Countries with little or no industry are called **less developed countries**.

DIAMOND-WATER PARADOX

A paradox is a statement or question that seems to contradict itself. The diamond-water paradox also seems to contradict itself. It states that water is more important to human existence (meaning it has a higher **utility**) than diamonds, yet the **price** of water is relatively low, while the price of diamonds is relatively high. If water has a higher utility than diamonds, why are diamonds more expensive than water?

The answer can be explained by defining two types of utility one called **marginal utility** and another called **total utility**. When an object or substance has great marginal utility, that means its **supply** is low, and an additional unit would bring a greater utility or satisfaction. When an object has great total utility, its supply may be plentiful and an additional unit would not be likely to bring additional satisfaction.

Water has a high total utility because it is necessary for so many things—drinking, cooking, washing—for the entire world's population. But since water is plentiful, it has a low marginal utility and people are not willing to pay a lot for it. Diamonds, however, have a low total utility—there are not many practical uses for diamonds except for jewelry, drills, etc. What is more, diamonds are not nearly as plentiful as water but are desired by many people. Therefore, consumers are willing to pay more for diamonds than water, so diamonds have a high marginal utility.

DIMINISHING RETURNS (LAW OF)

The law of diminishing returns is also known as the law of variable proportions. This law states that if some **factors of production** are fixed (such as buildings and machinery), production can be increased by adding more variable inputs (such as **labor** and materials). However, at some point, as more and more variable inputs are added, the extra production (which can be called the "returns") in relation to the amount of extra variables will diminish.

For example, if the machinery and the buildings for a factory remain fixed, but more workers and materials are constantly added, at first this increase in workers and materials will result in large increases in **production**. At some point, however, the returns will begin to diminish; that is an additional worker yields less and less additional **output**. In fact, at some point, an additional worker could cause output to fall.

DIRECT TAX

Some taxes are direct taxes and others are **indirect taxes**. A direct tax is one that is collected according to the wealth or **income** of individuals and **businesses**. The government collects these taxes in order to raise revenue. **Income tax**, inheritance tax, corporation tax, and **social security** charges are all examples of direct taxes.

Direct taxes are a form of **progressive taxation,** because the amount paid varies depending on the income and wealth of the taxpayer.

DISCOUNT RATE

A discount rate is the **interest rate** the **Federal Reserve System** charges to **bank**s. Sometimes banks need to borrow money to stay in business because much of their money is tied up in **investments**, **loans**, etc. In order for banks to have liquid **assets** (**money**) to loan to customers, the Federal Reserve System loans money to banks. Just as with other loans, **interest** must be charged for this money. The discount rate is the interest the Federal Reserve charges. By law, the discount rate is set by the board of directors of each Reserve Bank every 14 days, subject to the approval of the Board of Governors of the Federal Reserve.

DISCRETIONARY FISCAL POLICY

Discretionary fiscal policy is the use of government revenue (**taxation**) and spending to affect the ups and downs of the **economy**. The government has obligations to pay—so-called entitlements such as **social security**, **unemployment benefits,** and Medicare. There are also **interest** payments on the **national debt**. After these payments, about 25 percent of the **budget** is left to consider for tax cuts, paying down the national debt, or additional spending. Discretionary **fiscal policy** is the use of this 25 percent of the budget to affect the economy. For example, the government might increase **output, investments,** or spending, or perhaps it may increase personal **income** through tax cuts.

DISECONOMIES OF SCALE

Diseconomies of scale is the possible increase in long-run average cost that sometimes happens when a company's **production** of goods or services is also increased.

DISEQUILIBRIUM

Disequilibrium occurs when **equilibrium** has not been achieved. Sometimes if equilibrium has been achieved but is not maintained, it is also referred to as disequilibrium. If an economic system has a natural tendency toward disequilibrium, it is referred to as unstable.

DISGUISED UNEMPLOYMENT

Disguised unemployment refers to a situation where workers use less than their full capabilities. There may be self-employed workers who could easily perform more work than that for which they find customers, wage workers employed for only short work weeks who would like longer ones, and both self–employed and wage workers who are capable of more productive work than that which they are performing. The two types of less-than-full employment are called underemployment, and employment at less-than-full capability is called disguised unemployment. In less developed countries, people who live in rural areas may not have enough work and are therefore not adding anything to the work force. By moving to an urban area, however, they may find employment. (See **Lewis Model.**)

DISPOSABLE INCOME

Disposable income is the actual amount of total consumer **income** after income taxes and **social security** taxes are removed and government **transfer payments** (like **welfare**, social security benefits, or unemployment compensation) are added. Disposable income is often referred to simply as DI. Disposable income can be used for either **consumption** (spending) or savings.

DISPOSABLE INCOME					
	1995	**1996**	**1997**	**1998**	**1999**
Disposable personal income					
Total (billions of dollars)	5,422.6	5,677.7	5,982.8	6,286.2	6,639.2
Per capita (dollars)	20,613	21,385	22,320	23,231	24,305
Personal consumption **expenditures**					
Total (billions of dollars)	4,969.0	5,237.5	5,524.4	5,848.6	6,254.9
Per capita (dollars)	18,888	19,727	20,610	21,614	22,898
Gross domestic product **per capita (dollars)**					
Current dollars	28,131	29,428	30,968	32,373	33,857
Population (thousands)	263,073	265,504	268,046	270,595	273,161

Source: U.S. Department of Commerce, Bureau of Economic Analysis and Bureau of the Census

DIVIDEND

A dividend is a payment made to a company's shareholders. The dividend is a part of the after-taxes **profit** the company has made for the year (although often dividends are paid quarterly). The amount of dividend a shareholder receives is based on the amount of shares he or she owns. Based on one share of **stock** in the company, the dividend for that share for that quarter might be only 17 cents. However, if a shareholder owned 1,000 shares, the dividend would be 17 cents times 1,000 (0.17 X 1,000), or $170.

DOUBLE COINCIDENCE OF WANTS

Double coincidence of wants is a necessary element of **bartering**. In order for a successful barter to take place, both traders must want what the other has available to trade.

Since it is sometimes difficult to find two traders who want what the other has, **money** developed as a more convenient and efficient means of trade. Because everyone can use money, trading goods and services for money is not dependent on a double coincidence of wants.

DOUBLE COUNTING

When measuring the **Gross Domestic Product (GDP)**, it is necessary to avoid the counting of intermediate sales, because this amounts to double counting. An example of an intermediate sale is the sale of steel to the automobile industry. When the steel is taken and becomes part of an automobile, it is sold again as part of a complete machine. Sales of steel to the automobile indus-try are intermediate sales, while sales of automobiles to consumers are final sales. Intermediate sales are not counted in the gross domestic product, only final sales should be included.

DOUBLE TAXATION

Double taxation occurs when there is a **taxation** of **income** and profits both in the country where the income is made and again in the income earner's home country. Because most individuals and businesses do not want to pay double taxes, they are deterred from engaging in international **labor** and **capital**. For this reason, many nations have negotiated double taxation agreements with one another. These agreements typically limit taxation in the country where the income is earned.

DOW JONES INDUSTRIAL AVERAGE

The Dow Jones Industrial Average is a price average based on the **stock** prices of 30 of the biggest and most important industrial **corporations** in the United States listed on the **New York Stock Exchange (NYSE)**. This accumulated list is called the Dow Jones Industrial Average (DJIA) because it is compiled by Dow Jones & Co.

Some of the 30 companies that have been included in the Dow Jones Industrial Average are Alcoa, American Express, AT&T, Boeing, Coca-Cola, Disney, Eastman Kodak, General Electric, IBM, McDonalds, Proctor and Gamble, Sears, and Westinghouse. The DJIA is the most widely quoted and referenced **stock market** index

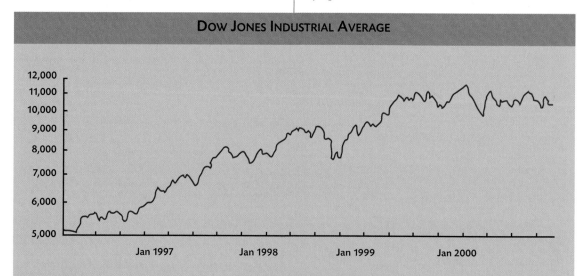

CHARLES DOW AND EDWARD JONES

Charles Dow was born in Connecticut in 1851. He began his career as a reporter in 1872, working for a variety of newspapers including the *Springfield Republican*, *The Providence Star*, and *The Providence Journal*, for which he reported on financial and economic stories.

Charles Dow

In 1880 Dow settled in New York City, where he continued to make a living reporting on financial stories for a couple of years. In 1882 Charles Dow joined with Edward Jones to create Dow Jones & Company. Together they produced news bulletins about the market called "flimsies." They distributed their flimsies to all of the financial companies on Wall Street. A year later their bulletin developed into a full-fledged daily paper called *The Wall Street Journal* (published officially under that name in 1889).

Edward Jones ran the office during the day, which included the task of overseeing a staff of copywriters (mostly 14- to 16-year-old boys) while Charles Dow provided the lengthier financial analysis as well as stock market news and gossip.

Edward Jones

Both men made many connections among the Wall Street financiers. It is said that Jones spent his evenings at the Windsor Hotel in 5th Avenue listening for gossip from such important financial types as William Rockefeller.

Dow, on the other hand, occupied most of his days and evenings compiling stock-price averages—a form of analysis he is credited with creating.

The Wall Street Journal became a success, and it soon was regarded as the most influential paper in its field. Dow's writing became the basis for an increasingly sophisticated analysis called the "Dow Theory" that many others would elaborate on over the years.

Dow Jones averages have remained one of the most trusted and relied-upon indicators of the stock market since the late 19th century.

Charles Dow was a member of the New York Stock Exchange from 1855 to 1891. He remained publisher and editor of *The Wall Street Journal* until 1901. He died in Brooklyn, New York, the following year.

today. This index is intended to represent the overall performance of the stock market as a whole over a given period of time. For example, the evening stock reports on the television news usually lead with the Dow Jones Industrial Average, reporting how much this average went up or down from the previous day. (See **NASDAQ** and **Standard & Poor's 500**.)

DUAL ECONOMY

A dual economy is found in less developed countries where **economic growth** is unbalanced. The country actually seems to have two economies. Some parts of the country are modern and efficient, while other parts are less developed and people may live in poverty.

DUMPING

Sometimes **businesses** will sell a product to a foreign **market** at a lower **price** than that charged to domestic buyers. This might be done to stay competitive in a foreign market. That is, consumers in a foreign market might not be willing and able to pay as much as domestic consumers do for a product. However, it would still be somewhat profitable to sell to these foreign markets, so businesses are willing to sell for a lower price. Other times, businesses might be willing to sell to foreign markets even if the sales price of a product is below **production costs** for that product, if the business has excess product it wants to get rid of, or if the business is trying to eliminate competitors in this foreign market. When businesses sell a product to a foreign market at a price lower than they would charge domestic buyers, this is called dumping.

DUOPOLY

A duopoly is a part of an **oligopoly**. It is a market with only two suppliers of a particular good or service. The two companies each sell to a large number of consumers. Therefore, each individual consumer is too small to affect the price of the goods or services being purchased.

E

EARNINGS

Earnings mean the **money** that is made from **factors of production**, including **wages**, salaries, fees and commissions, **profits**, rent, **dividends**, and **interest** payments.

ECONOMIC ANALYSIS

Economic analysis is a systematic way of studying the **economy**. Usually, economists first identify economic concepts (such as **supply** and **demand**, government policy, consumer spending and saving, etc.), then combine these various concepts to evaluate or analyze economic questions. Some economists study economic indicators such as the **Gross Domestic Product (GDP)**, **national income**, the **Consumer Price Index**, **unemployment rate**, **inflation**, **interest rates**, etc., and try to see what is happening with the economy and figure out where it is headed. Others may try to understand the impact of government policies or other economic events.

ECONOMIC BAD

A product or **service** that causes dissatisfaction or harm to consumers is sometimes called an economic bad. When a consumer is made worse off by a product or item, this is known as disutility. Therefore, an economic bad usually leads to disutility among consumers. Pollution and congestion are examples of an economic bad. People who are willing to pay to obtain an economic good, are also willing to pay to avoid an economic bad. (See **economic goods and services**.)

ECONOMIC DEVELOPMENT

Economic development is the process by which a community or a nation creates, retains, and reinvests wealth to experience **economic growth**. Economic development differs from economic growth in that the new wealth leads to generally higher **standards of living** for the population.

SIR W. ARTHUR LEWIS

Sir W. Arthur Lewis was a British economist born in 1915 on the island of St. Lucia in the British West Indies. In 1940 he received a Ph.D. from the London School of Economics. From 1948 to 1958, Lewis was a professor of **economics** at the University of Manchester. From 1963 to 1983, he was a professor of economics at Princeton University. Lewis specialized in the **economic theory** of developing countries. He also helped establish the Caribbean Development Bank. In 1979 he shared the Nobel Prize in Economics with American Theodore W. Schultz.

Lewis was the author of several important books, including *The Principles of Economic Planning* (1949), *The Theory of Economic Growth* (1955), *Development Planning* (1966), *Tropical Development 1880–1913* (1971), and *Growth and Fluctuations 1870–1913* (1978). Lewis was knighted in 1963. He died in Bridgetown, Barbados, in 1991.

ECONOMIC GOODS AND SERVICES

An economic good is a physical or tangible product used to satisfy people's needs and **wants**—that is, anything that people find useful or desirable. Usually, the term **economic goods** (or simply *goods*) is used with the term *services*.

Services are intangible items that satisfy people's needs and wants. A car is an economic good, while medical care from a physician is an economic service. Together, goods and services are all the things of value that an **economy** produces and constitutes the **Gross Domestic Product** and **Gross National Product**.

ECONOMIC GROWTH

Economic growth occurs when a nation increases the amount of goods it produces. A country's economic growth is measured by the change in **real gross domestic product** from one year to the next. Economic growth theorists explain the factors concerned with long-term economic growth over periods of a decade or more. (See **economic development**.)

ECONOMIC POLICY

Policy is a principle, plan, or course of action in order to achieve something. Economic policy is the government's plan or course of action to achieve one or more economic goals for the country. There are generally five economic goals for the country: **full employment**, stability, **economic growth**, **efficiency**, and **equity**. To achieve these goals government uses four basic types of policy: fiscal, monetary, regulatory, and judicial.

Fiscal policy includes all government actions that are used to influence economic activity through increases or decreases in federal **tax** revenues and increases or decreases in **subsidies** and **transfer payments**.

Monetary policy is the **Federal Reserve System**'s use of the **money supply** to stabilize the **business cycle** and/or to implement an increase or decrease in the **interest rate**. Unlike fiscal policy, which requires an agreement between Congress and the president, monetary policy requires only the actions of the seven members of the Board of Governors of the Federal Reserve System.

Regulatory policy is based on the government's ability to pass laws and enact regulations. Judicial policy is based on enforcement of laws and regulations through the courts (especially the Supreme Court).

ECONOMIC PROFIT

Economic profit is the difference between total **business** revenue (**income**) and **total cost**—that is, the revenue received over and above what it costs to produce a good. Simply put, it is the profit made on a product that is produced.

ECONOMIC RENT

Economic rent is similar to **economic profit**. The difference is that economic profit is the amount of a business's revenue above cost for products, while economic rent is revenue above

DAVID RICARDO

David Ricardo was a British economist, born in London in 1772. For the last four years of his life Ricardo was a member of the British Parliament. He died in 1823.

As an economist, Ricardo's major work, *Principles of Political Economy and Taxation* (1817), explored several theories based on his studies of the long-range distribution of wealth. One of these theories about rent was based on relative land productivity. Ricardo felt increasing population would lead to a shortage of productive land. Fertile land naturally produces more food than unfertile land, and as a result, fertile land commands a higher rent. The poorest land utilized for agriculture receives no rent, since all of its earnings go to cover labor and capital costs.

The difference between the **output** from the least fertile land (which can still be farmed) and that of very fertile land determines the source of rent on the better land. As the population increases, poorer land must be farmed in order to meet the growing demand for crops. This makes the cost of rent for good land go up. As the population increases, making rents increase, profits decrease. Since there is then less profit for reinvestment and growth, rising rent prices indirectly prevent economic progress.

cost for a **resource** such as **capital** or land. For example, if a land owner rents his land for $500 a month, but his **mortgage** and upkeep costs are just $300 a month, he has made $200 in economic rent

The **supply** of economic rent; is fixed; changes in **demand** therefore determine the amount of rent for a given amount of land. The demand is determined by several factors, including the price of the product grown on the land, the **productivity** of the land, and the prices of other resources combined with the land for **production**.

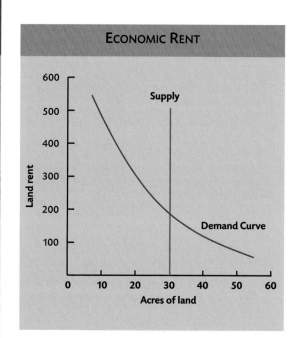

ECONOMIC RENT

Land rent: 600, 500, 400, 300, 200, 100

Supply

Demand Curve

Acres of land: 0, 10, 20, 30, 40, 50, 60

The graph above shows that the **demand curve** for land as a **factor of production** slopes downward, reflecting a fall in marginal productivity of land as more of it used.

ECONOMICS

Economics is a branch of social science that studies how wealth is produced, distributed, and consumed in a society. It also studies **labor**, finance, **taxation**, and other problems related to wealth. Economics is divided into two branches: **macroeconomics** and **microeconomics**.

ECONOMIC SYSTEM

Economic system is another name for an **economy**. An economy, or economic system, is the combined methods by which individuals or families, **businesses**, and governments make **production** and **consumption** decisions about how they will use limited **resources** to satisfy unlimited **wants** and needs.

Two of the most common economic systems in the world today are **capitalism** and **communism**. Each of these differs with regards to ownership and control of resources and production. With capitalism, ownership and control belong mainly to individuals, families, and businesses instead of the government. Private property rights is one of the most important aspects of capitalism. With communism, however, ownership and control belong mainly to the government. Individuals, families, and businesses have little or no private property rights.

ECONOMIC THEORY

A theory is a statement that attempts to explain basic principles and relationships that have been observed and verified to some degree. Economic theory attempts to explain basic economic principles and relationships at work in a nation's **economy**. Economic theory is constantly changing. At any given time, a variety of theories can be applied to a nation's economic situations. Each of these theories is designed to help economists understand how the economy works. Stable prices and full employment of resources provide a rising standard of living both for now and the future.

Classical theory, **Keynesian economics**, **neoclassical**, Marxian, and **neo-Keynesianism** are all examples of economic theories have been tested and continue to be debated by economists.

ECONOMIES OF SCALE

Economy of scale is the idea that when a business increases in size (scale), it can then produce goods more economically (at a lower cost). When the amount of goods produced is increased by increasing all the **factors of production** (**labor**, **capital**, land and entrepreneurship) then the cost of each item produced decreases. For example, a large firm might buy an expensive machine needed for **production**. If the firm makes a large quantity of goods, it may use the machine every day, so the cost of the machine per each item made is small. A smaller company would use this machine to make fewer items, so the cost of making each item would be more.

A large company is also more economical when it purchases raw materials on a large scale. Discounts are often given to those companies, which buy these raw materials in large quantities. A large-scale work force can also be more economical by having the work divided into specialized areas such as sales, accounting, assembly, etc. In a small company, one worker might have to do each of these jobs. In a large company, with a larger work force, a worker can specialize in assembly or sales, and be more efficient, thus lowering the costs.

Economist Alfred Marshall was the first to suggest that in the long run industries would experience lower costs and **prices** because of economies of scale resulting from increased **specialization**.

ALFRED MARSHALL

Alfred Marshall was a British economist, born in 1842 in Wandsworth, England. He is considered to be one of the most outstanding figures in the development of contemporary **economics**.

Marshall was educated at the University of Cambridge and later taught political economy there. His main contribution to economics was the development of the concept of **marginal utility** and his systematizing of classical economic theories. He stressed the importance of detailed analysis and adjustment of theory to emerging facts. His books include *Principles of Economics* (1890) and *Industry and Trade* (1919). In addition to his books, Marshall wrote many journal articles, public lectures, book reviews, and prefaces and chapters for books written by other authors. He always tried to express himself in the clearest, most simple language possible.

Marshall's most famous student was J. M. Keynes, who declared that Marshall was, " within his own field, the greatest in the world for a hundred years." Marshall died in 1924.

KEY POINT TODAY

Larger businesses tend to be able to produce goods and services more cheaply than smaller ones.

ECONOMY

An economy is the system a society uses to produce, distribute, and consume **economic goods and services.** The main job of any economy (no matter how simple or complex) is to produce useful goods and services from available **resources**, then distribute them to consumers. In order to operate effectively, all economies rely on **market** exchanges between buyers and sellers, and on government rules and regulations for these exchanges.

Capitalism is a form of economy that relies on markets, with minimal interference or control from the government. **Communism** and **socialism** are economies that rely heavily on government control. Examples of historical economies are feudalism and the barter system.

EFFICIENCY

Efficiency is one of five basic goals of any economy. Efficiency is obtained when the most possible satisfaction is derived from a given amount of **resources**. When the **price** buyers are willing and able to pay for a good is equal to the price sellers need to charge for that good, efficiency has been obtained. Efficiency is described as the maximum **output** for the least input.

ELASTICITY

Elasticity is the percentage of change in one variable in response to a percentage of change in another variable. **Price** and **demand** are two economic variables that affect each other. Price elasticity of demand (PED) measures the percentage of change in demand in response to a given change in price. For example, if the price of eggs goes up 20 percent and the demand for eggs goes down 30 percent, then the PED for eggs is -30 percent divided by 20 percent, or -1.5. The demand in this example is said to be price elastic. An example of price inelasticity would occur if the demand for eggs remained stable, even with a change in price of eggs.

EMERGING MARKET

The **World Bank** classifies economies with a **Gross National Product** (the total **output** of goods and services) per capita (per person) of $9,656 and above as high-income countries. An emerging market is a country whose **economic development** is in the group of nations below this income, but which is trying to use political and economic reform to become more economically advanced. Some of the reforms used might be turning over state-run **businesses** to private companies (**privatization**), removing obstacles to foreign investment such as excessive taxes, and the general public taking a bigger role in government (democratization).

Within the emerging market countries there is a wide range of economic development. These countries are not necessarily small or poor. Some examples of emerging markets are Argentina, Brazil, China, Chile, Egypt,

Hungary, Israel, Mexico, Nigeria, the Philippines, Poland, Russia, Thailand, and Vietnam. These countries and other emerging market countries get **loans** and other assistance from international groups such as the **World Bank** and the **International Monetary Fund**. They may also get aid from the wealthier nations like the United States. Sometimes the emerging **markets** band together in trading partnerships to increase their global competitiveness. The economic benefits to the emerging markets of better developed economies can be higher **income** levels, improved health and social services, and more stable government. The wealthier nations benefit by achieving a more stable worldwide **economy** and new markets for their products.

EMPLOYMENT RATE

The employment rate is the ratio of employed individuals to the total non-military adult population (16 years old and older) who are able to work. It is also called the employment-population ratio.

The employment rate does not affect nor is it changed by the **unemployment rate**, which goes up and down as people enter and exit the **labor** force. The labor force includes people who are working and those who are looking for work. When people who are looking for work get discouraged and decide to stop their search, the unemployment rate will decrease. However, when high school and college students begin to look for summer jobs, the unemployment rate goes up (as more people who are looking for jobs are without them), even though the employment rate does not change.

ENTITLEMENT PROGRAM

An entitlement program is a government program that provides personal financial benefits (or other government-provided goods and services) to individuals or organizations who are "entitled" to them because they meet eligibility requirements that are specified by law. Usually these recipients (or beneficiaries) are citizens or residents, but organizations such as business **corporations**, local governments, or even political parties sometimes have special entitlements under certain programs.

The most important federal entitlement programs in the United States are **Social Security**, Medicare and Medicaid, most Veterans'

A woman collecting her food stamps stands at a counter in the Social Services building.

Administration programs, federal employee and military retirement plants, unemployment compensation, food stamps, and agricultural **price** support programs. Since the middle 1980s, entitlement programs have accounted for more than half of all federal spending.

ENTREPRENEUR

The word *entrepreneur* is a French term which literally means "enterpriser" or "one who undertakes." In English the term has come to mean a person who is a risk taker and innovator who puts new ideas to practical use for the first time, turning inventions into new products, recognizing and using new qualities of old products, or using new processes of **production**. Simply put, an entrepreneur is a person who foresees a new opportunity to make substantial **profits** by creating new products or services and then takes the initiative in bringing together the necessary **factors of production** to make these products. Usually this is done by organizing a new business

Two young entrepreneurs operate a lemonade stand.

firm. In the 19th century the role of the entrepreneur was seen as the owner of a **business** or one who supplied all of the factors of production. Therefore, today the term entrepreneur is sometimes used incorrectly to mean any business owner or high-ranking manager, rather than a risk-taking innovator.

Because of the entrepreneur's essential role in initiating the process of production, entrepreneurship is identified by some economists as a "fourth factor of production," along with land, **labor** and **capital**.

EQUATION OF EXCHANGE

The equation of exchange is a mathematical formula used by economists to isolate the variables of **money**, velocity, **price**, and quantity of goods for separate study. This equation is not an **economic theory**, it is a mathematical truism. The equation of exchange divides the expenses of the country from the consumers on the one hand and producers on the other.

The equation of exchange is expressed like this (M = money) and (V= velocity of money): MV = P. MV is a measure of how much money consumers have and how fast they spend it. P equals the price, times the quantity of goods at that can be purchased at that price. (See **quantity theory of money.**)

EQUILIBRIUM

Equilibrium is a state or outcome when opposing forces are equal, so there is no tendency for change to occur. Some economists view equilibrium as a natural state that continues unless it is changed by outside forces. Other economists feel equilibrium is a goal that any **economy** pursues, though it might never be achieved.

These two views affect political policy. If equilibrium is a natural state, then government does not need to or should not interfere with economic factors. However, if equilibrium is a goal, then there is a definite need for government to intervene in order to obtain it. These

E

two views of equilibrium are a constant source of debate among economists.

In **economics**, equilibrium is often used to signify a situation in which supply equals demand, or no excess supply or demand. (See **disequilibrium.**)

EQUITY

Equity has two meanings in **economics**. The first defines equity as one of the economic goals of any nation. Equity as a goal involves the notion of fairness in **economic system**s. To be fair, or equitable, in an economic system is to be able to compete equally in a **market**. This would apply to companies competing in the selling of **economic goods or services** and to workers being able to find work that is emotionally and financially rewarding. The second meaning of equity is the value of something that is owned. For example, the **stock** in a company that shareholders own is equity in that company. Also, that part of a home **loan** that has been paid off is called the owner's equity in the house.

EUROPEAN COMMUNITY/EUROPEAN CENTRAL BANK/EURO

The European Union is currently a regional social and economic alliance of 15 European nations: Austria, Belgium, Denmark, Finland, France, Germany, Greece, Ireland, Italy, Luxembourg, the Netherlands, Portugal, Spain, Sweden, and the United Kingdom. The European Union is the result of cooperation that began in 1951 among six countries

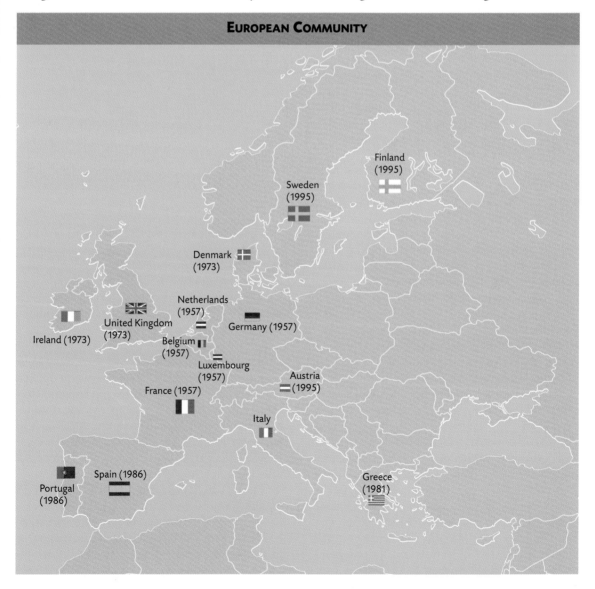

EUROPEAN COMMUNITY

Finland (1995)

Sweden (1995)

Denmark (1973)

Netherlands (1957)

Ireland (1973)

United Kingdom (1973)

Belgium (1957)

Germany (1957)

Luxembourg (1957)

Austria (1995)

France (1957)

Italy

Spain (1986)

Portugal (1986)

Greece (1981)

(Belgium, Germany, France, Italy, Luxembourg, and the Netherlands). The United Kingdom, Ireland, and Denmark joined the union in 1973, Greece in 1981, and Spain and Portugal in 1986. There is potential and probable **expansion** in the near future to eastern and southern European countries to join as well.

The European Union attempts to organize commerce and other activity among the European countries and their people in a way that is uniform, and strives to create a European identity as well as collective economic and social progress. To this end, the single European **market** was created in 1993 and a single **currency**, called the Euro, was introduced in 1999. Five institutions that were created with the European Union to facilitate its goals:

1) The European Parliament, elected by the people from each member nation.

2) The Council, which represents the governments of the member countries.

3) The Commission, which is the executive body of the European government and the part that can send legislation to the parliament.

4) The Court of Justice, which enforces compliance with the law.

5) The Court of Auditors, which keeps track of European Union governmental monetary receipts and expenses.

Other government bodies that have since been established are the Economic and Social Committee and the Committee of the Regions, the European Ombudsman, which deals primarily with citizens complaints; the European Investment Bank; and the European Central Bank, which is responsible for the **monetary policy** of the Euro.

The European Central Bank, along with the 11 member states' central banks, which have adopted the Euro, are the decision makers in regard to monetary policy concerning the Euro. It conducts foreign exchange, holds the **bank** reserves of member states, promotes smooth payment transactions between member states, and tries to maintain **price** stability and **economic development** within the European Union. Soon, some European currencies will be retired (or go out of existence) as the Euro takes over. The four member countries who have not adopted the Euro as of the year 2000, are Denmark, Greece, Sweden, and the United Kingdom.

EXCESS DEMAND

Excess demand is the same as a supply **shortage**. It means that the quantity demanded is greater than the quantity supplied at the existing **market** price. Excess demand is a condition of **disequilibrium** in a **competitive market**. When an excess demand exists, companies tend to raise **prices**. This increases the **supply**, decreases the **demand**, and diminishes the excess demand. This process continues until a price is achieved where supply equals demand and the excess demand is zero. This is called an **equilibrium**.

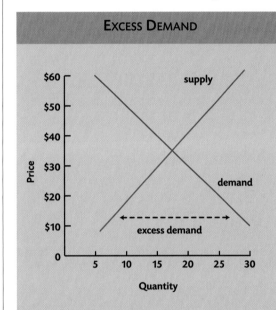

EXCESS SUPPLY

Excess supply means the same thing as a **surplus** of goods. It is a situation in which the quantity supplied is greater than the quantity demanded at the existing market **price**. Therefore, excess supply is a condition of **disequilibrium** in a **competitive market.** When an excess supply exists, companies will tend to lower prices. This increases the demand, decreases the supply, and diminishes the excess supply. This process continues until **supply** equals **demand**, or, an **equilibrium** is achieved.

EXCHANGE RATE

The exchange rate is the price of one nation's **currency** (**money**) in exchange for another nation's currency. That is, it is the amount of one currency that can be bought with another. When travelers go to a foreign country, they have to purchase the money in that country with the

E

EXCHANGE RATES DECEMBER 6, 2000		
Foreign Currencies	**To U.S. $**	**In U.S. $**
Australian Dollars	1.83554	0.54480
Belgian Francs	45.44317	0.02201
Brazilian Real	1.96700	1.43650
British Pounds	0.69614	0.65261
Canadian Dollars	1.53230	0.12082
Chinese Renminbi	8.27700	
European Monetary Union (Euro)	1.12651	0.88770
German Marks	2.20326	0.45387
Indian Rupees	46.78000	0.02138
Japanese Yen	110.42000	0.00906
Mexican New Pesos	9.40800	0.10629
Singapore Dollars	1.74300	0.57372
South African Rand	7.58200	0.13189
South Korean Won	1201.00	0.00083
Taiwan Dollars	33.05000	0.03026
Swiss Francs	1.70780	0.58555

money from their own country in order to buy things there. The amount of foreign money (currency) exchanged for their currency is the exchange rate. For example, if a person from the United States was traveling to Japan and wanted to have Japanese currency to spend there, he would trade American dollars for Japanese yen. The price of 100 Japanese yen might be one U.S. dollar. This would be the exchange rate of yen and American dollars.

The exchange rate is also called the foreign exchange rate. In addition to travelers, people who engage in foreign trade also have to exchange currencies as **imports** must be paid for with the currency of the country in which they are bought.

The table above shows some examples of exchange rates from around the world. It gives the exchange both in U.S. dollars and to the U.S. dollar.

EXCISE TAX

An excise tax is a **tax** on a specific good such as alcohol, tobacco, or gasoline. It is different from sales tax, which is a tax on all (or nearly all) goods sold. Excise taxes are used for one of two reasons: to discourage **consumption** of socially undesirable products such as alcohol or tobacco, for example (these are also called sin taxes), or to raise revenue from products people will continue to buy even though they are taxed (such as alcohol and tobacco).

It is important to note that excise taxes are placed on goods with inelastic demand and not on goods with elastic demand. That is because taxing inelastic goods is a better source of revenue for the government than taxing elastic goods. (See **elasticity.**)

EXCLUDABILITY

To exclude someone from something is to leave them out, shut them out, or prevent them from doing or having something. Excludability is the ability to exclude people from consuming certain goods or products if they do not pay for them. It is easy to exclude some people from using certain products. For example, if a person does not have the cash to pay for a new pair of shoes, then he is excluded from buying (and therefore using) a new pair of shoes. Other things, however, are more difficult to keep away from nonpayers. **Public goods** like oceans, fireworks displays, and air are difficult to keep from people who do not pay for them. Excludability helps distinguish between common-property goods, near-public goods, private goods, and public goods.

EXPANSION

Expansion is one of the phases of the **business cycle**. It is a general period of rising economic activity and the opposite of a **contraction**. The period of transition from expansion to contraction is called a peak. The period of transition from contraction to expansion is called a trough. Expansions tend to last an average of about three to four years, but this is uncertain. In the early 1980s a period of expansion lasted just one year. But the next expansion lasted over eight years, and the next has lasted more than ten years. Many economists call the early part of an expansion a **recovery**.

Many times expansions are indicated by an increase in **real gross domestic product** and a decline in the **unemployment rate**. The **inflation rate** also tends to rise, especially during the latter stages of an expansion phase.

EXPORT TABLE		
Countries	**Exports as a % of GDP**	**Imports as a % of GDP**
Belgium	70.0	64.9
The Netherlands	56.4	50.0
Canada	44.9	43.2
United Kingdom*	28.8	31.0
Italy	21.0	18.7
France	20.5	19.5
Germany*	14.0	12.1
United States	11.3	13.0
Japan**	9.9	7.6

*1997 data

**Estimate

Source: U.S. Department of Commerce, Commercial Country Guidelines

EXPECTATIONS

A major problem in **economics** is how to deal with the uncertainty about what the future holds. Expectations are basically anticipations of future events used in order to guide present economic situations. Therefore, much of **economic analysis** must incorporate expectations into various models as a given variable, usually with the assumption "other things being equal" (*ceteris paribus*).

Expectations have played a large role in **economic theory**, particularly in the work of **John Maynard Keynes**. Expectations are important in determining **business cycles.**

EXPORT PROMOTION

Export promotion is a popular strategy for promoting **economic development** and **economic growth** in national and global economies. The general philosophy of export promotion is that it is vital for stimulating and sustaining economic growth, with benefits reverberating throughout a country, helping to improve political and social health. Often export promotion has the potential to create a stronger **economy**, lower rates of **unemployment**, **globalization** instead of isolation, formation of strategic alliances, improved **balance of payments**, greater **exports**, and improved technology.

Governments around the world acknowledge the value of export-led development and have created agencies to promote their countries' products worldwide. (See **import substitution.**)

EXPORTS

Exports are the sale of **goods** or **services** to a foreign country. One country's **export** is another country's **import**, since an import is any good or service purchased from a foreign country. The difference between the amount of goods exported and the amount imported is the net exports.

EXTERNALITY

An externality is a cost or benefit that is not included in the price of a good or service. Air or water pollution are examples of negative externalities. If a factory causes air pollution, the cost of cleaning it up is not paid for by the factory but by society itself. Therefore, the **market price** the consumer pays for the goods produced by this factory does not include the cost of pollution. An example of an externality that is considered a benefit would be education, because society as a whole benefits when people are more educated, yet students pay for their education, not society.

The result of both externality costs and externality benefits is market inefficiency. Goods or services with externality costs will tend to be overproduced. Goods or services with externality benefits will be underproduced. (See **market failures.**)

F

FACTORS OF PRODUCTION

There are four basic factors of production—**labor**, **capital**, land, and entrepreneurship. Factors of production are simply the necessary elements used to produce **economic goods and services**. (See **resources**.)

FEDERAL DEPOSIT INSURANCE CORPORATION (FDIC)

The Federal Deposit Insurance Corporation (FDIC) is a program that was established by Congress in 1933 (the worst year of the **Great Depression**) to insure the deposits of failed **banks.** Just like an insurance company, the FDIC collects insurance premiums from its customers (the banks). In return, the FDIC assures the banks that it will be ready to pay off any deposits that the banks cannot. However, there are limits to the amounts the FDIC will pay back. Since the 1980s, that limit has been $100,000 per account. That means, a customer at a bank can have up to $100,000 in his account and it will be paid back by the FDIC, even if the bank fails. Since the FDIC guarantees bank deposits, it also has the authority to make inspections and see that banks are being properly managed.

FEDERAL FUNDS RATE

The Federal Funds Rate is the **interest rate** banks charge each other when loaning bank reserves through the federal funds **market**. Since this interest rate helps to determine banks' minimum cost of getting funds, it is a key interest rate in the **economy**. When the federal funds rate is high, **banks** usually raise the interest rates they charge for home **mortgages**, car **loans**, etc., as well as the **prime rate.**

FEDERAL RESERVE/FEDERAL OPEN MARKET COMMITTEE (FOMC)

The Federal Reserve Open Market Committee (FOMC) is made up of the seven members of the Board of Governors of the **Federal Reserve System**, the president of the Federal Reserve Bank of New York, and four memberships from a rotating selection of the presidents of the 11 other Reserve Banks. The four memberships each carry a one-year term. The FOMC is the federal government's most powerful **monetary policy**-making group. The FOMC has eight

A close-up of a U.S. five dollar bill. This bill comes from the 12th Federal Reserve District of San Francisco.

meetings per year where it discusses current and near-term economic and financial conditions, before it makes the decision whether to raise or lower short-term **interest rates** or to keep them the same.

FEDERAL RESERVE NOTES

Federal reserve notes are the paper **currency** (**money**) issued by the 12 Federal Reserve District Banks in the United States. These notes are issued in denominations of $1, $5, $10, $20, $50, and $100. Each of the 12 Federal District Banks supplies notes within its district, and each district **bank** has its own personal number and stamp (to the left of the portrait) that it puts on the notes it issues. For example, the number for the Boston District Bank is #1, while the number for the San Francisco District Bank is #12.

FEDERAL RESERVE SYSTEM

The Federal Reserve System is the organization that controls the United States **money supply** and conducts **monetary policy**. The Federal Reserve System was created by an act of Congress in 1913, during the presidency of Woodrow Wilson. Until 1980, only federally charted or state chartered banks that chose to join the system were part of the Federal Reserve. In 1980, due to many bank failures and fewer banks joining the system, a law was passed to make all banks subject to Federal Reserve regulations.

The Federal Reserve System is made up of 12 federal districts, each with a Federal Reserve **bank**. Each Federal Reserve bank is owned by the many member banks of that district. A bank becomes a member by purchasing **stock** in the district bank.

KEY POINT TODAY

The overriding goal of the monetary policy pursued by the Federal Reserve Board is for the **economy** to grow at a rate that is neither too slow nor too fast. Too-slow growth could lead to **recession;** too-rapid growth could cause **inflation**.

ALAN GREENSPAN

Alan Greenspan, the current Chairman of the Board of Governors of the Federal Reserve System, was born on March 6, 1926, in New York City. He attended New York University, where he received a bachelor of science degree in **economics** (summa cum laude) in 1948, a master's in economics in 1950, and a Ph.D. in economics in 1977. He has also received honorary degrees from Harvard, Yale, Pennsylvania, Leuven (Belgium), Notre Dame, Wake Forest, and Colgate universities.

From 1974 to 1977, Dr. Greenspan served as Chairman of the President's **Council of Economic Advisors** under President Gerald Ford. From 1981 to 1983, he was Chairman of the National Commission on Social Security Reform.

In 2000, Dr. Greenspan began his fourth four-year term as Chairman of the Board of Governors of the Federal Reserve System. He is also Chairman of the Federal Open Market Committee (FOMC)

12 FEDERAL RESERVE ECONOMIC DISTRICTS

Cleveland
Boston
Minneapolis
New York
9
Philadelphia
San Francisco
Chicago
2
Board of Governors
12
7
3
Richmond
Kansas City
4
St. Louis
10
1
Dallas
8
5
11
6
Atlanta

Alaska and Hawaii are part of the San Francisco District

The Federal Reserve System (popularly referred to as the "Fed") is run by its seven-member board of governors, who are nominated by the president of the United States and confirmed by the senate. The board of governors elects a chairman. Currently, this chairman is Alan Greenspan.

The Federal Reserve affects monetary policy through the **Federal Reserve Open Market Committee (FOMC)**. When the Federal Reserve buys government securities, more money is available in the member banks, so interest rates are pushed down. When they sell the securities, less money is available, and **interest rates** go up, slowing down the **economy**. Other ways that the Federal Reserve System affects the money supply is through setting the **discount rate** and determining the required reserve ratio.

FERTILITY RATES

Fertility means the reproduction capability of an individual, couple, group, or population. The fertility rate is the average number of children that would be born alive to a woman (or group of women) during her lifetime if she were to pass through her childbearing years meeting the age-specific fertility rates of a given year.

FIAT MONEY

Fiat money is **currency** that has no purpose other than the exchange of **economic goods and services**. It is the opposite of **commodity money,** which has a purpose in itself. Most **money** today is fiat money, including coins, paper money, and checks.

FINAL PRODUCTS/GOODS

Sometimes goods are purchased to make other goods, but final products are goods that are not purchased to make other goods. Rather, they are the final product the purchaser (consumer) will use. A car, a loaf of bread, a television set, and a computer are all final goods.

FINANCIAL INTERMEDIARIES

An intermediary is an agency or person who acts as a mediator, or go-between, between two people or organizations. A financial mediator is an agent connecting buyers and sellers of financial goods such as **stocks**, **bonds,** and **insurance**. **Banks** are very important financial intermediaries in the **economy**. Other intermediaries include financial planners, insurance companies, stockbrokers, and **mutual funds**.

FINE-TUNING

Fine-tuning is short-term government intervention through the use of fiscal or **monetary policy** designed to achieve the economic goal of stability and promote long-term **economic growth**.

A row of television sets are displayed on a store shelf. They are final goods for consumers.

FISCAL POLICY

Fiscal policy is a government action that affects spending and taxation in order to stabilize the **business cycle** or otherwise impact the **macroeconomy**. Although the government's fiscal **budget** is prepared every year and itemizes all expenses and **tax** revenue, fiscal policy is usually separate from this budgeting process. It typically involves special legislation to enact a change in taxes or spending. For example, if the **economy** is in a **recession**, the appropriate fiscal policy may be to increase spending through **transfer payments** and **subsidies**, or to reduce taxes (this is called expansionary policy). But during periods of high **inflation**, the appropriate fiscal policy may be contractionary policy (which is opposite from expansionary policy).

There are some inherent problems with fiscal policy. Mainly, fiscal policy may end up doing the wrong thing during the wrong time because it takes so long to get a bill through Congress. Other times, the measures taken in spending and taxing may either be excessive or fall short.

Fiscal policy can be contrasted with **monetary policy,** which is conducted by the Federal Reserve Board of Governors and **Federal Open Market Committee**.

FISCAL YEAR

A government's or **business's** accounting year is called a fiscal year. The fiscal year for the U.S. government begins on October 1st and ends September 30th of the following year. Different countries have different fiscal years that do not correlate with the normal calendar year.

FIXED ASSETS

Assets that are used for the long run rather than for resale, such as machinery and buildings, are fixed assets. Certain fixed assets, such as property, tend to **appreciate** in value over time.

FIXED COST

Fixed cost is any cost that does not change with changes in the quantity of products manufactured. For example, if a factory owner has a **mortgage** cost of $1,000 each month for the factory building, that cost remains the same each month, no matter how much product the factory manufactures or sells. Overhead costs, administrative salaries, **loan** repayment expenses, and some marketing costs are other examples of fixed costs.

FIXED EXCHANGE RATE

An **exchange rate** is the price of one nation's **currency** in exchange for another nation's currency—that is, the amount of one currency that can be bought with another. Sometimes governments create fixed exchange rates for their currency. They set a given rate of exchange and maintain this rate through government actions.

If a government wishes to fix the exchange rate for its currency, it must buy and sell its currency in the **foreign exchange market** in whatever amounts are necessary to maintain the fixed rate. For example, if a government sells its currency on the foreign exchange market, this will decrease the value of its currency. If it buys its own currency on the foreign exchange market, this will increase the value of the currency.

The graph below shows the exchange rate between the British pound and the U.S. dollar between 1949 and 1967. The British pound is fixed at $2.80 per pound. In order to maintain this fixed rate, Britain had to buy dollars and sell pounds when the British pound rose and fell.

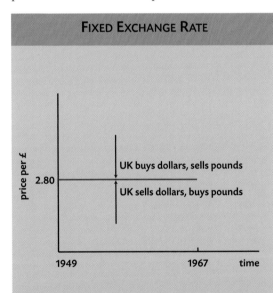

FIXED EXCHANGE RATE

price per £

2.80 — UK buys dollars, sells pounds

UK sells dollars, buys pounds

1949   1967   time

FLAT TAX

A flat tax is a system of **taxation** in which all levels of **income** are taxed at the same rate. This system can be compared with, or contrasted to, **progressive tax** or **regressive tax**.

FLEXIBLE EXCHANGE RATE SYSTEM

Exchange rate is the price of one nation's **currency** (**money**) in exchange for another nation's currency, that is, the amount of one currency that

F

can be bought with another. In a flexible exchange rate system, the rate of exchange is determined by the market forces of **supply** and **demand** and not by government action, as with fixed exchange rates. This system is also called the floating exchange rate system.

FLOATING DEBT

A floating debt is a short-term fixed-interest **debt**. A **treasury bill** nearing maturity is considered a government floating debt; a company's floating debt is a short-term **bank loan**.

FLOOR BROKER

A floor broker is a member of a **stock** or **commodity** exchange who can make orders for other brokers on the floor of the exchange.

FOREIGN EXCHANGE MARKET

A foreign exchange market is a **market** where the **currency** of one nation is traded for the currency of another nation and the **exchange rates** between currencies are determined. The foreign exchange market is not actually located in any one place. Transactions on the foreign exchange market take place all around the world, usually at **banks** and other financial institutions.

FOREIGN TRADE

Foreign trade refers to the exchange or trade of **economic goods and services** between countries (as opposed to trade within a single country). **Production**, exchange, and **consumption** are all fundamental parts of life in all countries. Foreign trade involves producers and consumers who live in separate countries.

Transportation is a big factor in foreign trade. As the cost of transportation has declined over the past few decades, foreign trade has increased dramatically, leading to a more global economy. Other factors affecting globalization and the increased amount of trade include the level of **tariffs** and **quotas** which inhibit the flow of goods across borders. (See **North American Free Trade Agreement.**; **exports**; **imports**.)

401(K) PLAN

A 401(k) is a type of retirement plan that allows

Venezuelan vice minister of foreign affairs Jorge Salero (left) and Indonesian foreign minister Alwi Shihab (right) sign a Memorandum of Understanding to create economic and trade relation in August 2000..

employees to save and invest for their retirement. Through a 401(k), an employee can authorize an employer to deduct a certain amount of money from his or her paycheck before taxes are calculated and invest it in a 401(k) plan. Money is invested in **investment** options chosen by the employee. The federal government established the 401(k) in 1981 with special tax advantages to encourage people to prepare for retirement.

> ### KEY POINT TODAY
> 401(k) plans often allow an employer to contribute to an employee's retirement account. Matching contributions encourage higher employee participation in these plans. 401(k) plans are also referred to as "employer match" or "matching dollars" plans.

FRANCHISE

A franchise is a contractual agreement, written or oral, by which a person or company permits the distribution of goods or services under his or her trademark, service mark, or trade name. During the course of the agreement, the franchisor (grantor) retains control over the franchisee and often gives the franchisee significant help.

Chain restaurants Kentucky Fried Chicken and McDonald's are examples of franchises. Individual franchises usually have to put up a large amount of **capital**, but in return the franchisee provides training, specialized equipment necessary for the **business**, advertising, marketing, and technical assistance.

FREE MARKET ECONOMY

A free market **economy** is a **competitive market** without government control or regulations like **price floors, price ceilings**, or taxes. In a free market economy the forces of supply and **demand** do away with any shortages and surpluses, so the market reaches **equilibrium** in price and quantity. Though no examples of a pure free market exist in the world today, countries that rely relatively little on government intervention in the marketplace are considered relatively free market economies.

FREE RIDER

When a person uses a good, often a **public good**, without paying for it, that is called a free ride. A free rider is the person who gets the free ride. Many public goods like the seashore in certain areas of the country, fireworks displays, and mountain views allow the public a "free ride," meaning individuals do not have to pay for these things in order to enjoy them. The government sometimes forces free-riders to pay for public goods through taxes, however.

FREE TRADE

Free trade occurs when there are no trade barriers or restrictions on **foreign trade**. Unrestricted free trade is usually beneficial to the country that is trading its goods (see **comparative advantage**) because it has a market for its products. Consumers benefit, too. They enjoy a greater selection of products and lower prices. However, producers in the country trading its goods usually receive lower prices and more **competition**. Completely unrestricted free trade is rarely seen anywhere. **Tariffs**, non-tariff barriers, and **quotas** restrict free trade to some degree everywhere.

FREE TRADE ZONES

A free trade zone is a geographic area established to promote industrial **production** of **economic goods and services,** first for exports and second for serving the domestic market. Free trade zones typically offer a number of **tax** incentives, foreign exchange benefits, and other incentives to producers. (See **European Community; North American Free Trade Agreement.**)

FRICTIONAL UNEMPLOYMENT

There are four sources (or types) of unemployment: cyclical, seasonal, structural, and frictional unemployment. Frictional unemployment occurs when **businesses** (employers) are looking for workers and workers are looking for work, and there is a time lag from one job to another, but the two don't find each other. This type of unemployment sometimes occurs when workers live far away from the businesses that are looking for workers, or there is limited information and workers don't even know about these jobs. Frictional unemployment also occurs when someone leaves a job to find another but has not yet found employment, or when a graduate or other individual enters the **labor force** for the first time and has not yet found a job.

FULL EMPLOYMENT

Full employment is one of the economic goals of any nation. In reality, 100-percent employment can never be achieved, because there will always be some unemployment due to job turnover, people looking for new jobs, and job losses due to trades that are declining and disappearing while new trades spring up to replace them. Full employment, therefore, does not mean that every person over the age of 16 in an **economy** is employed, but it does mean that full utilization of available **labor** and **resources** in the economy are at work to produce the limits of the potential **gross national product**.

Because there can never be 100-percent employment, most governments define their full employment goal as some targeted level of **unemployment**, such as 5 percent or less. This is because frictional and **structural unemploy-** ment exist even in a well-functioning economy. However, at full employment, there is not **cyclical unemployment**.

FUTURES MARKET

Futures are agreements to complete the sale of something at a set price at a set future date. For example, a farmer may want to insure that he'll get a certain price for his corn a year from now, so he'll make a futures contract for an amount of corn at a certain price to be sold at a set date. If the price of corn drops, the farmer has successfully avoided the lower price and still gets the price he set in the futures contract. If the price goes up, he has lost that **profit** but hopefully charged enough to make some profit. People who buy futures contracts bet that the price will go up in the future, so the corn they bought at the low price can be resold at a future higher price.

A Standard & Poor's futures trader signals a trade on the floor at the Chicago Mercantile Exchange.

G–H

GAME THEORY

The main points of game theory were developed in a book by John Von Neumann and Oskar Morgenstern called *The Theory of Games and Economic Behavior* (1947). Game theory is the mathematical theory of interactive behavior. It is concerned with actions and consequences that affect more than one person, with how groups of people or things interact strategically, and how the consequences of actions affect others. Game theorists make use of theoretical concepts and mathematical ideas to create hypothetical situations in order to analyze how the different "players" in a game interact. They attempt to formulate mathematical rules for this interaction that might predict the outcomes of interaction or decision making in everything from evolutionary biology to economic decisions by government.

GDP DEFLATOR

The GDP deflator is a **price index** based on **real gross domestic product**, that is used as an indicator of average prices in the **economy**. It is issued quarterly by the U.S. Department of Commerce, Bureau of Economic Analysis (BEA). The GDP deflator is nominal gross domestic product (GDP) divided by real (constant dollar) GDP X 100. Nominal GDP is the value of **output,** measured by prices prevailing in a specific accounting period. Real GDP is that output measured by prices prevailing in some base period. The value of the GDP deflator in the base period is always 100. When the GDP deflator increases over the course of a year, this means that the price level has risen, i.e. that **inflation** has occurred. Changes in another index, the **consumer price index (CPI),** is another way to measure inflation.

GENDER DEVELOPMENT

Women's economic contribution to families and nations is huge but often underestimated. Gender development focuses on the role of women in a society because women are crucial for every aspect of development, from quality of life to **economic growth** and **sustainability**. In countries where women enjoy equal rights, their children are healthier and better educated. **Fertility rates** are slower, and economic growth is usually faster. But where women are oppressed and undervalued, they suffer, their children suffer, economic growth is slower, and fertility rates are higher.

In 1995 the United Nations Development Program (UNDP) began to develop measures of gender development called the gender development index. The index takes the ratio of male to female average per capita **income**, literacy rates, and longevity (life expectancy) and compares them for all the countries in the world. The UNDP also measures a **human development** index.

Women learn to read in a literacy program sponsored by the United Nations.

GENERAL AGREEMENT ON TARIFFS AND TRADE (GATT)

The General Agreement on Tariffs and Trade, or GATT, is a treaty that was signed in 1947. The United States and 22 other countries agreed to reduce trade barriers. More than 100 countries have now signed this international treaty. Member countries have conducted negotiations through the years to further reduce trade barriers such as **tariffs** and **quotas on import.** This treaty has been very effective in lowering these trade barriers. A total of eight rounds of negotiations were conducted between 1947 and 1994.

GATT is now known as the **World Trade Organization (WTO).** The WTO was created during the 1994 Uruguay Round of Negotiations. It took effect January 1st, 1995. The biggest change resulting in the transition from GATT to the WTO is that countries that ratify (or sign) an agreement sponsored by the WTO are obligated to follow the terms of trade.

GINI COEFFICIENT

The Gini coefficient is a number used to measure **income** or wealth inequality. It shows how equal, or unequal, income and wealth are distributed among the population or across nations. The larger the coefficient, the higher the degree of difference in income or wealth.

According to the Gini coefficient, the distribution of income is considered to be relatively even if its value falls between 0.2 and 0.35 percent. Generally, more highly developed countries tend to have a lower differentiation of income (0.28 to 0.4). A high differentiation of income is characteristic of developing countries, where the Gini coefficient usually falls between 0.44 to 0.60 percent.

> **KEY POINT TODAY**
> Wealth is measured by the net **assets** an individual or household owns. It includes both financial and physical assets. In industrialized, capitalist countries wealth is not evenly distributed among its population.

GLOBALIZATION

Globalization is the move toward a globalized economy with increased integration flows of goods, investments, and labor among countries.

The primary economic framework of globalization is no longer tied to the concept of national boundaries. The core aspect of economic globalization refers to the observation that in recent years a quickly rising share of economic activity in the world seems to be taking place among people who live in different countries. The **World Bank**, **World Trade Organization**, and the **International Monetary Fund** have all played a large role in the world's increasing globalization.

GOLD STANDARD

Gold standard means a country uses gold as the standard for valuing its nation's **currency.** Usually, this means gold is used to back up paper **money** in circulation, which involves the use of a gold certificate. The number of certificates in circulation is in proportion to the amount of gold stored someplace (such as Fort Knox). The United States had this sort of gold standard in the late 1800s and early 1900s.

A gold standard can also use gold as the money in circulation. This was common in the United States West in the 1800s. Another way to have a gold standard is to use gold to fix the exchange price of paper currency in circulation. In 1934 the United States, France, and Britain fixed the price of gold at $35 per fine ounce as part of a monetary pact. This means that the price of gold was fixed in terms of dollars. In 1947 the **International Monetary Fund** officially adopted the fixed price set by the United States, France, and Britain. Until the early 1970s the fixed the price of gold remained at $35 an ounce.

The gold standard was abandoned by the United States and other countries in 1971, in favor of a floating **exchange rate system** where exchange rates are determined by fundamental economic conditions.

GOODS AND SERVICES

(See **economic goods and services.**)

GREAT DEPRESSION

The Great Depression was the period from 1929 to 1941, when the **economy** experienced high **unemployment**, low **production**, and limited **investment**. This period changed the way government viewed its role in **economic policy.** Economists still study and debate the causes and effects the **depression** had on the economy.

From 1929 to 1933, production of the nation's economy fell by half. Real **disposable income**

UNEMPLOYMENT IN THE GREAT DEPRESSION

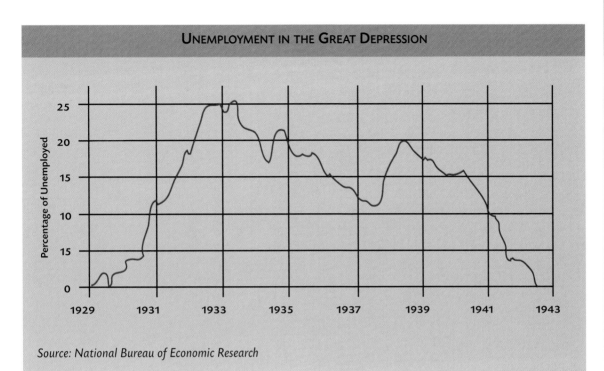

Source: National Bureau of Economic Research

dropped 28 percent. Stock prices fell to one-tenth of their value before 1929. The number of unemployed Americans went from the 1929 figure of 1.6 million to 12.8 million in only four years.

Many people say the Great Depression was caused by the **stock market** crash of 1929. However, that was only partly to blame. Although many people were prosperous throughout the 1920s, only a small percentage of the population was receiving the economic benefits of that prosperity. Wheat farmers, ship builders, and coal miners were among many whose **industries** were not thriving. The entire banking system was also vulnerable at the time due to minimal government regulation and excessive borrowing. When the stock market crashed, all of these economic weaknesses culminated to create a snowball effect of high unemployment and low production, thus creating the Great Depression.

KEY POINT TODAY

During the worst part of the Great Depression, an astonishing 25 percent of U.S. workers were unemployed.

GROSS DOMESTIC PRODUCT (GDP)

The gross domestic product (GDP) is the total market value of all new **economic goods and services** produced within the political boundaries of a country during a given period of time (usually one year). GDP is the United States government's official measure of how much **output** the U.S. **economy** produces. GDP is reported every three months by the Bureau of Economic Analysis, which is part of the U.S. Department of Commerce. Since the 1990s, GDP has largely replaced another measure of output—**gross national product (GNP)**.

GROSS DOMESTIC PRODUCT

	1995	1996
Gross domestic product	7,400.5	7,813.2
Total goods	2,798.1	2,951.3
Durable goods	1,239.8	1,331.9
Nondurable goods ·	1,525.3	1,589.4
Services	3,985.1	4,191.0
Structures	617.3	670.9

Source: U.S. Department of Commerce, Bureau of Economic Analysis

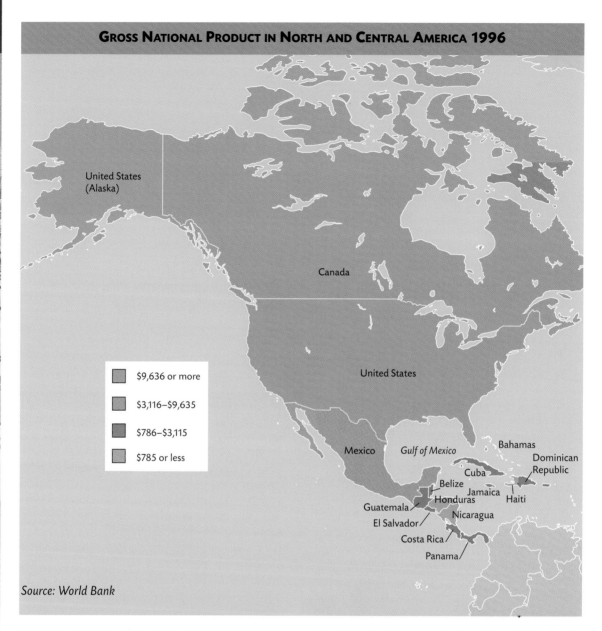

GROSS NATIONAL PRODUCT IN NORTH AND CENTRAL AMERICA 1996

United States (Alaska)

Canada

United States

$9,636 or more

$3,116–$9,635

$786–$3,115

$785 or less

Mexico

Gulf of Mexico

Bahamas

Dominican Republic

Cuba

Belize

Jamaica

Honduras

Haiti

Guatemala

Nicaragua

El Salvador

Costa Rica

Panama

Source: World Bank

GROSS NATIONAL PRODUCT (GNP)

The gross national product (GNP) is the total **market** value of all **economic goods and services** produced by a country during a given period of time (usually one year). GNP was once the federal government's official measure of how much **output** the United States **economy** produced. However, in the early 1990s, GNP was replaced by the gross domestic product (GDP). The two measures are the same except that GNP measures the value of output produced using resources owned by the citizens of a country, no matter where the production occurs. On the other hand, GDP measures all output produced within the political borders of a country.

HARD CURRENCY

Hard currency is a **currency** in which investors have confidence and are willing to accept in exchange for other currency. Countries that are economically and politically sound tend to have hard currency. Hard currency can be compared with soft currency, which investors do not have confidence in and therefore is not acceptable in exchange for currency of other countries.

HERFINDAHL-HIRSHMAN INDEX

The Herfindahl index is named after Orris C. Herfindahl, one of the first economists to use it to analyze **industry** concentration. However, another economist, Albert O. Hirschman, used this index earlier, so it is often called the Herfindahl-Hirschman Index (or HHI). This index is a mathematical standard that shows to what degree an industry is an **oligopoly**, as well as the relative concentration of **market** power held by the largest firms in that industry. This index is a better indication of the market control of the largest firms than the four-firm and eight-firm **concentration ratios.**

The HHI ranges from a low of 0, which indicates perfect **competition**, to a high of 10,000, which indicates a complete **monopoly**. Generally, concentration ratios between 80 percent and 100 percent have HHIs between 1,800 and 10,000. These are high-concentration industries, and the top firms have a great deal of market control. Industries with concentration ratios between 50 percent and 80 percent have HHIs between 1,000 and 1,800. These are medium-concentration industries. Industries with concentration ratios less than 50 percent have HHIs less than 1,000 and are low-concentration industries.

The formula for calculating the HHI is:

$$\text{HHI} = (\text{Share 1})(\text{Share 1}) + (\text{Share 2})(\text{Share 2}) + (\text{Share 3})(\text{Share 3}) + (\text{Share n})(\text{Share n}).$$

HIDDEN TAX

A hidden tax is a type of **indirect tax** that is a part of the price of a good or service, but the consumer is not aware of its existence. For example, the **excise tax** included in the cost of beer and cigarettes is normally unknown to the consumer. A **value-added tax**, on the other hand, is incorporated into the product at a specified known rate.

HISTORIC COST

The historic cost is the original cost of an **asset,** such as a piece of machinery in a factory. When the item is entered into the balance sheet for accounting reasons, it is listed at its original, or historic, cost. However, when working with a balance sheet, an allowance must be made for the replacement cost of the machinery, which may be much higher due to **inflation**.

HOUSEHOLD

In **economics**, a household includes a group of people whose economic choices (i.e., savings, purchases, etc.) are interrelated. Households play two important roles in an **economic system**. First, they function as buyers or consumers of **economic goods and services** in the marketplace. Second, they provide the **labor**, and at times the land and **capital**, to companies that produce goods and services. Labor done within the household is "unwaged"—that is, not counted in the **GDP**. The term *households* is generally used in **macroeconomics**, while "consumers" is used in **microeconomics**. (See **circular flow diagram; business.**)

HUMAN CAPITAL

Human capital is a person's education, training, knowledge, and experience, which make him or her more productive. There are many ways to increase human capital—by going to school and obtaining college degrees, taking training classes, getting on-the-job training, and even maintaining good health through good nutrition, exercise, and access to health care. Investment in human capital leads to future **economic growth**.

HUMAN DEVELOPMENT

Human development is a process of expanding people's choices. At all levels of development the three essential possibilities for human development are for people to lead long and healthy lives, to be knowledgeable, and to have access to the resources needed for a decent standard of living. If these three basics are not achieved, many choices are simply not available and opportunities remain inaccessible. Income is certainly one of the main means of expanding choices and well-being, but it is not the only important aspect of people's lives. (See **gender development.**)

HYPERINFLATION

Hyperinflation is an exceptionally high **inflation rate**. An inflation rate of 50 percent or greater per month would probably be considered hyperinflation. Unlike creeping inflation, which tends to have little negative effect on an **economy**, hyperinflation can cause people to panic and lose faith in the value of money. Often an economy will revert to a **barter** system; there is a serious concern for economic collapse at this point.

I–K

IMPERIALISM

Imperialism is the policy, practice, or advocacy of extending power and domination over a country through direct territorial acquisition or by gaining political and economic control. From the 15th through the 18th centuries, France, England, Spain, Portugal, and the Netherlands built imperialist empires in the Americas, India, West Indes, and Africa, primarily for **economic profit.**

The Age of Imperialism, which lasted from 1879 to 1914, marked the highest point in the scramble for control of Africa. European countries competed to make their informal colonies more formalized. Historically, economists have argued about the costs and benefits of imperialism to the countries that were under power. (See **colonialism.**)

IMPORT DUTY

An import duty is a tax imposed on a good that is being imported into a country. Import duties are **income**-producing taxes, and can be a barrier to trade. The import duty is paid by the buyer.

IMPORTS

Imports are goods and **capital** purchased from other countries. For example, when the United States buys bananas, coffee, cars, or computers from other countries, these are imports. Imports are the opposite of **exports**, which are **economic goods and services** sold to other countries.

IMPORT SUBSTITUTION

Import substitution is the process of substituting imported goods with goods produced locally by manufacturers. Import substitution is usually

The latest passenger car imports are on display at the Auto China 2000 exhibition in Beijing, June 2000.

accompanied by high **tariffs** on imported goods. It became a popular development strategy used by less developed countries in the 1960s, but it was more or less replaced by **export promotion** in the 1970s and 1980s.

INCENTIVE

An incentive is a cost or benefit that motivates consumers, **businesses**, or other participants in the **economy** to make a decision or take some action. **Prices** are one major incentive in the study of **economics**. When prices are high, buyers have the incentive to buy less, while sellers have the incentive to sell more. Sometimes the government creates incentives in order to achieve some desired result in the economy. For example, since the cost of **interest** on home **mortgages** is deductible from taxes, this increases the incentive to buy a home.

KEY POINT TODAY

An incentive plan is a system of rewarding an individual or group for increased effort or **production**. These reward systems include bonuses for reaching a set level of production. **Businesses** often provide incentive plans to their employees to bring about a desired behavior, and governments also provide incentives to businesses.

INCIDENCE OF TAXATION

In economic terms, the individual whose real income is reduced by a **tax** is the one who bears the burden of **taxation**. Incidence of taxation is the study of who bears the burden of a tax. This can be different from observing who pays tax to the government. For example, if a **business** must pay a tax but is able to increase the **price** of a good by the amount of the tax, the burden of the tax falls on the consumer in the form of higher prices. If the price cannot be increased, the burden is borne by the business in the form of lower net **profits.**

INCOME

Income is **money** earned or received by individuals or **households** that can be used for **consumption** or saving.

KEY POINT TODAY

Earned income refers to all the income individuals receive from working (both taxable and non-taxable). Taxable earned income includes: wages, salaries, and tips, or earnings from self-employment; union strike benefits; and long-term disability benefits received prior to retirement.

INCOME EFFECT

The income effect explains the way consumers have more or less purchasing power with the same amount of **money** depending on whether **prices** for **economic goods and services** go up or down. The term *income effect* is often used when discussing **wages**. For instance, usually a consumer has a set amount of money and plans his purchases according to that amount. Say a hot dog usually costs $1 at an amusement park. If the hot dogs go on sale and are suddenly priced at 50 cents, a consumer will probably buy more hot dogs at the lower price, rather than pocket the 50 cents savings he would have spent if he had bought a hot dog for a dollar. If prices go up, however, the consumer is likely to spend less because he has less purchasing power.

INCOME ELASTICITY OF DEMAND

In **economics**, **elasticity** occurs when one variable of an **economy** changes and causes another variable to change in response. Elasticity is measured in the percentage of change. **Price** and demand are two economic variables that directly affect each other. **Income** elasticity of demand is a change in demand due to a change in income. It is measured as the percentage change in **demand** due to a percentage change in buyer's income. Use this formula to calculate the income elasticity of demand:

$$\text{Income Elasticity of Demand} = \frac{\text{Percentage Change in Demand}}{\text{Percentage Change in Income}}$$

For a **normal good** this is positive. For an **inferior good** it is negative.

I

INCOME TAX

Income tax is a **tax** imposed by the government on the income (wages, rent, and **dividends**) received by **households**. Income tax is usually paid on a progressive scale; in other words, the higher an individual's income the higher percentage of tax he or she will pay. Changes in income tax rates can be used as part of **fiscal policy** to regulate **aggregate demand**.

Income tax increases tend to reduce **disposable income** for **consumption**, while income tax decreases act to increase **disposable income**.

INCREASING OPPORTUNITY COSTS (LAW OF)

The law of increasing opportunity costs states that the cost of producing a good increases as more of that good is produced. This is because the best suited (least expensive and/or most productive) **resources** for making the good are used first, so in later **production** the more expensive or less suited resources must be used.

INDICATORS (LEADING, COINCIDENT, AND LAGGING)

In **economics**, indicators provide information that can be used to assess or predict movements in **stock** prices or general economic conditions. There are three important indicators—leading indicators, coincident indicators, and lagging indicators.

Leading indicators, such as the Index of Leading Economic Indicators, consist of economic statistics that tend to move up or down a few months before the **expansions** and **contraction**s of the **business cycle**. Leading indicators include manufacturers' new orders, an index of vendor performance, orders for plant and equipment, **Standard & Poor's 500** index of stock **prices**, new building permits, durable goods, manufacturers' unfilled orders, the **money supply**, changes in materials prices, average workweek of production workers in manufacturing, changes in **business** and consumer **credit**, a consumer confidence index, and initial claims for **unemployment** insurance. They show what the overall economy is likely to do (as far as economic flucuations) in the next 3 to 12 months. If leading indicators rise today, then the rest of the economy is most likely to rise in the coming year. But, if leading indicators decline today, then the economy is most likely to decline within the next 3 to 12 months.

Coincident economic indicators are economic statistics that tend to move up and down during the expansions and contractions of the business cycle. These indicators move with the overall **economy**. When a contraction starts, coincident indicators decline. During an expansion, coincident indicators rise.

Lagging economic indicators are economic statistics that tend to move up or down a few months after the expansions and contractions of the business cycle. The key lagging indicators (as reported by the National Bureau of Economic Research) are unit **labor** costs, the prime **interest rate**, the amount of outstanding commercial and industrial **debt**, the annual change in **Consumer Price Index**, consumer **credit** as a fraction of personal **income**, duration of unemployment, and business inventories. These indicators show what the **economy** was doing a few months ago, that is why they are called "lagging." They lag, or come after, the turning points of the economy by 3–12 months. When lagging indicators are combined with leading and coincident indicators they tell economists a great deal.

Leading indicators predict a contraction, coincident indicators show that the contraction has arrived, and lagging indicators confirm that the contraction actually happened.

> **KEY POINT TODAY**
> Economists use indicators to forecast or predict future condition in the **economy**. As the world economy has grown larger and more complex in recent decades, forecasts generated by economists in private **industry**, government, and higher education have become increasingly important.

INDIRECT TAX

An indirect tax is a **tax** that is imposed on products at some stage in the **production**-distribution process. The government imposes indirect taxes as a way to raise revenue (**money**) and control the **fiscal policy**. These taxes are included in the final **prices** of **economic goods and services.** Sales tax and **excise tax** are an example of indirect tax. Unlike **direct tax,** which is a form of **progressive taxation**, indirect taxes are paid by all people regardless of wealth.

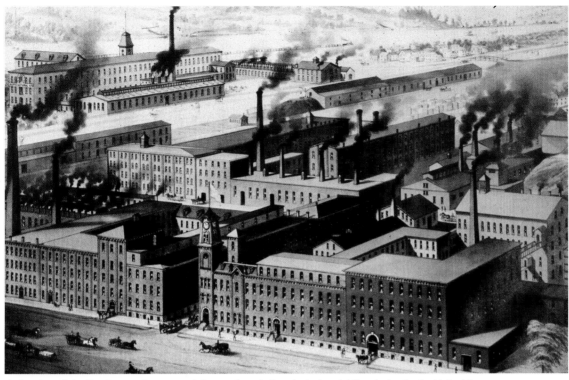

A drawing of the Remington Company of Connecticut during the Industrial Revolution in the United States.

INDUCED CONSUMPTION

Induced consumption is the amount of spending, or **consumption,** that is induced or brought about by an increase in income. For example, a worker is given a raise of $100 a month. He spends part of this extra money the first month to have some landscaping done at his home. This increases the landscaper's income, and the landscaper buys a shirt with the extra money. The landscaper's purchase, or consumption, was *induced consumption*—that is, induced by the increase in his or her income. (See **autonomous consumption.**)

INDUSTRIALIZATION

In **economics,** industrialization is the transition from a society based on agriculture to one based on **capital**-intensive **industry.** As a society moves away from an agrarian-based **economy** to one based on manufacture, incomes rise, and **production** increases, as well. With industrialization the population tends to move from rural areas to urban areas. People who once worked at home or on a farm now work in factories.

During industrialization, even agricultural practices grow more dependent on mechanization, but this also makes it possible to produce enough food for large urban popula-

tions, so increased agricultural productivity is necessary for modern industrial growth.

Modern industrialization began with the Industrial Revolution, which first took place in Great Britain in the late 18th century. In the early 19th century it spread to other parts of Europe and North America. The United States, the United Kingdom, and Japan are examples of some of the most industrialized countries in the world today.

INDUSTRY

Industry is a collective term that includes the manufacturers, producers, or providers of **economic goods and services** as a whole. These manufacturers, producers, and providers can be further divided into categories, based on the types of goods and services they make. Examples of different industries are the automobile industry, the steel industry, the food industry, and the entertainment industry.

INFANT INDUSTRY

Infant industries are those industries that are new to the **economy** as a whole, or new to a particular area— a developing country, for example. Some economists believe that infant industries should be protected from foreign **competition**

by **tariffs** and government **subsidies**. These economists argue that an industry must achieve a minimum size before it can compete with established companies.

INFERIOR GOOD

An inferior good is a good that people buy less of as their **income** increases. Many food products are inferior goods. Hamburger and beans or macaroni are common examples of products consumers buy when they have low **incomes**. These products provide "basic" satisfaction of a need or want. However, as consumer income increases, consumers want more satisfaction from the products they buy, so they eat more expensive foods like steak and fresh produce instead of hamburger and canned vegetables.

A long-distance bus pass might also be an inferior good. As a person's income increases, he is more likely to fly to a distant place, rather than travel by bus.

Inferior goods have a negative **income elasticity of demand**. That means the demand for these goods decreases as income increases. (See **normal goods**.)

INFLATIONARY GAP

An inflationary gap means that there is more

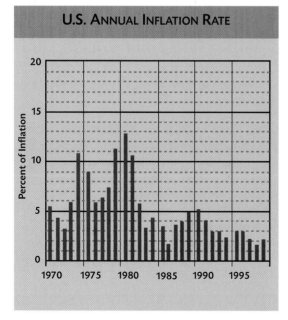

U.S. ANNUAL INFLATION RATE

demand for products than the **market** is willing to provide at the current price level (i.e., more demand than **supply**). This gap is inflationary because producers can now charge higher prices

for their goods since they are in such short supply. However, the gap may not be considered truly inflationary, because it is a temporary situation that will be corrected when **production** catches up to demand once again. The result may be a one-time price increase or a temporary price increase.

INFLATION RATE

Inflation is an overall increase in the **price** of **economic goods and services**. Inflation can be short-term or long-term. Short-term inflation can happen as a result of anything that causes overall **demand** to increase more than overall **supply**. Long-term inflation continues only through increases in the **money supply.**

The inflation rate is the percentage change in the price level from one period to the next. The inflation rate is measured by percent increases in the **Consumer Price Index (CPI)** and the **gross domestic product (GDP)** price deflator.

INFRASTRUCTURE

Infrastructure is the foundation or framework of an organization. In **economics**, methods of transportation, the ways in which **businesses** get their energy to run their machinery, and other **capital** are all examples of infrastructure. That is because economies cannot operate without these things being in place.

Government, or society, plays an important role in developing necessary infrastructure because of the cost and time needed to develop it and the fact that infrastructure has to be in place before businesses can operate efficiently. For example, a factory needs available electricity or other power in order to operate a factory, manufacture goods, and transport those goods to the consumer. Roads must therefore be built from factories to retail outlets or to other places where consumers can then purchase the goods made by these factories. Communications in the form of telephone lines are necessary for all facets of the business, including ordering supplies and taking orders for products.

Sometimes infrastructure is referred to as *social overhead*, because society already has to have it in place for a business to function. Not all infrastructure is provided by government or society, as businesses can create their own infrastructure.

Executives at AT&T Wireless Group ring the bell at the New York Stock Exchange on April 27, 2000, as the company marks the largest IPO in U.S. history.

INITIAL PUBLIC OFFERING (IPO)

Initial means first. An initial public offering (IPO) mea ... vately owr ... The sale o ... lic offering ... is being ma ... newer com ... raise **equity** ...

KEY ... After its I ... public. Pu ... stock at a ... capital. Th ... low-on, off ...

(handwritten notes) PEF 330 BOO Bookbinder, Steve The Dictionary of the global economy

INPUTS

Inputs include ... **labor, capital** ... combination to ... **ic goods and ...**

INSIDER TRADING

Insider trading includes any transaction dealing in **stocks** and **bonds** by an individual who has access to privileged information not yet available to the general investing public. A great deal of **money** can be made by insider trading.

INSURANCE

Insurance is a way to protect an individual or **business** against a financial **loss** or damage. General insurance protects **assets** from fire, flood, robbery, etc. Life and accident insurance protects the lives and limbs of individuals.

INTANGIBLE ASSETS

Intangible assets are **assets** that cannot be seen or felt but are still believed to have economic value to the owner. Things like goodwill, trademarks, patents, copyrights, **franchises**, etc., are examples of intangible assets.

INTEREST

Interest is a payment made by a borrower to a lender for the use of their money. Interest is charged on **loans** to finance **investments,** both physical and **portfolio**, as well as to finance **consumption** of a good or service.

SHORT TERM INTEREST RATE

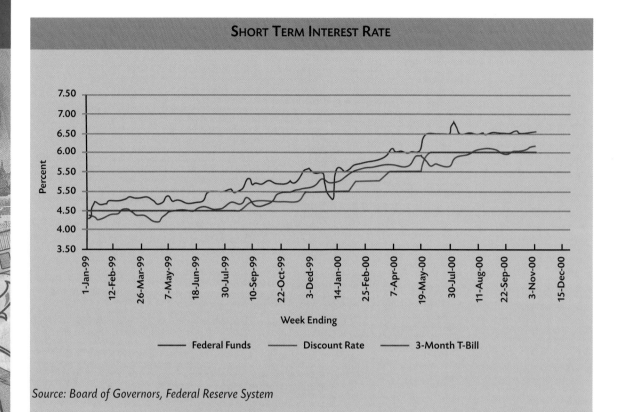

Percent

Week Ending

—— Federal Funds   —— Discount Rate   —— 3-Month T-Bill

Source: Board of Governors, Federal Reserve System

INTEREST RATE

The interest rate is the cost of borrowing funds and the payment received for lending. This amount is a percentage of the total amount loaned or borrowed, expressed as an annual percentage. For example, if someone borrows $100 from a **bank** and the interest rate of the loan is 10 percent, then that person will pay $10 in interest for borrowing the $100 for one year.

Different banks and lending institutions charge different interest rates for the same kinds of loans. The interest rate and other terms of the loan are listed in a contract that is signed by the person borrowing the money and by the institution or person loaning the money.

The less it costs to borrow money (i.e., the lower the interest rate), the more money consumers and businesses will **demand**. The higher the rate of interest, however, the greater the supply of loanable funds.

The graph above depicts the changing interest rates for three types of short-term **loans** over the course of a year: a **discount rate**, federal fund, and a three-month **Treasury bill.** (See **Federal Reserve System; discount rate.**)

INTERMEDIATE GOODS

Intermediate goods are goods that are used to make other goods. When intermediate goods are put together to make finished products, these are called **final goods**. However, sometimes goods that seem like intermediate goods are really final

Lumber used in manufacturing is considered an intermediate good.

goods. For example, lumber can be an intermediate good when it is purchased by a home builder. But if a homeowner buys lumber at a store like Home Depot, then this is considered a final good. Similarly, goods that seem like final goods can be intermediary goods. For example, if an individual buys a computer for home use, this is a final good. If a **business** buys the same computer to make **production** more efficient, then it is an intermediary good.

When measuring the **gross domestic product (GDP),** it is necessary to avoid counting the sales of intermediate goods as part of the final goods. (See **double counting.)**

INTERNAL REVENUE SERVICE

The Internal Revenue Service (IRS) is the branch of the U.S. Department of the Treasury responsible for for collecting all internal revenue, which includes **income** and **excise taxes.** The IRS also enforces all revenue laws.

INTERNATIONAL DEBT

People borrow **money** to buy, for example, supplies, equipment, or housing. Countries do basically the same thing—borrow money from private lenders, international financial institutions, and governments to pay for such things as roads, public services, and health clinics. This is international debt. Like individuals, countries pay back the **principal** and interest on the **loans** they take out. But unlike an individual, who receives the money directly and pays it back according to the terms and conditions of the loan, a country's debt is handled by the institutions of that country. Also, when a **business** or an individual cannot pay back a loan, over time he or she goes bankrupt. Countries cannot file for bankruptcy. When a country cannot pay back its debt, the creditors must decide how to go about reorganizing the debt or forgiving it.

INTERNATIONAL MONETARY FUND (IMF)

The International Monetary Fund (IMF) is an international organization of 182 countries, established in 1947 to promote international cooperation in **exchange rate** stability and financial exchange arrangements, to promote economic goals such as stable growth and high levels of employment, and to provide temporary financial assistance to countries. Structural

President Clinton speaks to world finance ministers attending the IMF annual conference, October 6, 1998.

Adjustment Loans (SALs) made by the IMF are usually linked to requirements that a country open its **economy** to the global market.

INTERNATIONAL LABOR ORGANIZATION (ILO)

The International Labor Organization (ILO) is a branch of the United Nations with 175 member countries consisting of workers, employers, and governments. It is the only international agency in which private sectors of society participate fully with government. The ILO's main goals are to promote decent work for all men and women through promoting basic principles and rights at work; provide more opportunities for women and men to find decent employment and income; promote better coverage and effectiveness of social safety nets (unemployment benefits for example); and encourage communication between government, **business**, and workers.

INTERNATIONAL TRADE

International trade is the exchange of **economic goods and services** between countries. The main advantage of international trade is that consumers have a wider variety of products to choose from, and **production** is more efficient as nations can specialize in goods that they can produce more cheaply (**comparative advantage**). Also, producers have more **markets,** or places to sell their products. Through trade, countries take advantage of their **resources** and economic strengths, and improve their living standards.

International trade benefits many countries, because they can improve their standard of living through increased trade. However, there can also be disadvantages to international trade. For example, if one country becomes dependent on another country for a certain product, and suddenly relations between those two countries are not good, one country may be forced to look elsewhere for the same product. New domestic industries can be hurt by foreign competitors before they become large enough to compete with them. And, importers can also practice "**dumping**"—selling surpluses on foreign markets for below the market **price**.

Developing countries have benefited least from world trading patterns. They tend to specialize in a narrow range of products for which there is little **demand** in the world market. Also, protectionist laws created by highly competitive industrial countries have worked against the interests of developing countries. (See **comparative advantage**.)

INTERNATIONAL TRADE TABLE		
	1997	**1998**
Exports (in billions of dollars)		
Canada	152.1	156.8
Japan	64.6	56.6
Western Europe	153.0	159.1
Australia, New Zealand, and South Africa	16.9	17.2
OPEC	24.2	23.4
Imports (in billions of dollars)		
Canada	170.1	175.8
Japan	121.7	121.9
Western Europe	175.8	194.0
Australia, New Zealand, and South Africa	9.0	10.1
OPEC	44.0	33.9
Balance (excess of exports +)		
Canada	−18.0	−19.0
Japan	−57.1	−65.3
Western Europe	−22.8	−34.9
Australia, New Zealand, and South Africa	7.9	7.2
OPEC	−19.9	−10.5

Source: U.S. Department of Commerce, Bureau of Economic Analysis

INVESTMENT

An investment is a purchase by a **business** that should result in a **profit** at some later date. Investments take many forms in the **economy**. To improve products and increase sales, **businesses** invest in research and advertising. Consumers invest in real estate or education to increase their future **income**. Government invests in highways and bridges, development,

and education to promote growth of the economy. Private investment is affected by **interest rates** (the cost of borrowing). (See **aggregate demand.**)

INVESTMENT BANK

Although investment banks are called **banks**, they are not really banks that have checking accounts and safety deposit boxes. Investment banks buy government securities, corporate **stock**s, **bonds**, and similar financial **assets** (at wholesale prices) in large blocks, and then turn around and resell them to the public in smaller amounts. Basically, investment banks "underwrite" stocks and bonds when they are first issued by guaranteeing to sell them at a predetermined price. However, if the public does not buy these items at the preset price, the bank loses its investment and usually a lot of money. This makes investment banking very risky. Millions of dollars can be made or lost overnight.

INVISIBLE HAND

Many economists believe that buyers and sellers will do what's best for the **economy**, automatically, without any government intervention, as if they were guided by an invisible hand. The concept of "invisible hand" was an essential part of the **economic analysis** of **markets** in Adam Smith's book *The Wealth of Nations*.

KEYNESIAN ECONOMICS

Keynesian economics was developed by John Maynard Keynes and presented in his book *The General Theory of Employment, Interest, and Money* (1936). Keynes proposed that **aggregate demand**, or the lack of it, is the main cause of **business cycle** instability. This theory came about in the **Great Depression,** when the **economy** seemed to have reached an **equilibrium** at a high **unemployment** level. Keynes argued that the low economic activity was caused by the lack of aggregate demand in the economy. One component of aggregate demand is investment. Since the private sector was not investing **capital**, Keynes argued that the government could boost the economy by providing capital—that is, the government should increase spending.

Keynesian economics was a guide for federal government policy until the 1960s, but in the 1970s and 1980s **monetarism**, **neoclassical economics**, **supply-side economics**, and rational expectations became more widely accepted.

However, Keynesian economics and **Neo-Keynesianism** still have a strong following in academic and policy-making circles today. Some important components of Keynesian economics are:

1) the **consumption** function or the positive relationship between household consumption and **disposable income**.

2) the marginal propensity to consume— **households** will consume a fraction of extra income and save the rest.

3) the **multiplier effect**—this captures changes in gross **output** resulting from a change in aggregate demand;

4) the use of **fiscal policy** and **monetary policy** to stabilize **business cycle** fluctuations.

JOHN MAYNARD KEYNES

John Maynard Keynes was one of the most influential economists of the 20th century. In fact, an entire branch of **economics** is named after him.

Born in Cambridge, England in 1883, Keynes was educated at Eton College and Cambridge University. He began his career in the India Office of the British government. In 1913 he published a highly regarded book called *Indian Currency and Finance* (1913).

In 1919 Keynes wrote *The Economic Consequences of Peace*. During the 1920s he thought the conventional analysis of economic situations did not adequately explain the economic problems England was suffering at the time. In fact, he became so convinced that deflationary policies were the cause of the problems that he published (among other works) two important volumes about **money** called *The Treatise on Money*.

In 1936 Keynes published what many authorities consider to be one of the most significant theoretical works of the 20th century: *The General Theory of Employment, Interest and Money*. Keynes died in 1946.

L

LABOR

Labor is the activity produced by the work force, both by hand, as in the construction of a building; and mentally, as in medical research. Labor is one of the four **factors of production**, along with natural **resources**, entrepreneurship, and **capital**.

> ### ⊚ KEY POINT TODAY
> Labor includes all human efforts, such as those provided by clerks, technicians, professionals, managers, and company presidents.

LABOR FORCE

The labor force is the total number of people (16 years of age and over) who are willing and able to work or are working in an **economy**. Labor force is another term for the economy's total labor **supply**. Generally, the labor force excludes anyone in the military. The quality of labor, size of the labor force, **labor force participation rate**, and **capital** stock make up a country's **aggregate supply** potential.

LABOR FORCE PARTICIPATION RATE

The labor force participation rate (LFPR) is a ratio of the total civilian labor force (16 years of age and older) to the total civilian population (16 years of age and older). The data used to estimate the LFPR is obtained from the monthly Current Population Survey conducted by the Bureau of the Census for the Bureau of Labor Statistics.

Use this formula to calculate the LFPR:

$$\text{(LFPR)} = \frac{\text{Civilian labor force X 100}}{\text{Total non institutionalized civilian population}}$$

LABOR MARKET

This is a **market** where **businesses** and individuals buy or supply the services of the **labor force**. When the labor market is weak, there is a lot of labor (workers) available, and that labor will tend to be cheap (workers will work for low wages). When there is a "tight" labor market, on the other hand, this means that there are few workers available for the amount of work demanded, and therefore they will command relatively high **wages** for their work.

LABOR FORCE PARTICIPATION RATE			
Year	All Civilian Workers	Males over 16	Females over 16
1960	59.4%	83.3%	37.7%
1970	60.4	79.7	43.3
1980	63.8	77.4	51.5
1990	66.5	76.4	57.5
1998	67.1	74.9	59.8

Source: U.S. Bureau of Labor Statistics

AFL-CIO president John Sweeney speaks at the launch of the "Ask a Woman" campaign, February 17, 1997.

LABOR UNION

A labor union is an organization of workers or employees who join together to negotiate with their employers over **wages**, **fringe benefits**, working conditions, and other aspects of employment. The main role of labor unions is to protect the interests of workers. Big **businesses** do not always welcome labor unions, however.

In the late 1700s, labor unions struggled for the right to legally organize and negotiate with employers. Unions' earliest attempts were met with negative reactions from both government and businesses. Even the courts viewed union activity as criminal conspiracy. It was not until the 1930s and the **Great Depression** that labor unions became powerful. Today, some prominent labor unions include the United Auto Workers, various teachers' unions, the United Mine Workers, and the umbrella labor organization—the American Federation of Labor and Congress of Industrial Organizations (AFL-CIO).

LAISSEZ-FAIRE

Laissez-faire is a French term that literally means "let do." In English it has come to mean "leave alone." In **economics** it refers to the belief that government should should allow economic agents to act with little government involvement, as long as they respect the personal and property rights of others. The laissez-faire philosophy can be contrasted with government intervention, which is the belief that government should regulate **business** and other aspects of the **economy**. Laissez-faire is also associated with **conservatism**.

> ### ⟳ KEY POINT TODAY
> Laissez-faire is the belief in **free trade** and market **competition** that has been around since Adam Smith. According the the laissez-faire doctrine, free trade, **private enterprise**, and largely unrestricted **international trade** will lead to greater consumerism and a rising **standard of living**.

LAND TENURE

Land tenure refers to the right, manner, or terms of holding land. Wealth, **income** distribution, and social and political influence are partly determined by the laws governing land tenure. These laws specify the forms of tenure and the privileges and responsibilities that go with them. They define land ownership and the extent to which the owner can freely get rid of land and of the income made from its use. In this sense, the form of tenure determines the wealth and income distribution based on the land. If private ownership is permitted, class differentiation is unavoidable; in contrast, public ownership eliminates such distinctions. The forms of tenure range from temporary, conditional holding, to ownership in 'fee simple,' which means total rights of control and disposal over the land

LATIN AMERICAN FREE TRADE AGREEMENT (LAFTA)

A group of Latin American countries formed the Latin American Free Trade Agreement (LAFTA) in 1960 with the aim of establishing a **free trade** area among the countries. This aim was never achieved, and LAFTA was replaced in 1980 with the Latin American Integration Association (LAIA). LAIA has the more limited goal of encouraging free trade but with no timetable for achieving it.

LAW OF DEMAND

The law of demand states that if other things are constant (**ceteris paribus**), then **demand** will increase if **prices** are lower. However, demand will be lower as prices go up.

Income effect and substitution effect help explain the law of demand. With income effect, a change in the price of a good affects the purchasing power of an individual. Therefore if a good is priced less than usual, an individual has more purchasing power with the same amount of money. With substitution effect, if the price of one good changes, it makes this good more or less attractive in relation to the price of other goods. For example, if hot dogs and hamburgers start at the same price, but the price of hot dogs goes down, then they are relatively more attractive to the buyer, who will be likely to substitute hot dogs for hamburgers when making a purchase. (See **law of supply.**)

LAW OF DIMINISHING MARGINAL UTILITY

The law of diminishing marginal utility states that as more of a good is consumed, eventually each additional unit of that good has less and less value to the consumer. When an object or substance has great **marginal utility**, an additional unit would lead to a large increase in consumer satisfaction. As the **supply** increases, its marginal utility goes down. Therefore the more of a good that is consumed the more its marginal utility will diminish.

LAW OF SUPPLY

The law of supply states that if other things are constant (*ceteris paribus*), then the higher the price of a good or service, the more of that good or service will be produced during a certain period of time. This means that manufacturers tend to produce more of a product for which they can get a high **price** for it. (See **law of demand.**)

LEFT-WING/LEFTIST

Left-wing or leftist are terms used to generalize varied political ideologies, such as **socialism**, **communism**, social democracy, etc., that denounce social and economic inequality. Leftist or left-wing individuals advocate greater government intervention to redistribute wealth by reducing private **property rights**, limiting rights to inherit wealth, and by putting a higher tax burden on the rich and wealthy in order to provide more payments and services to the poor. Leftists around the world have been critical of the **World Trade Organization** and the **International Monetary Fund** for their policies, which leftists feel benefit the already wealthy and take advantage of poorer countries.

LEGAL TENDER

Legal tender is a country's **currency** (**money**) that must be nationally accepted as payment for a **debt**. It is designated by law that a debtor may offer, and a creditor must accept, legal tender as payment for a debt or settlement of financial obligations.

LENDER OF LAST RESORT

A nation's **central bank**, such as the **Federal Reserve** in the United States, has the authority and financial resources to act as "lender of last resort" by extending credit to commercial **banks** or to other groups in unusual circumstances involving a financial crisis or national emergency, where failure to obtain credit would have a severe adverse impact on the **economy**.

LESS DEVELOPED COUNTRY

In the 1950s and 1960s the term "less developed country" was used interchangeably with the term "developing countries." Today, at least 36 of the world's poorest countries are considered by the United Nations to be the "least developed" of the less developed countries (LDCs). They have low **income** and literacy levels, few natural **resources**, poor health care, unsanitary drinking water, and barely enough food to feed their population. These countries face many difficulties achieving rapid **economic development** in the near future. In order to experience **economic growth,** an increase in income would have to be attained and maintained. This would require sustained increases in **investment** from domestic savings, foreign investments, or loans.

According to the Human Development Index released by the United Nations Development Program (UNDP), in 1999 some of the middle income LDCs include Colombia, Thailand, and South Africa. Among the least developed countries listed are the Democratic Republic of the Congo, Nigeria, and Haiti. (See **human development**; **gender development**; **developed country.**)

An Ethiopian woman works outside her home with her children in the background. Ethiopia is one of the world's poorest countries.

LEWIS MODEL

The Lewis Model was developed by Sir Arthur Lewis in the 1950s. It is the theory of how to use **disguised unemployment** or underemployment in rural areas of less developed countries by creating incentives for rural populations to migrate to urban areas. In cities this rural population would provide the basis for a cheap pool of labor for a growing industrial sector. The profits made in the industrial sector would be reinvested into the country's **economy,** providing a higher level of **economic growth.** (See **rural-urban migration.**)

LIABILITY

A liability is a claim on the **resources** of an individual or company in regard to **money** borrowed. For example, property, **stocks**, savings, or objects such as a car are considered a liability.

LIBERALISM

Liberalism today refers to a political viewpoint that favors government intervention to redistribute wealth, regulate the **economy,** control **profit**-seeking **businesses**, and provide equal opportunities for all citizens regardless of race, age, gender, or ethnic origin.

> **KEY POINT TODAY**
> Liberalism was initially a school of thought from the late 18th century that promoted liberal values, the active development of the freedom of the individual, and economic activity.

LIQUIDITY

Liquidity is the ease of converting an **asset** into **money**, with little or no loss of **value**. If an asset is easy to convert to money, it has a high degree of liquidity. Savings accounts, checking accounts, **certificates of deposit**, and **money market** accounts are considered highly liquid, while **stocks** and **bonds** are not as liquid because it takes longer to convert them to money, and there are expenses such as brokerage fees and transactions fees, which tend to reduce their value in the process. Physical assets like houses, cars, furniture, etc., are even less liquid because it takes more time to convert them to money.

LIQUIDITY TRAP

A liquidity trap is created when **interest rate**s fall so low that **demand** does not increase. Normally, low interests rates would stimulate demand because the cost of borrowing money is low, so **businesses** and individuals could borrow money to invest in **capital** and other resources of **production**. But if the interest rates get too low, there is an expectation of a looming rise in interest rates, which makes people act as if they had already risen. People therefore want to hold on to their money in the form of cash (liquidity).

One example of the **Keynesian** economist's solution to the liquidity trap is to use **fiscal policy** to increase government spending which in turn will increase demand and stimulate the **economy**.

LOAN

A loan is the **money** that is advanced by **banks** and other institutions to **businesses** and individuals. The money is borrowed to help pay for either physical or financial **investment**s and purchases of current **economic goods and services**. Typically there is both an agreed time frame for the borrower to pay back the money loaned and an agreed **interest rate**.

LOCATION OF INDUSTRY

Location of industry is the geographic distribution of economic activity within an **economy**. Many factors influence a company's decision to locate their **business** in one place or another, including availability of **labor**, raw materials, proximity of **markets**, and availability of trained scientists or engineers. Once an **industry** is established in a particular area, it tends to attract other businesses. An example of a location of industry is Silicon Valley in California.

LONG RUN

Long run is a term used in **macroeconomics** to indicate an indefinite period long enough for all **factors of production** to become variable (changing in response to something else). Land, **capital**, **labor**, and entrepreneurship are the

four **factors of production,** and it takes time for any of these factors to change. There is no specific time period for the long run. It can range from months to decades. The long run differs from the **short run,** in which one or more production costs are fixed.

LONG-RUN AGGREGATE SUPPLY CURVE

The long-run **aggregate supply curve** is a graphical representation that plots the overall supply against the change in **price** level over a long run period. This curve is represented by a vertical line at the **full employment** level of **output**.

LONG-RUN COST

There are three kinds of long-run costs: long-run average cost, long-run **total cost**, and long-run **marginal cost**. Long-run average cost is the per unit cost of producing a good or service in the long run when all **factors of production** (land, labor, capital, and entrepreneurship) are variable (changing).

The long-run average cost is found by dividing the long-run total cost by the quantity of total **output** produced.

Long-run total cost is the opportunity cost for all of the factors of production used in the **long run** to produce a particular good or service. This includes everything from **wages** paid to **labor**, rent paid for the land, **interest** paid to **capital** owners, and a **normal profit** paid to **entrepreneurs**.

Long-run marginal cost is the change in the long-run total cost of producing a good or service as the result of a change in the quantity of output produced. It is also the result of changes in the cost of all **inputs** or factors of production.

LONG-RUN INDUSTRY SUPPLY CURVE

The long-run industry supply curve is a graphic representation that plots the overall **supply** against the change in **output** (**production**). It is a line or curve showing that as **prices** increase, the supply also increases. The line or curve can take one of three different paths depending on the overall changes that have taken place in costs during the period being examined. The three paths are a decreasing cost **industry**, an increasing cost industry, or a constant cost industry.

In the case of decreasing cost industry, the long-run industry supply curve is downward sloping. As an industry grows bigger, the cost of production falls. This situation occurs if, for example, the increase in the size of an industry means that a better network of suppliers is developed, and thus the cost for each producer is lowered.

When the long-run industry supply curve is upward sloping, it signifies an increasing cost industry. This occurs if industry growth makes some **factor of production** more scarce, so its **price** goes up. Thus, production costs rise for all the producers in the industry. An example might be the lumber industry—as trees grow scarce, the prices go up.

The third possibility is the constant cost industry. In this case, the long-run industry supply curve is flat. Thus the cost of production does not change as industry grows.

LONG-RUN SUPPLY CURVE

The long-run supply curve is a plot on a graph that shows the relationship between the **price** of **economic goods and services** and the quantity supplied by **businesses**. The period of time (considered to be long-run) has to be long enough for businesses to enter or leave the **market**. The time frame also has to be long enough to allow for companies to adjust all four of the factors of production—land, **labor**, **capital**, and entrepreneurship.

LORENZ CURVE

The Lorenz Curve is a graph showing the percentage of total **income** being received by the various income groups in society. It highlights the equality or inequality in an **economy** of the distribution of wealth. The **Gini coefficient**, which is a single number that represents this equality or inequality, is derived from the Lorenz Curve by measuring the distance of the curve from a line of perfect equality. The graph below shows what equal income distribution looks like in the form of a straight blue line, while the curved red line (Lorenz Curve) depicts the actual proportion of income earned by a cumulative percentage of the population.

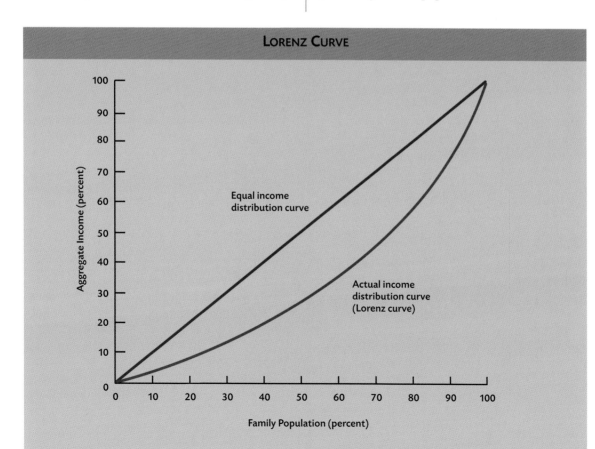

LORENZ CURVE

Equal income distribution curve

Actual income distribution curve (Lorenz curve)

Aggregate Income (percent)

Family Population (percent)

M

M1 MONEY SUPPLY

The M1 money supply is the most narrow measure **money supply** in the U.S. **economy**. It is the total sum of **currency, demand deposits, checkable deposits,** and travelers checks. These are money items that can be used directly to make purchases.

M2 MONEY SUPPLY

The M2 Money Supply is the second most narrow **money supply** measure in the U.S. economy. This money supply includes the **M1 money supply,** plus money in savings. It includes **savings deposits,** small **certificates of deposit, money market** accounts, and other items. This money supply is typically four times as much as M1.

MACROECONOMICS

Economics is divided into two branches—macroeconomics and **microeconomics.** *Macro* means using relatively large quantities, or "on a large scale." Macroeconomics is the study of the entire **economy**—that is, all **businesses,** all consumers, and their impact on the economy—especially focusing on topics like gross **production, unemployment, inflation,** and **business cycles.**

MANAGED EXCHANGE RATES

A managed **exchange rate** is a system that allows the value of a **currency** to be determined in the international currency **market** but still gives the **central bank** powers to regularly intervene to stabilize the local currency.

M1 Money Supply		M2 Money Supply	
Month/Year	**Amount (billions $)**	**Month/Year**	**Amount (billions $)**
September 1990	817.53	September 1990	3254.68
September 1991	866.45	September 1991	3353.48
September 1992	983.08	September 1992	3407.92
September 1993	1099.33	September 1993	3453.41
September 1994	1146.60	September 1994	3489.58
September 1995	1138.58	September 1995	3607.43
September 1996	1091.75	September 1996	3759.22
September 1997	1059.87	September 1997	3958.15
September 1998	1070.94	September 1998	4257.09
September 1999	1087.25	September 1999	4560.47
September 2000	1089.27	September 2000	4843.41

Source: San Francisco Federal Reserve Bank

Men and women work on electronic equipment at one of the many maquiladoras in Tijuana, Mexico.

MAQUILADORAS

Maquiladoras are assembly plants located along the border of northern Mexico that manufacture finished goods for **export** to the United States. The maquiladoras are generally owned by non-Mexican corporations. They take advantage of low-cost Mexican **labor**, beneficial **tariff** regulations, and close proximity to U.S. **markets** to produce items such as home appliances and automobiles. Starting on a small scale in the mid-1960s, the maquiladoras grew dramatically after Mexico substantially changed its economic regulations concerning foreign investment in the early 1980s. From 1983 to 1990, the maquiladora industry grew at approximately 20 percent annually, and it grew even more with the creation of the **North American Free Trade Agreement** (NAFTA) and the U.S. economic boom in the late 1990s. In 1999 more than 3,500 plants employed approximately 1.2 million workers.

MARGINAL ANALYSIS

In **economics** the word margin means "change." Marginal analysis providees a way for economists to study and analyze small, incremental changes in key economic variables, as opposed to broad, overall changes. In so doing, they can reveal interactions, implications, and conclusions about the **economy** that are not so obvious when one looks only at the "big picture." Usually, when one variable in the economy changes, another variable changes as a result. Marginal analysis lets economists see the relationships between these changes.

MARGINAL BENEFIT

Marginal benefit is the increase (or decrease) in an activity's overall benefit, due to a unit increase (or decrease) in the level of that activity, *ceteris paribus* (all else being equal). The additional benefit obtained by consuming the last (or next) unit of a **commodity**.

MARGINAL COST

Marginal cost (MC) is the change in **total cost**, or total variable cost, that results from a change in the quantity of **output** produced by a manufacturer in the **short run**. Marginal cost shows how much total cost changes for a given change in the quantity of output. Since changes in total cost are matched by changes in total variable cost in the short run, MC is the change in either total cost or total variable cost. Use this formula to

determine MC:

$$MC = \frac{\text{change in total cost (TC)}}{\text{change in quantity of output (Q)}}$$

Since any change in total cost is also an equivalent change in total variable cost in the short run (fixed cost does not change), this second formula can also be used to determine MC:

$$MC = \frac{\text{change in total variable cost (TVC)}}{\text{change in quantity of output (Q)}}$$

MARGINAL PRODUCT

Marginal product (MP) is used to show how the total product of a producer changes by adding the last unit produced. To find marginal product, use the following formula:

$$MP = \frac{\text{change in total product}}{\text{change in variable input}}$$

If the MP of **labor** in a doughnut shop is 25 doughnuts, then it is possible that hiring the last worker caused the total product to increase by 25 doughnuts. But this does not necessarily mean the last worker hired produced 25 doughnuts him- or herself. It means that having this added person working caused total product to increase by 25 doughnuts.

MARGINAL PROPENSITY TO CONSUME/SAVE

The marginal propensity to consume (MPC) refers to the fraction of an increase in **disposable income** that is spent for **consumer goods**. In other words, if a consumer's income increased, how much of this increase would he or she be inclined to spend or consume? The answer depends on the MPC. For example, if **income** is increased by $100 per month, and consumer spending is increased by $70 a month, then the MPC would be 70/100 (0.7).

The marginal propensity to save (MPS), on the other hand, is the fraction of an increase in income that is not spent for consumer goods. If a consumer's income increased, how much of this increase would he or she be inclined to save? In the example cited above, the consumer ended up with a 70/100, or 70 percent, marginal propensity to consume; the MPS based on the same income and MPC, would be 30/100 (0.3).

MARGINAL PROPENSITY TO IMPORT

The marginal propensity to import (MPI) is the change that occurs in spending on **imports** as national **income** changes. A nation can import more **economic goods and services** when there is more income to spend. Likewise, a nation will import less when the national income is less. MPI can be shown with this formula:

$$MPI = \frac{\text{change in spending on imports}}{\text{change in income}}$$

MARGINAL RATE OF TRANSFORMATION

Marginal rate of transformation is a ratio that shows how much of one product must be given up in order to release enough **inputs** or **resources** to produce one additional unit of some other product. The marginal rate of transformation gives the **opportunity cost** of a unit of that good in terms of the other good. In an **economy**, the most successful national **output** is achieved when the marginal rate of transformation of the goods produced is equal to the ratio of their **prices**.

MARGINAL REVENUE

Marginal revenue is the change in **total revenue** resulting from a change in the quantity of **output** sold. Note that for a perfectly competitive firm, marginal revenue is equal to **price**. Use this formula for marginal revenue:

$$MR = \frac{\text{change in total revenue (TR)}}{\text{change in quantity of output (Q)}}$$

MARGINAL REVENUE PRODUCT

Marginal revenue product is the change in **total revenue** that occurs when a unit change of one input is made by a company in order to produce and sell additional units of **output.** An input can be one of the **factors of production**: land, **capital**, **labor**, or entrepreneurship. The marginal revenue product combined with the marginal factor cost lets a company know how many factor inputs it needs to maximize **profits.**

As seen in the graph below, each additional worker, or unit of labor, adds to the company's total revenue in the form of marginal revenue product.

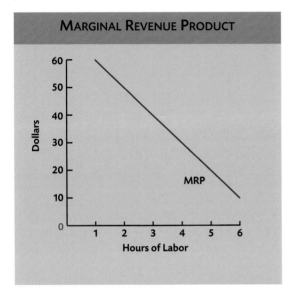

MARGINAL REVENUE PRODUCT

(y-axis: Dollars — 60, 50, 40, 30, 20, 10, 0)
(x-axis: Hours of Labor — 1, 2, 3, 4, 5, 6)
MRP

MARGINAL UTILITY

Marginal utility is the increase in satisfaction of **wants** and needs obtained from the **consumption** of one additional unit of a good or service. For example a person's **total utility** (satisfaction) will increase if he or she buys a new CD. Marginal utility is the change in total utility divided by the change in quantity.

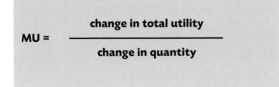

$$MU = \frac{\text{change in total utility}}{\text{change in quantity}}$$

William Stanley Jevons developed the utility theory in his book *The Theory of Political Economy* (1871). Jevons believed that goods are valuable only if they provide total utility (satisfaction).

WILLIAM STANLEY JEVONS

William Stanley Jevons was an English philosopher and scientist, born in Liverpool in 1835 and educated at University College in London. In 1866 he was appointed to a chair of political economy at Owens College in Manchester, England. In 1876 he moved to University College in London. Jevons wrote many works on logic and scientific methods. His book *Principles of Science* (1874) is probably the most important. His other notable works on **economics** include *The Theory of Political Economy* (1871), and *The State in Relation to Labour* (1882).

Jevons rejected the idea that the exchange value of a good depends on costs spent to produce the good. Rather, the value depends on what the consumer's evaluation of the utility of the good.

Jevons is credited with developing the marginal utility theory of consumer choice. Jevons was also one of the founders of Econometrics, the application of statistical and mathematical methods used to study economics.. He was particularly interested in linking statistical analysis with theoretical analysis in economics. Jevons died in 1882.

MARKET

A market is when and where buyers and sellers come together to exchange **resources**. and **economic goods and services.** Markets involve voluntary exchanges, and most modern markets involve a good or service being exchanged for **money.** Markets address the problem of **scarcity.** Unlimited **wants** and needs are the source of market **demand**, while limited resources are the source of market **supply.** A market can be a **stock market**, supermarket, the mall, or a farmer's market, etc.

All economies use markets and government to allocate resources. Economies that rely heavily on markets are called market-oriented economies, **capitalist** systems, or **free market economies.** **Competitive markets** have large

Shoppers mill through the Pacific Mall on Hong Kong Island. A mall is one of many types of markets.

numbers of buyers and sellers so that no one has control over **price**.

MARKET FAILURE

A market failure occurs when a **market** does not efficiently allocate resources into the **production**, distribution, or **consumption** of a good to achieve the greatest possible consumer satisfaction. There are four main types of market failures: **public good,** market control, **externality**, and imperfect information.

A public good is something like clean air or a beach. It is difficult to keep nonpayers from consuming the good, and one person's use of it does not prevent someone else's use.

In the case of market control there are many buyers and only one seller of a particular good or service. A **monopoly** would be an extreme example of market control.

An externality is a cost that the producer of a good does not have to pay but which has to be paid by others—cleaning up pollution, for example.

The last main market failure is imperfect information, meaning that either the buyers or the sellers do not have all the relevant information for make an informed decision in trade.

MARKET POWER

Market power is the amount of influence buyers or sellers have over the **price** or quantity of a good or service exchanged in a **market**. Market power depends on the number of competitors on each side of the market. A market with few buyers but many sellers means buyers have more market power than sellers (because there is limited demand for the product). The opposite is true in a market with many buyers and few sellers—sellers have more market power. Another name for market power is market control. A monopolist is an extreme example of market power. In general, any buyer or seller who can take actions to change a market price has some market power.

MASS PRODUCTION

Mass production is the **production** of very large quantities of products using the principles of **specialization**, division of **labor**, and standardization of parts. With mass production, industries try to attain high rates of **output** at low unit costs, with lower costs expected as volume increases. Mass production involves the use of tools, machinery, and other equipment (which is usually automated) to make standard interchangeable parts and products. This form of

Cars are produced at a Ford plant in Michigan.

production has resulted in improvements in the cost, quality, quantity, and variety of goods around the world.

According to some historians, mass production began around 1800 with Eli Whitney's firearms factory. Mass production reached its highest level with the automobile industry of the early 20th century. Henry Ford was the first industrialist to make full use of this system of production; it therefore became known as Fordism. Mass production allowed factories to hire unskilled or semiskilled laborers who would perform the same small tasks over and over again to produce one part of a product on an assembly line.

MEANS TEST

Means testing is the granting or denial of benefits or services based on one's **income** or **assets** (one's means). It often determines whether or not one has the "means" to pay for something, as in financial aid for college, etc.

Social Security and Medicare are **entitlement programs** in which there is some movement toward more means testing. **Money** for these programs is raised through taxes in the form of payroll deductions, when a person reaches retirement age he or she receives money back. Payroll deductions, and the return of money, take place whether a person is rich or poor. So far this does not describe a means test

system. Within this system, however, a form of means test could take place if the poor have less money deducted from their payroll and/or if they receive proportionately more in benefits when they retire.

MEDIUM OF EXCHANGE

A medium of exchange is anything that functions as **money**. It is an object that is exchanged for **economic goods and services**. It does not have to have any other **value** or use, just value in exchange. The main function of money (**currency** and checks) is to act as the medium of exchange. Buyers exchange their money for goods and services, and sellers give their goods and services in exchange for money. (See **fiat money; legal tender**.)

MERCANTILISM

Mercantilism was a popular economic approach in Europe during the 16th, 17th, and 18th centuries under which governments controlled **industry** and trade. Mercantilism was characterized by the view that **exports** were desired above trade within a country and above **imports**.

MERGER

A merger occurs when two or more companies mutually agree to join together into one. There are three main types of merger: the horizontal merger, the vertical merger, and the conglomer-

The chairmen of Exxon and Mobil announce the giant merger of their companies in 1998.

ate merger.

The horizontal merger takes place when two competing companies in the same market join together as one. The vertical merger occurs between companies that have a supplier/customer relationship. The conglomerate merger happens when two companies in unrelated markets combine in order to diversify their production.

KEY POINT TODAY
A takeover, like a merger, is the joining together of two companies. However, unlike a merger, a takeover often involves one company buying out the other company without full agreement of the acquired (bought) company. For this reason, many takeovers are often referred to as a "hostile takeover."

MICROCREDIT

Microcredit is the extension of small **loans** to very poor people for self-employment projects that create an **income**, allowing them to care for themselves and their families. These people, often women, are **entrepreneurs** who are too poor to qualify for traditional **bank** loans. Microcredit has proven an effective and popular measure in the ongoing struggle against poverty, particularly in **less developed countries**, enabling those without access to lending institutions to borrow at bank rates and start small **businesses**. For example, a woman in Bangladesh who is loaned the equivalent of 50 U.S. dollars might be able to buy enough supplies, such as soap and other household items, to start her own small supply store in her village.

Although definitions of microcredit vary from country to country, some of the overriding criteria used include size, target users, use of the loan, and terms and conditions. Loans are micro, or very small in size. The target users are microentrepreneurs and low-income **households**. The use of funds are not only for **income** generation and enterprise development but also for community use—for example, health, education, etc. Most terms and conditions for microcredit loans are flexible, easy to understand, and suited to the local conditions of the community.

MICROECONOMICS

There are two branches of **economics**—**macroeconomics** and microeconomics. Microeconomics is the branch that studies identical units of the **economy**—**business** and consumers—and covers such topics as **markets**, **prices**, **industries**, **demand**, and **supply**. Microeconomics is concerned with understanding the market process and how it works and therefore studies the decision makers in households, businesses, and governments who determine the process of demand, supply, and price formation.

MIXED ECONOMY

A mixed economy is one that relies on both **markets** and governments to allocate **resources**. Most economies in today's world are mixed. But in other economies, markets allocate resources through voluntary choices made by the people, and government forces allocation by involuntary taxes, laws, restrictions, and regulations.

MONETARISM

Monetarism is a school of economic thought that was pioneered by Milton Friedman. Monetarism places the primary emphasis of its analysis on the size of the **money supply** and the influence of **money** in the functioning of the **economy**. According to monetarists, the rate of change in the money supply is the most important variable in determining economic **output** and **inflation**.

MILTON FRIEDMAN

Born in New York City in 1912, Milton Friedman is perhaps the country's best-known living economist. He received a B.A. in 1932 from Rutgers University, earned an M.A. in 1933 from the University of Chicago, and a Ph.D in 1946 from Columbia University.

From 1935 to 1940 and from 1941 to 1943, Friedman worked as an economist with various federal agencies. In 1946 he joined the economics department at the University of Chicago, where he remained until 1976.

Friedman was awarded the 1976 Nobel Prize in economic science. In 1988 he was awarded the Presidential Medal of Freedom and the National Medal of Science.

Friedman is considered the leader of the Chicago School of monetary economics. It stresses the importance of the quantity of money as an instrument of government policy and as a determinant of **business cycles** and **inflation.**

Friedman's books about economics include *Capitalism and Freedom* (1962); *A Monetary History of the United States, 1867–1960* (1963); *Dollars and Deficits* (1968); *A Theoretical Framework for Monetary Analysis* (1971); and *Free to Choose* (1980), which was written with his wife Rose.

MONETARY BASE

Monetary base is the **currency** held by the public (as opposed to **banks**) and reserves held by banks. It is sometimes referred to as "high powered money."

KEY POINT TODAY

Keynesian economists do not place great significance on changes in the **money supply**. Monetarists, on the other hand, focus on changes in the money supply as the center of their school of thought. Monetarists are more likely than Keyensians to rely on market **competition**, rather than government intervention, to promote a healthy and stable economy.

MONETARY POLICY

Monetary policy is a collective term to mean all the actions taken by **central banking** authorities (the **Federal Reserve System** in the United States) to stabilize the **business cycle**, maintain a low percentage of **unemployment**, achieve **economic growth**, and control the **interest** and **inflation rates**.

The Federal Reserve System determines the total amount of **money** circulating in the economy. The main tools of monetary policy include adjustment to the reserve requirements on deposit accounts, changes to the **discount rate** that affect **bank** borrowings, and **open-market operations** that involve the buying and selling of U.S. government securities in the secondary market thus affecting bank **liquidity**. Open-market operations is the policy measure that is most effective and most often used.

Monetary policy does not require an agreement between Congress and the president as **fiscal policy** does. It requires only the actions of seven people who serve as the Board of Governors of the Federal Reserve System or the **Federal Open Market Committee**.

The Board of Governors is the policy-making group of the U.S. Federal Reserve System. The Board includes seven members, each serving 14-year terms, with one term expiring every two years. This Board, when joined by five Federal District Bank presidents, forms the Federal Open Market Committee. The Chairman of the Board of Governors is considered to be one of the most powerful figures in directing the U.S. **economy**.

Monetary policy received greater emphasis in the late 1970s and early 1980s due to the problem of **stagflation** and the growing influence of the Chicago School and **Milton Friedman**.

M

MONETARY POLICY

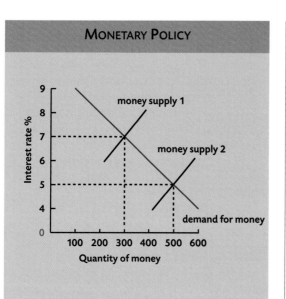

As seen in the graph, if the Federal Reserve wants to raise the interest rate from 5 percent to 7 percent, it can do so by reducing the money supply from money supply 1 to money supply 2.

MONEY

Money is anything that is generally accepted as payment for **economic goods and services**. Goods, services, and other **assets** are priced in terms of money and are exchanged using money rather than exchanging one good for another as in a **barter** system. That means the key role of money is to act as a **medium of exchange**, but it also functions as:

1) a store of value—meaning money must retain its value (discounting for inflation) for future spending on goods and services.

2) a standard unit of account—meaning it is used for measuring purchasing power and for comparing the **value** among various goods and services.

3) standard of deferred payment.

In most economies today, money takes the form of paper **currency**, metal coins, and balances in checking accounts. Throughout history, however, a wide variety of materials have been used as money—everything from colored beads to chocolate bars. Tangible items can make the best money because they have durability, divisibility, transportability, and are not easily counterfeited. Money affects the **economy** because when there is too much money, inflation occurs. (See **commodity money; legal tender.**)

MONEY MARKET

A money market is a financial **market** for short-term borrowing and lending. It trades U.S. **Treasury bills**, commercial paper, and other short-term (maturities of one year or less) and

Dealers trading at the Tokyo foreign money market in 1999.

highly liquid financial instruments.

For example, **businesses** often use money markets when they need short-term funds to pay operating costs that are due before revenue can be collected from product sales to pay for these operating costs. The **Federal Reserve System**, commercial **banks**, and many different kinds of companies are all involved in the money market which can be compared with **capital** market.

MONEY MULTIPLIER

Money multiplier is the amount of money that is created when a **bank** makes **loans** from its deposits. Since a bank only has to keep a certain percentage of its deposits in the **Federal Reserve System,** that leaves the rest of the deposits available for loans. The loans that the bank gives out increase the **money supply**. The increase in the money supply will be greater than the amount of **money** initially loaned because this money, or a part of it, will be used and will end up as a deposit in a bank, 90 percent of which can again be used for a loan.

MONEY SUPPLY

The money supply is the total amount of **money** in circulation in an **economy**. Money can actually be defined in several different ways. For example, in the United States the money supply is defined by the **Federal Reserve System** in the following four ways:

1) M1: the sum of **currency**, **demand deposits**, travelers' checks, and other **checkable deposits** (OCDs).

2) M2: M1 plus retail money market mutual fund (MMMF) balances, **savings deposits** (including **money market** deposit accounts, or MMDAs), and small **time deposits**.

3) M3: M2 plus large time deposits, repurchase agreements (RPs), Eurodollars, and institution-only money market **mutual fund** (MMMF) balances.

4) L (Liquidity): M3 plus other liquid **assets**.

These measures differ in low **liquidity**, or how close to cash the included items are. The U.S. money supply is controlled by the Federal Reserve through its **monetary policy**.

MONOPOLISTIC COMPETITION

Monopolistic competition is one of four basic **market** structures. The other three are **perfect competition**, **monopoly**, and **oligopoly**. Monopolistic competition is a market with a large number of small firms which sell similar, but not identical, products and in which there is a relative freedom to enter into and exit out of this **industry**. There are also many buyers (consumers) in a monopolistic competition.

A monopolistic competition is similar to a **perfect competition,** which has a large number of small firms with absolutely no market control. A monopoly is one firm with complete market control. Monopolistic competition is actually a mix of these two, because it is a market that contains a large number of extremely competitive firms, each with its own little monopoly because of product differentiation. Product differentiation means that although every firm supplies basically the same good, each firm's product offers something unique or special. These differences make it possible for these firms to act

JOAN ROBINSON

Joan Robinson was one of the most prominent economists of her time. Born in 1903 in Surrey, England, she was educated at the University of Cambridge, receiving a degree in **economics** in 1925.

In 1931 Robinson began teaching at Cambridge, remaining there until 1965. In 1979 she became the first female honorary fellow of King's College.

In her 1933 book *The Economics of Imperfect Competition*, Robinson introduced the theory of imperfect competition. Edward Chamberlin, another economist at that time, had discovered a similar theory.

During the 1930s Robinson was involved with the development of John Maynard Keynes's revolutionary **economic theory**. She not only taught Keynesian theory but also wrote several books and study guides on economic theory. In the early 1940s, however, she introduced aspects of Marxist economics in books such as *An Essay on Marxian Economics* (1942).

Robinson's unorthodox views made her the subject of considerable controversy throughout her career. She died in 1983.

EDWARD CHAMBERLIN

Edward Hastings Chamberlin, a U.S. economist born in 1899, was known for his theories on industrial monopolies and **competition**. He studied at the University of Iowa under the economist Frank H. Knight and received his Ph.D. from Harvard in 1927, where he subsequently spent his academic career.

Chamberlin's *Theory of Monopolistic Competition* was published in 1933, at the same time that economist Joan Robinson's theory of imperfect competition was made known to the world. These theories were very similar, and Chamberlin spent the rest of his life trying to differentiate his theory from Robinson's and defending it against critics.

Chamberlin is credited with introducing the term **product differentiation** into economic literature. Chamberlin's work was considered a major landmark in the development of the theory of industrial competition. He died in 1967 in Cambridge, Massachusetts.

like little monopolies. The best examples of monopolistic competition are businesses such as restaurants, clothing stores, and convenience stores. Each has some, but not extensive, **market power.**

MONOPOLY

A monopoly is a **market** structure with only a single seller of a unique product and no close substitutes. This means a monopoly has no **competition**. Monopoly is one of four basic market structures (the other three are **perfect competition**, **oligopoly**, and **monopolistic competition**). A firm with a monopoly has extensive market control (the ability to control the **price** and/or quantity of the good sold) because the **demand** for a monopoly firm's **output** is the only market demand. However, while a monopoly can control the market price, it cannot charge more than the maximum demand price buyers are willing to pay and it will usually find it optimal to charge a price below the maximum demand price. A monopoly does not generate an efficient allocation of **resources**. In the United States, monopolies are usually illegal, as they violate **antitrust laws**.

MONOPOLY RENT

Monopoly rent is the **income** or **profits** received by a **monopoly**. Rent in **economics** is the monetary return to any **factor of production** above the **price** of its **supply**. The factors of production are land, **capital**, **labor,** and entrepreneurship. Any of these can receive rent and the returns to a monopoly are called monopoly rent.

MONOPSONY

A monopsony is a **market** structure where there is only one buyer, making it the buyer equivalent to a monopoly. Just like a monopoly seller, a monopsony buyer is a **price** maker with complete market control. A monopsony does not generate an efficient allocation of **resources**. The price paid by a monopsony is lower and the quantity exchanged is less than if the market were perfectly competitive.

MORAL HAZARD

A moral hazard means a person changes his or her behavior in such a way as to adversely affect another person after an agreement between these two parties has been reached. Moral hazard is a problem faced by **insurance** companies when people who buy insurance later change their behavior in such as way that it increases the probability of a loss occurring. This will result in the insured party collecting insurance payments. Insurance companies usually do not know that this change in behavior has occurred. For example, after a person buys health insurance, he or she might stop exercising or not have regular medical exams, because they know their insurance company will pay for any medical expenses they get as a result. Another example fo a moal hazard is a person who qualifies as a safe driver, gets insurance, and then becomes more careless at driving. Moral hazard is a problem because the person making the decision is not responsible for his risky outcome.

MORTGAGE

A mortgage is when a borrower, or mortgagee (the person who receives the mortgage), uses an **asset** (such as a house) as security for a **loan**. The mortgagor (lender) and mortgagee sign a contract that outlines the payment schedule and amount of the mortgage. The mortgagor does not have the right of possession of the asset used for security unless the mortgagee does not keep up his or her payments.

MULTINATIONAL CORPORATION

A multinational corporation is a company that both produces and sells **economic goods and services** in a number of countries. A multinational company is different from a company that produces something in one country and **exports** that product to overseas markets, because it both produces and sells in more than one country. Typically, multinational corporations benefit from overseas **production** due to greater cost effectiveness.

MULTIPLIER EFFECT

The multiplier effect explains the impact of a change in any component of **aggregate demand**. According to the multiplier effect, an increase in the use of **money** will have an effect larger than the amount of the initial increase. When **income** increases, only a part of the increase is usually saved, while the rest is spent. Whoever receives a portion of the spent money will also save part and spend part, and so on. The total amount that is spent overall will be greater than the initial change (increase) in income. The multiplier effect is not instantaneous; rather, it is a cumulative process that occurs as a series of successive additions to an income.

For example, a government spends $1,000 on a computer, and the computer vendor saves some share of that income (money), say 30 percent, and spends the remaining 70 percent of the income from the sale of the computer. He may buy a digital camera for $700, which creates an increase in income of $700 for the camera seller. The camera seller may then spend 70 percent of this income on a stereo for $490. The stereo salesman then has a $490 increase in income. He may save 30 percent of that income and spend 70 percent, etc. Thus, the initial government expenditure has a multiplied effect on spending as a whole in the economy.

In order to tally this change in total spending, use the following equation:

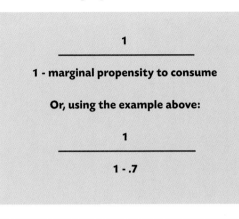

$$\frac{1}{1 - \text{marginal propensity to consume}}$$

Or, using the example above:

$$\frac{1}{1 - .7}$$

> **KEY POINT TODAY**
>
> The accelerator principle holds that small changes in consumer spending can result in large percentage changes in **investment** by **businesses**. The accelerator principle has been built into many **business cycle** theories, and is often used to explain shifts in investment.

MUTUAL FUND

A mutual fund is an investment company that combines, or pools the funds of many individuals to purchase corporate **stocks**, **bonds**, or other financial **assets**. When funds are pooled, transaction costs are reduced and individuals are given the opportunity to participate in financial **markets** that are typically closed to smaller investors (because of the greater amount of pooled money). Mutual funds also give consumers the chance to get higher **interest rates,** or returns on their **investments** than they would get at **banks,** and to diversify their **portfolio**.

> **KEY POINT TODAY**
>
> The most common types of mutual funds are "open-ended." That means there are no limits on the number of shares issued. "Close-ended" mutual funds issue a fixed number of shares that are then traded around.

N

A high tech expert for CNN, the cable news network, explains the ups and downs of the NASDAQ market on the air.

NASDAQ

NASDAQ stands for the National Association of Securities Dealers Automated Quotation. In 1971 NASDAQ was created to automate and trade **over-the-counter (OTC)** securities. Before then, dealer quotations were circulated by paper copy only. These copies were printed on pink-colored paper, which is why OTC securities

> **KEY POINT TODAY**
> NASDAQ stands for National Association of Securities Dealers Automated Quotation. It is a composite index based on the prices of 5,000 over-the-counter stocks.

are often referred to as "pink sheet" **stocks**. The "Pink Sheets" are still published weekly by the National Quotation Bureau. An electronic version of the Pink Sheets is also updated once a day and circulated by market data vendor terminals.

NATIONAL DEBT

National debt is also called public **debt**. It is the total amount of government debts due to government borrowing from the population, from foreign governments, or from international institutions. These debts are often created by issuing **interest**-paying **loans** in the form of **bonds**, bills, or notes. The government incurs these loans when there is a **budget deficit**. The government must repay these loans just as an individual must repay any loans he incurs.

NATIONAL DEBT, 1990–2000	
Years	**National Debt**
09/29/2000	$ 5,674,178,209,886.86
09/30/1999	$ 5,656,270,901,615.43
09/30/1998	$ 5,526,193,008,897.62
09/30/1997	$ 5,413,146,011,397.62
09/30/1996	$ 5,224,810,939,135.73
09/30/1995	$ 4,973,982,900,709.39
09/30/1994	$ 4,692,749,910,013.32
09/30/1993	$ 4,411,488,883,139.38
09/30/1992	$ 4,064,620,644,521.66
09/30/1991	$ 3,665,303,351,697.03
09/30/1990	$ 3,233,313,451,777.25

Source: U.S. Department of the Treasury

National public debt became a regular element in a country's **economy** when sources of **income** became available to provide funds to repay loans, a monetary system was fully formed, and an organized **money market** came into operation. The first public debt occurred in the late 17th century in Europe. Today the U.S. debt is divided into marketable and nonmarketable loans. Marketable loans are made up of bills, notes, and **bonds** that can be traded. Nonmarketable loans are U.S. savings bonds, securities owned by foreign governments, and government account securities that are redeemable but not tradable.

NATIONAL INCOME

National income (NI) is the government's official measure of how much **income** is generated by the **economy**. It is the total income earned by the nation's citizens as a result of their ownership of **resources** used in producing **final goods** and services during a given period of time (usually one year).

Every three months, three income measures are reported in the national income and product accounts by the Bureau of Economic Analysis. National income is the broadest of these three income measures. The other two are personal income (PI) and **disposable income** (DI).

NATIONALIZATION

When a national government takes over the ownership of a private **business** or **industry,** this is called nationalization. Nationalization was a common practice in the 1950s, 1960s, and 1970s—as when the United States tried to nationalize passenger train service with the establishment of Amtrak in 1970.

Nationalization has often gone hand-in-hand with the implementation of communist or socialist forms of government, as was the case in the transfer of industrial, banking, and insurance enterprises to the state in Russia after 1918; and the nationalization of the coal, electricity, gas, and transportation industries in Great Britain and France between 1945 and 1950. More recently, nationalization has been sparked by a resentment of foreign control over industries that the state may be largely dependent on, such as the nationalization of the oil industries in Mexico in 1938 and Iran in 1951, and in the nationalization of foreign businesses in Cuba in 1960. Another motive for recent nationalization is the belief in some developing countries that state control of various industrial operations is at least temporarily necessary because of the lack of a developed **capital** market or supply of **entrepreneurs** in the domestic private sector. In the 1980s the nationalization trend began to be reversed with the emergence of **privatization**.

Conservatives tend to favor privatization—market allocation and private ownership of **resources**. Liberals are more likely to favor paternalistic government allocation and ownership of resources—nationalization.

NATURAL MONOPOLY

A natural monopoly is an **industry** in which technical factors make it more efficient for a single firm to provide the goods. It can therefore lower its **price** when it produces and sells a larger quantity. This ability occurs because a natural monopoly uses a great deal of **capital**. Since capital carries an up-front cost that must be paid regardless of **production**, a natural monopoly can spread these costs over a larger quantity **output**. The larger the quantity sold, the lower the cost for each unit. Therefore, a single natural monopoly can produce and supply a good at a lower cost and price than two or more firms. In other words, if two or more firms try to supply the same good, the market will "naturally" end up with just one.

Telephone companies, electrical utilities, gas distributors, and cable television systems are all common examples of natural monopolies. To some degree, airlines, railroads, and other transit companies are also natural monopolies. Many such monopolies, especially those that supply essential products or services (like electricity), are allowed to legally operate as monopolies but are heavily regulated, controlled, or entirely operated by the government to prevent any of the abuses that monopolies might inflict on consumers.

NATURAL RATE OF UNEMPLOYMENT

Unemployment means the proportion of the **labor force** (16 years of age and older) that is looking for employment (a job) but is not currently employed. The natural rate of unemployment is the rate that exists when the **economy** is at **full employment**. This rate is primarily composed of **frictional** and **structural unemployment**.

NEGATIVE INCOME TAX

Negative income tax is a system for collecting taxes on **income**. With this system the government gives **tax** credits or pays **money** to people whose incomes are below a certain level or who have no income, and collects taxes from people whose incomes are above that level. Advocates of the negative tax system point to the advantages it has in encouraging people to work and making the **labor** markets more flexible. The negative income tax system has never been used in the United States.

NEOCLASSICAL ECONOMICS

Neoclassical economics was built on the school of economic thought called **classical economics** that developed during the 18th and 19th centuries. Classical economics tried to explain the way **markets** and market economies worked. In the late 19th century economists tried to solve some of the problems with classical economics and classical theory, and they developed what became called neoclassical economics ("neo" means "new"). The introduction of marginalist theory was the new basis of economic thought.

Neoclassical is often linked with American economist Paul Samuelson. Samuelson's method of **economic theory,** illustrated in his book *Foundations of Economic Analysis*, is said to characterize the neoclassical school of thought.

PAUL SAMUELSON

Paul Samuelson was born in Gary, Indiana in 1915. He went to college at the University of Chicago and received his Ph.D. from Harvard. He joined MIT as an assistant professor in 1940 and by 1947 was made full professor. In 1991 MIT established the Paul A. Samuelson Professorship in Economics in his honor.

Samuelson's most famous work, *Foundations of Economic Analysis* (1947), helped to revive neoclassical economics and to initiate the era of mathematization of **economics**. In 1948 Samuelson published the most successful and widely used economics textbook ever, *Economics*. Since its publication, 17 editions have been produced, with more than 3 million copies sold in the English language. It was the first book to explain the principles of Keynesian economics.

In 1970 Paul Samuelson became the first American to be honored with a Nobel Prize in Economics. During his long and prolific career, he served as an adviser to Presidents Kennedy, Johnson, and Carter.

NEO-KEYNESIANISM

John Maynard Keynes was a British economist who developed revolutionary theories about **monetary** and **fiscal policy** during the **Great Depression**. Keynes felt the government and the **central bank** should be used as tools in solving the **depression** and stabilizing the **business cycle**. After World War II, an American group of economists interpreted and formalized Keynes' classical theories; and this interpretation became known as Neo-Keynesianism. (See **John Maynard Keynes**, page 71.)

NET EXPORTS

Net exports is the difference between **exports** (**economic goods and services** produced by the domestic economy and purchased by foreign economies) and **imports** (goods and services produced by foreign economies and purchased by the domestic economy). Exports and imports are combined into a single measure called net exports in order to show the overall interaction between foreign economies and the domestic economy. If exports exceed imports, then net exports are positive. If imports exceed exports, then net exports are negative. (See **balance of trade.**)

NET NATIONAL PRODUCT (NNP)

Net National Product (NNP) is the total **market** value of all **final goods** and services produced by an **economy** during a given period of time (usually a year), after adjusting for the **depreciation** of **capital**. Just like net domestic product (NDP), NNP is a measure of the net production in the economy. NNP has the same relation to NDP that **gross national product (GNP)** has to **gross domestic product (GDP)**.

NEWLY INDUSTRIALIZED COUNTRIES

During the 1960s and 1970s, the Republic of Korea (South Korea) and the Republic of China (Taiwan) experienced periods of dramatic **economic growth,** which was brought on largely by the adoption of an **export promotion** strategy of development. These two countries, along with the city-states of Hong Kong and Singapore, made up the group of export-oriented **industrialization** success stories known as the "Four Asian Tigers," also referred to as newly industrialized countries (NICs).

NEW YORK STOCK EXCHANGE

The New York Stock Exchange (NYSE) is the largest **stock market** in the United States. It is located on **Wall Street** in New York City and is often called the "Big Board." When the United States was just starting out in the 1790s, the New York Stock Exchange was established to help new **corporations** raise **money** needed for capital **investment**. A group of 24 brokers signed the

> **KEY POINT TODAY**
> A "member" of the NYSE is a company or individual who owns a "seat" on the trading floor. The number of seats has remained at 1,366 since 1953.

Buttonwood Agreement, which offered them specified commission and equal preferential treatment. Consequently only members could participate in the **stock** auctions that were held under the buttonwood tree (an actual tree that grew in lower Manahttan) or, in bad weather, in a nearby coffeehouse. In 1817 the Buttonwood Group became the NYSE. Today, millions of transactions take place on the NYSE each day. All of these transactions are made by NYSE members. There are over 1,000 members of the exchange, and the only way to get a seat is from a member who is retiring or has recently died.

NOMINAL GDP

Nominal GDP is the nominal **gross domestic product (GDP)**. It is the total market **value** (measured in current **prices**) of all new **economic goods and services** produced within the political boundaries of an **economy** during a given period of time (usually one year). It is important to note that nominal GDP is measured in current, or actual prices—the prices buyers actually pay for the goods and services they purchase. Nominal GDP is also referred to as the current gross domestic product. (See **real GDP.**)

The New York Stock Exchange

A waiter points something out on a menu to a customer. Dining out is a normal good.

NOMINAL INTEREST RATE

The nominal interest rate is the **interest rate** that is shown on the face and in the body of a **bond**. This is the **rate of return** on a deposit, bond, or a **loan** that does not take into account the **inflation rate**. It is contrasted to the **real interest rate.**

NOMINAL VALUE

A **stock** is a certificate representing one unit of ownership in a **corporation**, **mutual fund**, or a limited partnership. When such a share has been offered for sale by a **corporation,** it is said to have been issued. Nominal value is the **value** of such a share when it is issued. Later, the share can go up or down in value. Nominal value is expressed in terms of current dollars

NORMAL GOOD

A normal good is one whose **demand** increases with an increase in **income**. That is, as incomes rise people will purchase more of that good. Therefore, we say a normal good has a positive **income elasticity of demand**.

Some examples of normal goods would be cars, houses, entertainment (such as movie tickets, dining out, cable TV, sporting events, etc.), and additional educational opportunities. When people experience a rise in income, they have more **money** they can spend on these things.

The opposite of a normal good is an **inferior good**. As people make more money, the demand for inferior goods decrease.

NORMAL PROFIT

Normal profit is a return, or profit, on the production of **economic goods and services** that is just sufficient to keep the existing firms in an **industry**. If there were more than normal profit, other firms would enter the **market**. If there were less than normal profits, existing firms would leave the market. Normal profit is also the **rate of return** that would be achieved in an industry under **perfect competition.**

NORMATIVE ECONOMICS

Normative economics is the branch of **economics** that uses ideals for the way the **economy** should operate, rather than actual proof. As the policy side of economics, it is based on value judgments that cannot be proven right or wrong.

Normative economics is used to recommend ways to change the world, to improve it, and to make it a better place. Normative economists might say something like "the price of wheat should be $5 a bushel to give farmers a higher living standard and to save the family farm," or, "People who earn a high **income** should pay more **income tax** than people who earn a low income." But these are value judgments. No authority can say unerringly the way things "should be" regarding farmers or incomes. (See **positive economics**.)

NORTH AMERICAN FREE TRADE AGREEMENT (NAFTA)

The North American Free Trade Agreement (NAFTA), is an agreement that calls for the gradual removal of **tariffs** and other trade barriers on almost all goods produced and sold in North America. NAFTA took effect in Canada, Mexico, and the United States on January 1, 1994. This agreement forms the world's second largest **free trade zone**, connecting over 365 million consumers in Canada, Mexico, and the United States in an open **market**. However, this agreement has been quite controversial. Critics say the treaty is filled with concessions to special interests protecting their markets, and U.S. workers feared that their companies would lay off their highly paid U.S. **labor** and move their factories to Mexico in favor of the cheaper labor there. Supporters claimed that Mexico's **economy** was too small a market and labor pool to harm the United States. Despite the controversy, most economists firmly support NAFTA.

NAFTA has eliminated duties on half of all

KEY POINT TODAY

NAFTA did not affect the phase-out of tariffs between Canada and the U.S. under the Canada-U.S. Free Trade Agreement (FTA), which was completed on January 1, 1998. Since then, virtually all tariffs on Canada-U.S. trade in goods were eliminated. Some tariffs remain in place for Canada's supply-managed sectors (e.g. dairy and poultry), as well as sugar, dairy, peanuts and cotton in the United States.

U.S. goods to Mexico and has called for the phasing out of other **tariffs** over 14 years.

NORTH-SOUTH INCOME GAP

The North-South **income** gap refers to the growing inequity between the incomes of industrialized countries and less developed countries. The North-South income gap earns its name from the fact that most industrialized nations are in the Northern hemisphere.

Labor activists and workers in El Paso, Texas, protest their loss of jobs—a loss they blame on NAFTA.

OLIGOPOLY

The four basic **market** structures are **perfect competition**, **monopoly**, **monopolistic competition**, and oligopoly. An oligopoly is a market structure where a small number of large firms, selling either identical or differentiated products, dominate the market. There are also significant **barriers to entry** into the **industry**.

Today, about half of the output produced in the world **economy** comes from oligopolistic industries. Everything from breakfast cereal to cars, from computers to aircraft, from television broadcasting to pharmaceuticals, from petroleum to detergent are produced in oligopolistic industries. Since each major firm in an oligopolistic industry is relatively large, each has a substantial degree of **market power**.

With oligopoly, each of the firms in an industry is interdependent—that is, the actions of one firm depend on the actions of another. In both **perfect competition** and **monopolistic competition**, the actions of one firm have no effect on other firms. Each firm is so small in relation to the overall market that firms are independent of one another. Since a monopoly is the only firm in an industry, interdependence is not relevant.

OPEN ECONOMY

An open economy is an **economy** with a great deal of **foreign trade**. A completely open economy has no trade barriers at all. Most nations have a relatively open economy (as opposed to a completely open economy) due to some trade restrictions.

> **KEY POINT TODAY**
>
> In an open economy, international trade, **exports**, and **imports** are all large in comparison to the size of the economy's **national income**.

OPEN-MARKET OPERATION

Open-market operation refers to the **Federal Reserve System**'s buying and selling of government securities to try to alter **bank** reserves and therefore the nation's **money supply**. These actions are under the direction of the **Federal Open Market Committee** and are the Federal Reserve System's most effective and most often used tool of **monetary policy**. For example, if the Federal Reserve wants to increase the money supply (called "easy money"), it buys government securities. The Federal Reserve pays for these purchases by adding reserves to the banking system. The reserves are then used by banks for **loans** to consumers and **businesses**. This results in an increase in the total of checking account balances in the **economy**. Since checking accounts are three-fourths of the money supply, the Federal Reserve increases the money supply this way instead of printing money.

If the Federal Reserve chooses to reduce the money supply (called "tight money"), it sells some government securities. This reduces bank reserves, restricts the ability of banks to make loans, and therefore decreases the money supply.

OPPORTUNITY COST

The opportunity cost of any good or service is the cost of foregone opportunities—that is, it is the value of other goods or services that are given up in order to produce it. For example, if a certain amount of **labor** is used to make televisions, then that labor is already in use and cannot be used to make CD players. In deciding whether to make televisions or CD players, it would be necessary to decide what the value of the CD players that could be made would be in comparison to the televisions. Of course, all the **factors of production** would have to be considered.

Generally, the opportunity cost of any action is the value of the action not taken. For example, if you choose to work or visit a friend after school, the opportunity cost of working is the value you place on visiting a friend.

Iranian President Mohammad Khatami surveys an offshore oil rig in the Persian Gulf in March 2000.

ORGANIZATION OF PETROLEUM EXPORTING COUNTRIES (OPEC)

The Organization of Petroleum Exporting Countries (OPEC) is a **cartel** dedicated to the stability and prosperity of the petroleum **market**. Membership in this organization is open to any country that is a substantial exporter of oil and shares the ideals of the organization. OPEC became the major petroleum pricing power in 1973, when ownership of oil **production** in the Middle East transferred from the operating companies to the governments of the producing countries or to their national oil companies. Algeria, Gabon, Indonesia, Iran, Iraq, Kuwait, Libya, Nigeria, Qatar, Saudi Arabia, the United Arab Emirates, and Venezuela are all members of OPEC.

OUTPUT

Output refers to the **economic goods and services** created by using a combination of **factors of production**. (See **production**.)

OVER-THE-COUNTER (OTC) MARKET

Over-the-counter (OTC) market is a term that refers to a secondary **stock** market for company stocks and securities that are not listed on an organized **stock exchange**, such as the **New York Stock Exchange** (NYSE) or the **American Stock Exchange** (AMEX). These securities are sold mainly over the telephone or over computer networks.

Many companies have insufficient shares outstanding, stockholders, or **earnings** to warrant an application for listing on a major exchange, so their securities are traded instead over the telephone between dealers who act either as principals or as brokers for customers.

Trading rules in the OTC market for broker-dealers are established and enforced by the National Association of Securities Dealers (NASD). The OTC is a high-speed computerized network called **NASDAQ** (National Association of Securities Dealers Automated Quotations).

P

PARADOX OF THRIFT

A paradox is a statement or question that seems to contradict itself. The paradox of thrift states that if people try to be thrifty and save more, this will make things worse because the **economy** will slow down and some people will lose their jobs. With no **income** they may wind up saving less than before. This is a paradox because we tend to think of saving as good for the individual. However, if all save, it can be harmful. Neverhteless, if savings by individuals are borrowed by **business** to finance **investment** spending, saving does not cause **demands** to fall, and the paradox is resolved.

PARTNERSHIP

A partnership is one of the three basic forms of **business** organization. The other two are **corporations,** and proprietorships. A partnership is a business owned by two or more partners. Legally, the owners and the business are considered to be one and the same. This means that each owner can be held personally responsible for any and all of the business's **debts**, including those debts made by the other partner. This is called unlimited **liability**. Lawyers, accountants, dentists, and physicians often form partnerships in order to do business.

PERFECT COMPETITION

Perfect competition refers to an ideal **market** structure that has a large number of small firms selling identical products, with freedom of entry into and exit out of their **industry.** Perfect competition is one of four basic market structures that also include **monopoly**, **oligopoly**, and **monopolistic competition**.

Perfect competition is an ideal market structure, but it does not exist in the real world. However, it does provide a perfect reference point that can be used to analyze real-world market structures. Perfect competition allocates **resources** efficiently.

PHILLIPS CURVE

The Phillips curve is a graphic representation showing the relationship between **inflation** and **unemployment**. It comes from the economist A. William Phillips, who in the 1950s developed the idea that there is a **trade-off** between a low **employment rate** and the rate of inflation. In other words, when unemployment levels rise, a **demand** for jobs also rises. Meanwhile, the demand for products decreases as people cannot afford to buy as many things. A drop in demand creates a rise in **prices** or an increase in inflation. Economists often debate the existence of a trade-off between inflation and employment.

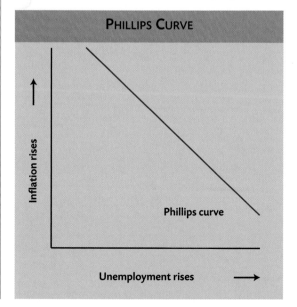

PHILLIPS CURVE

Inflation rises

Phillips curve

Unemployment rises

PLANNED ECONOMY/CENTRAL PLANNING

A planned economy is an **economic system** that relies almost entirely on government planning and control in all its phases. The government decides how many goods should be produced, who will produce them, and at what price they will be produced.

A planned economy can be contrasted with a market-oriented economy, or a **capitalist** society that relies primarily on the decisions of a large number of independent buyers and sellers to determine the answers to **production** and pricing questions. The former Soviet Union and China are the best-known examples of planned economies.

POLITICAL BUSINESS CYCLE

A political **business cycle** is an **expansion** or **contraction** in the **economy** that is caused by political leaders trying to achieve a personal political goal—in many cases, to be reelected to office. In order to be reelected, politicians might be tempted to stimulate the economy to grow through **fiscal policy** such as increased government spending or **tax** cuts. Whether fiscal policy is politically motivated or motivated by what is best for the nation as a whole is up to the voters to decide.

PORTFOLIO

A portfolio is the combined holdings of **loan** securities and other **assets** by an individual or an institution. A portfolio may contain assets such as **bonds**, **common stocks**, **preferred stocks**, government securities, and others. The purpose of having a diverse group of **investments** in a portfolio is to reduce the risk that any single investment will lose money. This strategy of maintaining different types of investments is called diversification. A portfolio may also include some investments that offer high **short run** dividends and others that offer **long run** capital growth.

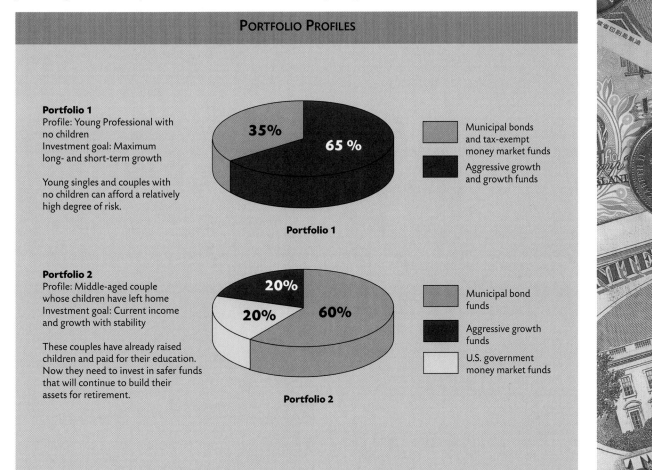

PORTFOLIO PROFILES

Portfolio 1
Profile: Young Professional with no children
Investment goal: Maximum long- and short-term growth

Young singles and couples with no children can afford a relatively high degree of risk.

35%
65 %

Municipal bonds and tax-exempt money market funds

Aggressive growth and growth funds

Portfolio 1

Portfolio 2
Profile: Middle-aged couple whose children have left home
Investment goal: Current income and growth with stability

These couples have already raised children and paid for their education. Now they need to invest in safer funds that will continue to build their assets for retirement.

20%
20%
60%

Municipal bond funds

Aggressive growth funds

U.S. government money market funds

Portfolio 2

POSITIVE ECONOMICS

Positive economics is the branch of **economics** that tries to explain the way the **economy** actually operates rather than how it ought to. This can be contrasted with **normative economics,** which tries to explain the way the economy should ideally operate. With positive economics, scientific methods are applied to economic situations to verify hypotheses.

If one says, "an increase in the price of corn to $10 a bushel gave farmers a higher living standard and helped save 1,000 family farms from bankruptcy," this is a positive statement because it can be verified by checking corn **prices** to see if they did in fact increase to $10 a bushel. One can also examine farmers' living standards (measured by per capita income), and check if 1,000 family farms that might have gone bankrupt are still operating. Verifying such a statement can be quite involved, but the fact that it *can* be verified makes it a positive statement.

POVERTY LINE

The poverty line is the official measure of the **income** needed by a family based on family size, location, and characteristics of the head of the **household**. When a family makes an amount of

money below this line, then they are living below the poverty line. There is no official number used in the United States to distinguish those living below the poverty line, although a guideline was created. In 2000 that guideline was set at an annual income of $17,050 or less for a family of four living in any state except Hawaii and Alaska. The income varies depending on the size of the family.

> ### KEY POINT TODAY
> Poverty is an area of economic research that is increasingly demanding more attention. There are many **social costs** linked with the number of people who live below the poverty line—for example, the costs of crime, poor health, and low levels of education.

PRECAUTIONARY MOTIVE/TRANSACTION MOTIVE/SPECULATIVE MOTIVE

According to **Keynesian economics** there three reasons, or motives, to keep money in a liquid (easily changed to cash) form. The precautionary

Two children stand outside of a house in Tunica County, Mississippi, one of the poorest counties in the United States.

motive drives people to keep cash on hand to take care of unforeseen circumstances such as illness, **unemployment,** or other emergencies. The transaction motive reserves cash for daily or frequent expenditures, such as commuting costs or lunch money, that occur between the intervals of income.

The **speculative motive** involves the desire to have a certain amount of cash or other liquid **assets** on hand in order to be able to easily invest in the **bonds** or securities **markets**. It involves an uncertainty as to future **interest rates** and **stock** prices, and whether the rates will rise and fall, because the **investments** one would want would be different in each of those cases. The term comes from the fact that prediction of future interest rates is highly speculative.

PREFERRED STOCK

Preferred stock is a type of ownership share in a **corporation**. Usually **stock** is divided into two types—**common stock** and preferred stock. Preferred stock has first claim to the corporation's net **assets**. Common stock has second claim. If a corporation has no preferred stock, then common stock has all claim on the net assets. (See **blue chip.**)

PRESENT VALUE

Present value is the amount of **money** today (after **interest** is added) that would have the same **value** as an amount some time in the future. For example, $100 today plus 10 percent interest ($10) would have a value of $110 in one year and a value of $121 at the end of two years. This also works in reverse: $110 in one year, given a 10 percent **interest rate** ($10) would be equivalent to $100 today.

The process of translating a future payment into its present value (such an amount to be received when a **bond** reaches maturity) is called discounting.

PRICE

Price is the value of the **asset** that a person pays or a **business** receives in a **market** transaction in exchange for another asset. For example, **money** is usually the item or asset that is exchanged for something else. The amount of money given up for an item is its **price**.

Price relates to both **supply** and **demand**. It relates to supply because the price of a good or service reflects the **opportunity cost** of **production** (the supply price). It relates to demand because the price reflects the ability of the buyers to purchase a good or service that is based on

A variety of prices are displayed to the consumer at a fish market in New York's Chinatown.

the satisfaction received (the demand price). **Equilibrium** price occurs when the demand and supply prices are equal. This also means that the quantities demanded and supplied are equal, and the market has achieved equilibrium.

Prices play the major role in balancing supply and demand in market exchanges and eliminating **shortages** and **surpluses** because price changes separately cause changes in quantity demanded and quantity supplied. A rising price decreases the quantity demanded and increases the quantity supplied, thereby eliminating a shortage. A falling price increases the quantity demanded and decreases the quantity supplied, thereby eliminating any surplus.

PRICE CEILING

A price ceiling is a legally set maximum price for goods or services. The government will sometimes set a maximum **price** for a good to keep it from rising too high. That way, it will stay affordable for people with less **money**. Things like apartments, gasoline, and natural gas often have price ceilings. There are often problems with price ceilings, however. Since more people can afford items with fixed prices, this usually results in a **shortage** of these goods. As a result of this shortage, a **black market** may be created, and the good is then sold illegally above the price ceiling. (See **price floor.**)

PRICE DISCRIMINATION

Charging different prices according to different buyers for the same good is called price discrimination. Suppliers who have achieved some degree of **market power**, especially those with a **monopoly**, will often practice some kind of price discrimination.

Electricity rates, long-distance telephone charges, movie ticket prices, airplane ticket prices, and assorted child or senior citizen discounts are all subject to price discrimination. The buyers for these items cannot trade back and forth, so they are willing to pay different prices. On an airplane, for example, business travelers often pay more for identical service.

For a **business** (or individual) to practice price discrimination effectively, not only must it have market control, it must also identify two or more groups that are willing to pay different prices, and then keep the buyers in one group from reselling the good to another group.

PRICE ELASTICITY OF DEMAND

In **economics**, **elasticity** is a term that means the measure of the percent change in one variable in response to a percent change in another variable. The price elasticity of demand (PED) is the change in quantity demanded in response to a relative change in price. Specifically, it is the percentage change in quantity demanded due to a percentage change in demand price. The price elasticity of **demand** should be compared with the price elasticity of **supply.**

Use this formula to calculate price elasticity of demand (PED):

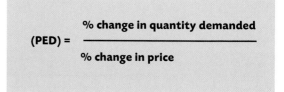

$$(PED) = \frac{\% \text{ change in quantity demanded}}{\% \text{ change in price}}$$

PRICE ELASTICITY OF SUPPLY

In **economics**, **elasticity** is a term that means the measure of the percent change in one variable in response to a percent change in another variable. Price elasticity of supply (PES) is the change in quantity supplied in response to a relative change in price. Specifically, it is the percentage change in quantity supplied due to a percentage change in supply price. The price elasticity of supply should be contrasted with the price elasticity of demand.

Use this formula to calculate price elasticity of supply (PES) :

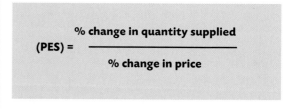

$$(PES) = \frac{\% \text{ change in quantity supplied}}{\% \text{ change in price}}$$

PRICE FIXING

Price fixing means that two or more firms in an **industry** agree on the **price** to charge for a product or service and thus avoid competing with each other. Price fixing is one of the reasons **cartels** are started; it is also a violation of the U.S. **antitrust laws.**

PRICE FLOOR

A price floor is a legally established minimum **price** for a product or service. The government will sometimes set price floors to maintain the price of a good at a higher level because suppliers believe they are not getting enough **income** for the product or service they sell. Farm products and workers often have price floors (a minimum wage, for example). The problem with price floors is that they usually result in a **surplus**. This means that many times surplus food rots in warehouses, or surplus workers do not have jobs. Sometimes the government steps in and buys up the surplus food and other items at the minimum price. This food may then be stored or it may given away or sold to another country. Ultimately, however, the cost of buying the surplus and disposing of it is borne by the taxpayers. (See **price ceiling.**)

PRICE INDEX (CONSUMER PRICE INDEX AND PRODUCER PRICE INDEX)

A price index is a measure of the average of a group of prices, calculated as a ratio to prices in a given time period (that is, a **base year**). A price index is primarily used to compare changes in the group prices over time. Such an index is an indicator of overall price trends.

The **Consumer Price Index** (CPI) is a "weighted" index of prices of **economic goods and services** usually purchased by people in cities (urban population). This index is compiled and published each month by the Bureau of Labor Statistics (BLS). The BLS obtains data for this index from a survey of 25,000 retail outlets and quantity data generated by the Consumer Expenditures Survey. The CPI is used to indicate the current price level. Increases in the CPI measure **inflation.** It is also used to adjust **wage** and **income** payments (such as **Social Security** or **welfare** payments) to keep pace with inflation.

The Producer Price Index (PPI) is an index of the prices domestic producers receive from selling their products. This index is compiled and published monthly by the BLS. The PPI most seen in the various media is the Producer Price Index for All Commodities. There are thousands of PPIs reported for various industries or combinations of industries and for specific products. The Wholesale Price Index came before the Producer Price Indexes and tracked wholesaler to retailer sales. The prices in the old Wholesale Price Index are now shown in the Finished Goods Price Index.

PRICE TAKER

A price taker is a buyer or seller with so little **market power** that he or she has no control over the price of a good and must "take" or accept it at the going market **price. Perfect competition** is a **market** structure with many price takers.

PRICE WAR

A price war occurs when rival **oligopolies** (companies that compete to sell the same prod-

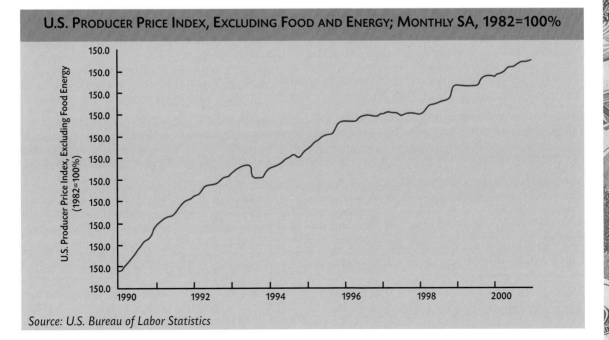

U.S. PRODUCER PRICE INDEX, EXCLUDING FOOD AND ENERGY; MONTHLY SA, 1982=100%

U.S. Producer Price Index, Excluding Food Energy (1982=100%)

Source: U.S. Bureau of Labor Statistics

A salesgirl slashes prices during a price war between the former rival department stores, Macy's and Gimbels.

uct) reduce their **prices** below those of their competitors (and maybe even below their own cost).

Two examples of companies that might do this would be Coca-Cola and Pepsi-Cola or Burger King and McDonald's. Since Coca-Cola and Pepsi-Cola are products that are very much alike, and Burger King and McDonald's both sell hamburgers, each pair of these companies are rivals. They might try to underprice the other in order to attract more business. If a customer likes Coca-Cola, but Pepsi-Cola is less expensive, he or she might start buying Pepsi instead of Coke.

Price wars also typically break out when there is a fall in **demand** for a certain product but an **excess supply**.

PRIMARY MARKET

A primary market is a financial **market** for newly issued securities—that is, the first opportunity investors have to buy a newly issued security. After these first purchases, trading occurs in the **secondary market**.

When government securities are sold to primary dealers, this is considered a primary market. These primary dealers may then resell the securities to investors in the secondary market. There are primary markets for nonfinancial goods as well.

PRIME RATE

The prime rate is the **interest rate** that **banks** charge their best customers. It is somewhat lower than other commercial interest rates, but is offered only to **blue chip** companies with the highest **credit** ratings. The prime rate is one of the key interest rates in the **economy**. This rate is watched closely by government policy makers, **businesses**, and financial advisors. Consumers should also pay close attention to the prime rate if they have **loans** with adjustable rates, like credit cards that are adjusted according to the prime rate. When the prime rate changes, these adjustable rates also change.

PRINCIPAL

A principal is the original amount of **money** in a **savings deposit** in a **bank**, or the original amount that a borrower borrows before the **interest** sets in.

PRINCIPLE AGENT PROBLEM

A principle agent problem often occurs in large **businesses** and governments because those making decisions (called agents) have different goals from those affected by these decisions (called principals). A **corporation**'s management and its shareholders provide a good example of a principle agent problem. As the owners of the corporation, the shareholders are the principals interested in earning a **profit**. The managers of the corporation act as agents. As such, they are supposed to do what is best for the shareholders. However, they might be tempted to employ more workers than they actually need or to increase their own salaries, which takes away from shareholders' profits.

A man stands in the doorway of his small shop. The shop is his private enterprise.

Shareholders probably do not know what the managers do. A principle agent problem is a source of inefficiency in business operations.

PRIVATE ENTERPRISE

Private enterprise is any business, no matter what its size, run by private individuals or **corporations** for **profit** or other private benefit. This is in contrast to enterprises owned and run by various governments. Private enterprises are considered the key components of **free market** or capitalist economies. They provide the competitive **supply** of goods the consumers will trade for in the **market**.

PRIVATE SECTOR

The private sector includes transactions between individuals, institutions, and **business** in the **economy** and combines them into a single group. The private sector can be contrasted with the **public sector** (which is also called the government sector.)

Private ownership and control of **resources** for voluntary allocation decisions come from the private sector, while the public sector gives government much of the power to make those decisions. Most economies are a combination of allocation decisions made by both the private sector and the public sector. Together the private and public sectors make up a country's domestic economy, and with the foreign sector added, they make up a country's national economy.

PRIVATIZATION

While **nationalization** gives government control over **production** activities, privatization does just the opposite. It is the process of converting government-owned **assets**, properties, or production activities to private ownership. Privatization became popular in the 1980s, along with business deregulation and a movement toward greater use of **markets**. Those who favor privatization argue that **competitive markets**, guided by the **"invisible hand"** and private ownership of property, tend to create the most efficient system. Many government functions cannot be performed efficiently by the private sector, however.

Privatization is usually favored by conservatives who advocate the market allocation and private ownership of **resources** from this philosophical view of **economics**. Liberals, however, usually favor nationalization, or government allocation and ownership of resources.

PRODUCER GOODS

Producer goods are goods such as fuel and chemicals that are used in the **production** of another product. They are not goods that are sold directly to the consumer.

PRODUCER SOVEREIGNTY

Producer sovereignty can be contrasted with **consumer sovereignty**. Producer sovereignty asserts that in a particular **economy** or sector, producers' preferences and decisions determine what will be produce, and how, and what consumers will use. This might be because producers control consumers' perceptions through advertising, or because professional expertise backed by legal restrictions on consumer behavior enables producers to control actual decisions. Economists used to believe that consumer preferences determined the **market**. Today many

P

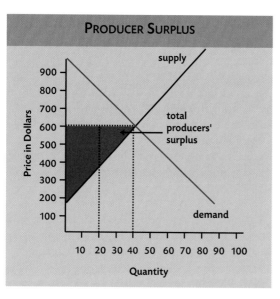

PRODUCER SURPLUS

supply

total producers' surplus

demand

Price in Dollars

900
800
700
600
500
400
300
200
100

10 20 30 40 50 60 70 80 90 100

Quantity

believe that from Microsoft on down to toothpaste, it is actually the producers that control the market.

PRODUCER SURPLUS

When producers obtain extra **money** from selling a good over and above the **opportunity cost** of **production**, this extra money is called producer **surplus.** Producer surplus is the difference between the minimum **supply** price sellers would be willing to accept for a product and the **price** they actually receive. For example, if Sears is willing and able to accept $200 for a new dishwasher (the supply price), but the going **market** for dishwashers is $300, and Sears receives $300 for every dishwasher sold, then they have a producer surplus of $100 per dishwasher.

PRODUCTION

Production is the process of transforming raw materials, **factors of production**, and natural **resource**s into **economic goods and services** that satisfy consumers. Living standards are enhanced by taking things that do not provide consumer satisfaction in their natural state and converting them into goods that provide more consumer satisfaction. For example, minerals, iron ore, and other materials that are used to make a car are much less satisfying to consumers on their own than when made into something that can be driven—like a Porsche or a Cadillac. On a more basic level, wheat and other grains are not very satisfying, but when they are used to produce bread, they become a product all consumers can appreciate.

Recently harvested wheat is poured into the back of a truck to be transported.

PRODUCTION COSTS

Production costs include the amount of money that is spent in manufacturing **economic goods and services.** The various costs of manufacturing a product may include raw materials, worker's **wages**, taxes, electricity, maintenance of equipment, etc.

PRODUCTION POSSIBILITY FRONTIER

The production possibility frontier shows those combinations of **economic goods and services** that a **business**, **industry**, or nation could possibly achieve with the existing fixed **resources** and technology. It is often represented by a graph that illustrates **production** possibilities when resources are fully employed. When the resources of production are not fully employed, the production quantity falls.

This graph shows the difference in production possibility when there are two people picking apples versus four people. With two people working, the maximum amount of apples they can pick in six days is 400 pounds. When four people are working together, however, the maximum amount of apples they can pick is 600 apples. In other words, when more people work together on a job, production increases.

PRODUCTIVITY

Productivity is the average amount of **economic goods and services** produced, per period, by a unit of a **factor of production**. Productivity increases when a worker produces more of a good in the same amount of time.Productivity increases primarily through the use of more efficient workers and higher quality equipment.

PROFIT

Profit is the amount of **money** a **business** has left over after all **production** costs, including taxes, have been paid. Types of profit include payment to **entrepreneurs** for the assumption of risk, and **interest** payments to capitalists for **loans**. (See **economic profit**.)

PROGRESSIVE TAXATION

Progressive taxation is a form of **taxation** (imposing taxes) that takes a larger percentage of a larger **income** and a smaller percentage of a smaller income. This means that people with a higher income pay a larger percentage in taxes. For example, if you earn $20,000 a year and your boss earns $40,000, you pay $2,000 (10 percent) in taxes, while your boss pays $8,000 (20 percent) in taxes. The U.S. **income tax** system is progressive, but all the loopholes and deductions keep it from being truly progressive in practice. **Direct taxes** are a form of progressive taxation. (See **regressive taxation**.)

PROPERTY RIGHTS

Property rights are the legal ownership of **resources**. This ownership entitles the owner to receive the benefits or pay the cost of the productive activities of these resources. Property rights originated with the ownership of land and its natural resources, but today it is just as important for **labor** and **capital** resources.

PROPORTIONAL TAXATION

Proportional taxation is a form of **taxation** that takes the exact same percentage of all incomes (no matter how large or how small). For example, if you earn $20,000 a year and your boss earns $40,000, you pay $2,000 (10 percent) in taxes a year, and your boss pays $4,000 (10 percent) in taxes a year. Taxation is then said to be proportional. (See **progressive taxation; regressive taxation**.)

PROTECTIONISM

Protectionism is a government policy that protects domestic producer-sellers from the **competition** of foreign sellers. Protective **tariffs**, **quotas**, and other non-tariff barriers designed to stop foreigners from selling in domestic **markets** are all elements of protectionism.

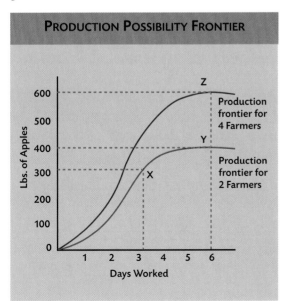

PRODUCTION POSSIBILITY FRONTIER

Lbs. of Apples / Days Worked

Production frontier for 4 Farmers

Production frontier for 2 Farmers

P

A fireworks display over the Statue of Liberty is an example of a public good.

PUBLIC GOOD

A public good is a good or service that is available to everyone. Public goods are those that are difficult to keep nonpayers from using (non-excludability). In addition, the use of the good by one person does not prevent use by others (non-rivals).

The national defense, fireworks displays at public events, and a clean environment are all examples of public goods. The government provides many public goods, because a private business could not profitably produce these kinds of things. They cannot charge a **price** and keep "free riders" (non-paying people) away. The government pays for public goods through taxes.

PUBLIC SECTOR

The public sector includes all of the transactions made by the government sector; in the United States that includes the federal, state, and local governments. The public sector is contrasted to the **private sector,** which includes **households** and **businesses**.

Government ownership and control of **resources** for allocation decisions come from the public sector, while the private sector gives private businesses and consumers much of the power to make those decisions on their own.

Most economies are a combination of allocation decisions made by both the public sector and the private sector. (See **mixed economy.**)

PURCHASING POWER

Purchasing power is the ability to purchase goods or services. Purchasing power declines as **prices** rise. For that reason, **inflation** severely reduces purchasing power. For example, if you usually buy a hot dog at a vendor's stand for 50 cents, but today the hot dogs are $1.00, you have less purchasing power than you did when hot dogs were just 50 cents. The other element that affects purchasing power is not how much one dollar will buy, but how many dollars you have. If a bicycle cost $50 forty years ago and the average annual income was $3,000, and an identical bicycle now costs $100 but the average annual income is $10,000, then purchasing power has increased. The old annual income ($3000) could have bought 60 bicycles, but the new annual income ($10,000) can buy 100 bicycles.

PURCHASING POWER PARITY

Purchasing power parity is a method of adjusting **incomes** in different countries to reflect differences in the purchasing power of that income. It provides a more accurate measure of national income differences between countries.

Q–R

QUALITY CONTROL

Quality control means detecting problems in products and services before they reach consumers. While **businesses** try to produce as much as possible as cheaply as possible, it is important that they also focus on quality control in order to improve their relationships with consumers and, by extension, their **market** positions.

QUANTITY DEMANDED

Quantity demanded refers to the maximum quantity of a good or service that buyers are willing and able to buy at a specific **demand price**. The specific quantity demanded is paired with a specific price. If 1,000 candy bars are sold for $1 each, then the price-quantity demanded pair is $1 and 1,000 candy bars. If 600 are sold when the price is $2 each, then the price-quantity demanded pair is $2 and 600 candy bars. (See **demand curve.**)

QUANTITY SUPPLIED

Quantity supplied refers to the maximum quantity of a good or service that sellers are willing and able to sell at a specific **supply** price. The specific quantity supplied is paired with a set price. If 1,000 candy bars are produced and sold for $1 each, then the price-quantity supplied pair is $1 and 1,000 candy bars. If 600 are produced and sold when the price is $2 each, then the price-quantity supplied pair is $2 and 600 candy bars. (See **supply curve.**)

QUANTITY THEORY OF MONEY

The quantity theory of money says that a percentage change in the **money supply** will lead to an equal percentage change in nominal gross domestic product (**nominal GDP**). This theory was derived from the **equation of exchange** and explains the **monetarists'** view of **macroeconomics**.

In order to translate the equation of exchange to the quantity theory of money, one assumes that the velocity of money is constant (not affected by things like **output, price** level, and money supply). The quantity theory of money has important implications on the concepts of **economic growth**, **inflation**, and the role of **monetary policy** to both stabilize prices and produce maximum non-inflationary economic growth.

QUOTA

There are two types of quotas, and both deal with limits on quantity. The first type of quota is the maximum limit on a quantity. For example, an **import** quota is a limit on the amount of goods that can be imported into a country. Import quotas are designed to reduce **competition** for domestic producers. They are a barrier to trade. The second type of quota is a minimum acceptable quantity. This type often deals with employment, as in affirmative action. For example, certain jobs may have quotas for minority workers (African Americans, Hispanics, women, etc.). This means that at least a certain number or percentage (the quota) of certain minorities must hold these positions.

RATE OF RETURN

The rate of return is often referred to as the rate of **interest**. It is the payment that lenders or creditors require for letting others use their money and the payment borrowers are willing to pay to use someone else's money.

The rate of return is the ratio of additional annual **income**, or **profit**, created by an **investment**, to the cost of that investment. For example, if building a new factory will cost $10 million, but it will provide an extra $1 million in profit each year, then its rate of return is 10 percent.

This rate of return must be compared with the rates of return on other **investment** projects or **interest rates** in the financial **markets**. In order for a **business** to maximize **profits,** it must use that $10 million to obtain the highest rate of return or interest rate. There can be complica-

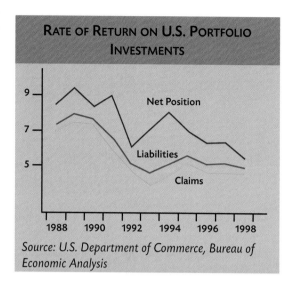

RATE OF RETURN ON U.S. PORTFOLIO INVESTMENTS

Net Position

Liabilities

Claims

Source: U.S. Department of Commerce, Bureau of Economic Analysis

tions in determining the rate of return. The biggest complication is an uncertain future. One never knows for certain how much extra **profit** or income one will get in the future.

REAL GROSS DOMESTIC PRODUCT

Real gross domestic product refers to the total **market** value (adjusted for **inflation**) of all **economic goods and services** produced within the political boundaries of an **economy** during a given period of time (usually one year). It is measured in constant **prices**—those for a specific **base year**. Real gross domestic product is also called constant dollar gross domestic product, and it adjusts gross domestic product for inflation. Real gross domestic product can be

U.S. REAL GROSS DOMESTIC PRODUCT (BILLIONS OF DOLLARS)	1993	1994	1995	1996	1997	1998
Gross Domestic Purchases:						
Personal Consumption Expenditures	4,343	4,486	4,605	4,752	4,913	5,151
Gross Private Domestic Investment:						
Non-Residential Fixed Investment	600	648	710	776	859	961
Residential Fixed Investment	242	267	256	275	282	312
Change in Business Inventories	22	60	27	30	63	58
Total Gross Private Domestic Investment	864	986	995	1,082	1,205	1,331
Government Consumption Expenditures:						
National Defense	354	336	323	319	308	300
Non-Defense	151	149	146	146	148	152
Total Federal:	505	486	470	465	458	453
State and Local	746	765	783	802	827	844
Total Government Consumption Expenditures	1,252	1,252	1,254	1,268	1,285	1,297
Total Gross Domestic Purchases:	6,459	6,712	6,855	7,101	7,396	7,766
Net Exports of Goods and Services	(70)	(104)	(96)	(111)	(136)	(238)
Imports	728	817	889	971	1,106	1,223
Exports	658	712	792	860	970	985
Total Gross Domestic Product	6,389	6,610	6,761	6,994	7,269	7,552
Final Sales of Domestic Product	6,368	6,551	6,731	6,961	7,203	7,490
Gross National Product	6,408	6,619	6,779	7,008	7,266	-
Real Gross Domestic Product Index	102.3	105.8	108.2	112.0	116.4	120.9

Source: U.S. Department of Commerce, Bureau of Economic Analysis

compared with nominal gross domestic product (**nominal GDP**), which means total **output** in current prices.

REAL INTEREST RATE

The real interest rate is the stated or nominal rate of **interest** adjusted for inflation. This means that if the stated interest rate is 10 percent and the **inflation rate** is 3 percent, then the real interest rate is 7 percent—the difference between these two rates.

If a person lends $100 to someone for one year at 10 percent interest, then the lender gets $110 one year from when the money was loaned. If the inflation rate is 0 percent, this person can buy 10 percent more with his $110, so the "real" return is 10 percent. If, however, the inflation rate is 10 percent, he can buy no more now than he could with $100 a year ago, so the "real" return on his money is zero.

REAL VALUE

The "real" value expresses the change in **value** that occurs over time. For example, the **gross** national product is corrected for changes in **price** levels over a period of time, so that it expresses value in terms of constant prices.

RECESSION

A recession is one of the phases of the regular **business cycle**. It occurs when the **gross domestic product (GDP)** shows negative growth over two consecutive quarters. It is not as severe an economic decline as a **depression**. During a recession, real GDP may decline by 10 percent or so, while **unemployment** may rise from **full employment** (5 percent) up to 6 to 10 percent. **Inflation** is usually low or nonexistent during a recession. Recessions can last from 6 to 18 months, but one year is most common.

RECESSIONARY GAP

A recessionary gap means that the aggregate **supply** of a country is greater than the aggregate **demand**. It is measured by the amount of actual **output** that falls short of what output would be if all **resources** and **factors of production** were fully employed.

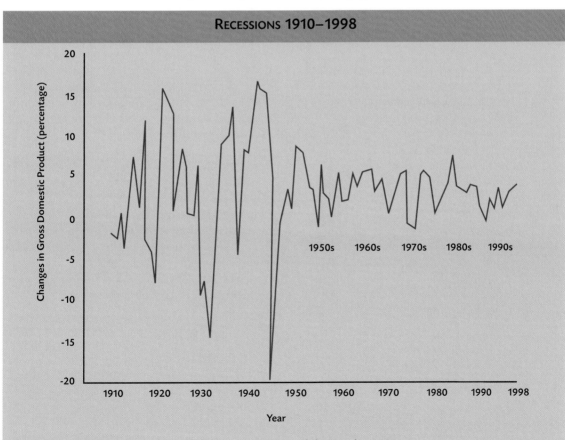

RECESSIONS 1910–1998

Source: U.S. Bureau of the Census and the Economic Report of the President, 1999

RECOVERY

Recovery is one of the phases of the regular **business cycle** characterized by a rise in economic activity. It is an early expansionary phase that occurs shortly after a **contraction** has ended, but before complete **expansion** begins. The **unemployment rate** remains relatively high early in recovery. **Real gross domestic product** begins to increase as well. Recovery tends to last from six months to a year, but because it is really just the early part of an expansion, there is no clear-cut end to this phase.

REGRESSIVE TAXATION

Regressive taxation is a form of **taxation** in which people with more **income** pay a smaller percentage in taxes. Examples of regressive taxes include **indirect taxes** such as sales tax and **excise tax**. For example, say you earn $300 a week and buy something that costs $100. The sales tax on the item is 10 percent, or $10. If a person who earns $600 a week buys the same item, the 10 percent sales tax for him or her is much less of his or net pay for the week. Therefore, the burden of of taxation is proportionally less for wealthier people. (See **progressive taxation.**)

RENT-SEEKING BEHAVIOR

People exhibit "rent-seeking" behavior when they try to get higher **wages**, more **profit**, or any other payment over and above the minimum they would be willing to accept. This term comes from the idea of **economic rent**, which is a payment over and above the **opportunity cost**. An example of rent-seeking behavior is spending **resources** to lobby lawmakers to pass laws and regulations restricting **competition**.

RESERVE BASE

The reserve base is made up of **currency** and **demand deposits** held by **banks**, plus the **money** held by the public. The reserve base is sometimes called "high-powered" money, because an increase in bank reserves, or money in circulation that enters the banking system, creates an expansion of money and credit.

RESERVE REQUIREMENT

The rules set up by the **Federal Reserve System** which determine the amount of **bank** reserves that banks must keep in order to back up their deposits are called reserve requirements.

Legal reserves, **money**, and checks that are counted as reserves must be in the bank or on deposit in a Federal Reserve bank. These legal reserve requirements were established to prevent banks that practice fractional-reserve banking from making too many **interest**-paying loans and not keeping enough reserves on hand to pay their depositors. This practice forced many banks to close down in the 1800s, and it created several **economy**-wide bank panics.

In principle, the Federal Reserve can change reserve requirements to control the **money supply**. In practice, however, it prefers to use **open-market operations** or the **discount rate**. Reserve requirements are 0 percent for deposits of up to $4 million, 3 percent from $4 million to $51.9 million and 10 percent for deposits above $51.9 million. In addition, the Federal Reserve can impose an extra 4 percent reserve requirement if it needs it to control the **money supply.** The Federal Reserve can also impose higher requirements in emergencies for up to 180 days.

RESERVES

Reserves are funds that are set aside to use for some future obligation, such as a balloon payment on a real estate **mortgage loan**. Reserves are also **bank** cash and deposits by banks with the **Federal Reserve System.** Primary reserves are those monies set aside by a commercial bank to operate the bank. Secondary reserves are those monies set aside to meet **liquidity** requirements. (See **reserve requirements.**)

RESIDUAL CLAIMANT

A residual claimant is the person or party who receives anything left over after the other claimants of production, such as the landlord, investor, **entrepreneur**, or **labor** have been paid.

In a **corporation**, the suppliers receive their payment and the **bond**holders receive their **debt** plus interest. The stockholders' claim is to the balance, so they are the residual claimants.

RESOURCES

Resources are the **factors of production— labor, capital**, land, and entrepreneurship—used by society to produce **economic goods and services.** Land provides the basic raw materials to produce goods (natural resources). Labor is the resource that does the work of transforming these raw materials into goods. Labor also includes both the physical and mental efforts of

An overview of the East Continental Pit Copper mine, operated by Montana Resources, Inc.

workers who help in the **production** of products. Capital includes all the tools, equipment, buildings, and vehicles used in production of goods. The one thing that sets capital apart from the other resources is the fact that it has itself been produced. Things like socket wrenches, oil drilling rigs, office buildings, and delivery trucks have all been produced using land, labor, capital, and entrepreneurship. Capital's main job in the production process is to make labor's job easier, so that labor becomes more productive.

While land, labor, and capital are each vital to production, entrepreneurship is also vital because it bears the risk of bringing the other resources together to begin the production process.

Another important point to remember about resources is that they are limited in supply. Limited resources, combined with unlimited wants and needs, creates the economic problem of **scarcity**.

RETURNS TO SCALE

Usually, "returns" are revenue, or **income**, received for the sale of **economic goods and services**. Returns to scale are a bit different, being neither revenue nor income. Instead, returns to scale are changes in **production** that occur when all **resources** proportionately increase. Returns to scale can be found in one of three different forms: *increasing*, *decreasing*, and *constant*.

Increasing returns to scale result when a given increase in resources causes a relatively greater increase in production. For example, if all resources are increased by 20 percent, and **output** increases by more than 20 percent, this is an increasing returns to scale. Decreasing returns to scale result when a given increase in resources causes a relatively smaller increase in production. If, for example, all resources are increased by 20 percent, and output increases by less than 20 percent, this is a decreasing returns to scale. Constant returns to scale result when a given increase in resources causes the same increase in production. For example, if all resources are increased by 20 percent, and output also increases by 20 percent, this is a constant returns to scale.

RIGHT-WING/RIGHTIST

Right-wing and rightist are terms used to generalize varied political ideologies such as unrestricted **capitalist**, **conservative**, nationalist, and militarist. Rightist or right-wing individuals advocate less government intervention in **business** matters. Generally, a rightist favors less government spending and more **tax** cuts.

RURAL-URBAN MIGRATION

Unproductive land, few employment opportunities, and the simple need to survive often lead to the breakup of rural communities. Many people head for the cities to look for work. Cities in **less developed countries** are known for the pressure urban migration can bring on housing and the environment. Often people arrive from rural areas and find a living on the streets while staying in temporary sub-standard homes, before they can establish themselves and their families more permanently. This results in the swelling of slums in many cities. (See **disguised unemployment; Lewis Model**.)

S

SAVINGS AND LOAN INSTITUTION

A savings and loan institution is a depository first established to help home owners with low-cost **mortgage loans** using **savings deposits.** Due to changes in state and federal banking laws, savings and loan institutions have expanded their activities and most of them offer most of the same services that traditional **banks** do, including checking accounts.

SAVINGS DEPOSITS

Savings deposits are accounts at **banks, savings and loan associations, credit unions**, and mutual savings banks that pay **interest** but cannot be used directly as **money.** They let customers set aside a portion of their liquid **assets** that could be used to make future purchases. However, in order to make those purchases, money has to be transferred to **checkable deposits** or **currency.** Since it is easy to do this, savings deposits are often called "near money." Savings accounts make up a sizable portion of the **M2 money supply** in the United States.

> **KEY POINT TODAY**
>
> Savings is the amount of **income** that is not spent on current **consumption.** In a simple **circular flow diagram,** savings is a withdrawal taken by **households.**

SAVINGS IN THE U.S. (BILLIONS OF DOLLARS)						
YEARS	**1993**	**1994**	**1995**	**1995**	**1996**	**1998**
GROSS SAVING						
Gross Private Saving						
Total private saving	1,039.4	1,155.931	1,155.9	1,257.5	1,349.3	1,646.0
Personal saving	350.8	5.5	315.5	302.4	272.1	229.7
Total gross business	808.6	883.8	883.8	963.6	1,018.3	1,141.5
Gross Government Saving						
Total government saving	−120.0	−43.4	−43.4	−8.5	58.9	274.8
Total federal saving	−195.4	−130.9	−130.9	−108.0	−51.5	134.3
Total state and local saving	75.4	87.5	87.5	99.4	110.4	140.5
Total Government and Private Savings	1,039.4	1,155.9	1,155.9	1,257.5	1,349.3	1,646.0

Source: U.S. Department of Commerce, Bureau of Economic Analysis

The ATM (automatic teller machine) is one of the most commonly used services in the service sector.

SCARCITY

Scarcity is a consequence of the fact that there are limited **resources** that can be used to produce **economic goods and services** to meet the unlimited **wants** and needs of the world's population. This means that some people will have to do without something they want or need. It also means that when a **business** uses resources to produce one product or good, it is forced to give up producing something else for which these same resources could be used.

SECONDARY MARKET

A secondary market is a financial **market** where previously issued securities and **debt** obligations are traded. That means the secondary market involves the trading of **stocks, bonds,** and other financial instruments after **corporations** have issued them. When corporations issue new stock, they are sold in the primary market. The **over-the-counter (OTC) market** and the **New York Stock Exchange** are examples of secondary markets. There are also many other types of secondary markets for nonfinancial goods. For example, the used car market is a secondary market for cars.

SERVICE SECTOR

The service sector is that part of the **economy** that deals with the supply of services instead of goods. Telephone and insurance services are in the service sector, as are dentists, lawyers, doctors, teachers, resume writers, landscape designers, architects, etc.

SHAREHOLDER (STOCKHOLDER)

A shareholder or stockholder is a person who owns shares of **stock** in a company or **mutual fund**. Individuals and businesses that own shares of a company help to finance the business in return for shares of the company. A shareholder or stockholder receives **dividends** that a company declares and also can vote on some company matters, including the board of directors.

SHORTAGE

A shortage is a **market** condition that exists when the quantity demanded for a good is greater than the quantity supplied at the existing price. Sometimes a shortage is also called **excess demand** or a sellers' market. A shortage leads to an increase in the **equilibrium** price.

SHORT RUN

In **macroeconomics** (the overall study of the **economy**), short run refers to a period of time when some **prices** (particularly **wages**) are inflexible or unchanging.

In **microeconomics** (the study of the of individual units in the economy), a short run is a period of time when at least one **input** or **resource** is fixed and one is variable or changing. The term *short run* can vary greatly depending on the **industry**. For example, it may take a large oil company years to build and begin a new operation, while it may take a small boutique one month to rent a space and begin business.

SHORT-RUN MARKET SUPPLY CURVE

A **supply curve** shows the relationship between the **supply** price and the quantity supplied on a graph. The supply curve shows several things:

1) As the **price** of a good or service increases, the quantity supplied also increases.

2) Maximum quantities and minimum prices.

3) Supply is a whole range of quantity supplied at a range of prices. When a different quantity is supplied at a different price, then this is a different point on the supply curve.

4) Hypothetical prices and quantities.

The short-run market supply curve shows the relationship between price and supply within an **industry** when one or more of the **factors of production** and the number of firms are fixed. The short-run market supply curve is equal to the sum of the individual short-run supply curves of all firms currently in the industry.

SHORT SELLING

Short selling occurs when an investor borrows (instead of buys) **stock** from a broker and immediately sells it. This is done because the investor is anticipating a decline in the **price** of the stock, and he wants to sell the stock at the existing price before it declines and is worth less money. If the price of the stock does decline, then he simply replaces the borrowed shares by buying them at the cheaper price; he has then made a **profit**. However, if the price of the stock rises instead of declines, the investor suffers a loss.

SOCIAL COST/SOCIAL BENEFIT

Social cost and social benefit are basically **externalities** or side effects. They are costs or benefits of a transaction to someone other than the one

Motorists line up for gas during the gas shortage in the 1970s.

making the transaction. For example, pollution could be considered a social cost. Society in general pays the cost of pollution clean-up when a **business** produces pollution as it manufactures its goods. Education would be considered a social benefit. A student usually pays for his or her education, but society as a whole benefits from the population being better educated. In this regard, social costs and social benefits are like externalities. Government uses taxes and **subsidies** to try to correct for some of the negative externalities and other social costs.

SOCIALISM

Socialism is an **economic system** that emphasizes government ownership of **resources** (rather than individual), widespread public ownership of key **industries**, worker influence within the government, and **income** based on need rather than on ownership of resources or contribution to **production**. Karl Marx viewed socialism as the transition between a **capitalist** economic system and a communist one. Modern socialism tries to correct the inefficiencies of **market failures** to obtain more equal wealth and income distributions, and to equalize economic opportunities.

A 1934 poster advertises social security benefits.

Over the past century and a half, there have been countless socialist doctrines, experiments, and programs. The primary tenets of socialism are often difficult to identify, but they lean toward a **mixed economy** rather than pure communism. The emphasis has been on collective rather than private ownership and management of resources—whether that means government ownership of selected utilities or centralized planning of all economic activity. (See **communism**.)

SOCIAL SECURITY

Social security is a system for providing financial aid to the poor, elderly, and disabled. In the United States, this system was established by the Social Security Act of 1935, to help with the problems of the **Great Depression**. Today's social security system has several parts. They are:

> **KEY POINT TODAY**
> The federal government is in charge of some social security programs, while state and local governments administer others. They are paid for by taxes to which both employers and employees contribute.

1) Old Age and Survivors Insurance (OASI) provides benefits to anyone who has reached a certain age and has paid taxes into the program while employed. It also provides benefits to qualified recipients' survivors or dependents. This means that a widow, a widower, or orphaned children can qualify for monthly checks.

2) Disability Insurance (DI) provides benefits to workers and their dependents in the case of physical disabilities that keep them from working.

3) Hospital Insurance (HI) or Medicare. Medicare provides two types of benefits—hospital coverage for anyone in the OASI or SSI part of the system, and supplemental medical benefits that require a monthly insurance premium.

4) Supplemental Security Income (SSI)—SSI pays monthly checks to people who are 65 or older, are blind or have a disability, and do not own much or have a lot of **income**. SSI is not just for adults. Monthly checks can go to disabled and blind children as well. People who get SSI usually also get food stamps and Medicaid.

SOFT LOAN

A soft loan is a **loan** that has an **interest rate** substantially below the interest rate that is typically charged on a loan for a similar purpose. Soft loans are usually offered to developing countries and other international **businesses** as a form of economic aid. (See **World Bank.**)

SOLE PROPRIETORSHIP

A sole proprietorship is one form of **business** organization. It refers to an unincorporated business owned and controlled by one person. With a sole proprietorship, the owner is personally responsible for any legal **debts** or **liabilities** incurred by the business.

SPECIALIZATION

Specialization occurs when the **resources** of a person or a business are devoted (at least primarily) to specific tasks. **Labor** is divided into many limited, specified tasks. If a person specializes in an activity, that person is likely to be more efficient than if he or she performed many tasks. Specialization is a fundamental concept in the study of **economics**. Limited resources can be used more effectively in the production of eco-nomic **goods and services** when resources are specialized. When you go to McDonald's, for example, usually several people work as cashiers, while others cook the food. If each worker tried to cook the food, sell the food, and clean up, things would not be done as efficiently.

SPECULATION

Speculation is guessing or predicting what certain **assets,** such as **money, stock,** or **currencies,** will be worth in the future. Investors speculate with the intent to buy an asset at a low **price** today and sell it at a later date for a higher price. Speculators buy these assets in the hope of reselling them to make a **profit**. Speculation is very common in many financial **markets**. It is often considered to be quite risky, since an investor may make a lot of money when the price of an asset rises but also stands to lose a lot of money when the value of an asset goes down. (See **arbitrage.**)

SPECULATIVE MOTIVE

The speculative motive is one of the three reasons to keep accumulated wealth in a liquid (easily changed to cash) form or as **money** itself. The other two are the transaction motive and the

There are many specialized tasks that need to be performed during the construction of a building.

precautionary motive. The speculative motive involves the desire to have a certain amount of cash or other liquid **assets** on hand because of uncertainty about the fluctuating value of other assets.

SPOT MARKET

A spot market is a **market** where things can be bought and sold immediately, or "on the spot." Most stores are spot markets. Buyers give the store **money** to pay for a product and immediately take the product home with them. (See **futures markets**.)

STABILIZATION POLICY

Stabilization policy is a collective term for the economic actions that a government takes to stabilize the **business cycle** and prevent both high rates of unemployment and **inflation**. These are also called counter-cyclical policies. Expansionary policies that promote increasing economic activity are used to counter a **contraction (recession)** and high **unemployment rates**, while contractionary policies are used to counter inflationary expansion.

STAGFLATION

Stagflation is a term that combines the two words "stagnation" and "inflation." Stagflation refers to high **inflation rates** that occur at the same time the **economy** has high un**employment rates** (stagnation) and a depressed level of **production**.

Throughout U.S. history during an expansion, inflation has usually been higher and unemployment is lower. The opposite has usually occurred during a **recession**. But in the 1970s, inflation got worse at the same time the economy dropped into a recession. This led economists to develop the term "stagflation" and to reevaluate the how the economy works.

> **KEY POINT TODAY**
>
> Economists who were accustomed to seeing a **trade-off** between inflation and employment and relied on the **Phillips curve** were perplexed by the economic conditions of the 1970s. Many turned to alternative approaches to **economic theory**. In the United States, many economists turned to **supply-side economics**.

STANDARD & POOR'S 500

Standard & Poor's 500 is a market-value-weighted index (meaning shares outstanding are multiplied by their stock price) of 500 stocks that are traded on the **New York Stock**

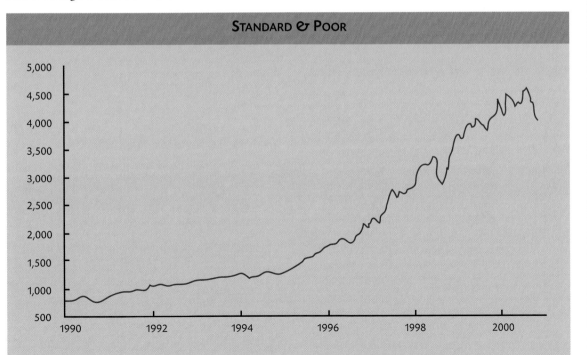

STANDARD & POOR

Exchange (NYSE), the **American Stock Exchange** (AMEX), and the **NASDAQ** National Market System. The weightings make each company's influence on index performance directly proportional to that company's **market** value. This characteristic has made the Standard & Poor's 500 Index the **investment** industry's standard for measuring the performance of actual **portfolios**.

In 1860 Henry Varnum Poor published *The History of Railroads and Canals of the United States* and began supplying financial information at a time when Europe wanted to know more about the newly developing **infrastructure** in the United States. In 1906 the Standard Statistics Bureau was formed to provide previously unavailable financial information on U.S. companies. In 1941 Poor's Publishing and Standard Statistics merged to form the Standard & Poor's Corporation.

> **KEY POINT TODAY**
>
> Companies selected for the Standard & Poor's 500 Index are not chosen because they are the largest companies in terms of market value, sales, or profits. Instead, the companies included in the Index are representative of the most important industries within the U.S. **economy** and many are the leaders of their **industry.**

STANDARD OF LIVING

A country or specific population's standard of living is the normal level of monetary **income** or the **consumption** of **economic goods and services** to which it is accustomed. The **Gross National Product (GNP)** and per capita give objective but imperfect measures for comparing the living standards of two or more countries.

Elements that make up a country's standard of living include goods consumed, educational opportunities, and the amount of **money** spent for health and recreation. While standards of living may vary greatly among groups within a country, it also varies from nation to nation, and international comparisons are sometimes made by analyzing GNPs, per capita **incomes**, or any number of other indicators from life expectancy to clean water. Overall, industrialized nations tend to have a higher standard of living than developing countries. In the United States, the standard of living has been rising steadily over the years. However, when **prices** rise faster than per capita income (as in the late 1970s), the standard of living may actually decline. (See **purchasing power parity.**)

> **KEY POINT TODAY**
>
> It is difficult to assess a standard of living because different individuals' styles of living cannot be compared in terms of economic **value.** For example, two people may have the same income, but one may live in the country, where she enjoys clean air and land, while someone living in the city may not have land but instead enjoys theater, art galleries, and museums. Although in monetary terms these two individuals may share identical salaries, their standard of living seems quite different.

STICKY PRICES

"Sticky prices" is a term used to describe **prices** that adjust slowly in response to market **shortages** or **surpluses**. "Sticky" in this case means rigid or inflexible. **Prices** may be the most sticky in resource **markets,** like **labor** markets, and less sticky in financial markets. Product markets are sometimes considered somewhere in between these two, in terms of their "stickiness." The stickiness of wages is sometimes used as an explanation of **unemployment**.

An AT&T stock certificate for 3 shares at 33.3 dollars per share dated October 24, 1961.

STOCK

Stock is a share in a **corporation** issued by that corporation or the government as a way to raise long-term **capital**. However, stock is really a measurement that just tells how much something is worth for an instant in time (as opposed to a period of time). For example, a share of corporate stock tells how much a share of that corporation is worth at the instant it is purchased. Later, the **value** of that share may increase or decrease depending on the company and **market**. Population, **employment, capital,** and **business** inventories, as well as **money,** are also important stock measures.

STOCK MARKET

A stock market is a financial **market** that trades ownership shares, called corporate stock, in **corporations.** The **New York Stock Exchange**, the **American Stock Exchange**, and the National Association of Securities Dealers are the three best-known national stock markets in the United States. The Chicago, Philadelphia, and Pacific exchanges are some notable regional markets that trade stock on a smaller scale.

Tokyo, Japan; London, England; Toronto, Canada; Frankfurt, Germany; Paris, France; and many other major cities also have stock markets. In recent years stock markets around the world have become increasingly interdependent as multinational **business** has grown as well.

STORE OF VALUE

Store of value is one of the four basic functions of **money**, including **medium of exchange**, measure of value, and standard of deferred payment. Store of value refers to how money is used for later satisfaction from future use or **consumption** of goods or services. The value is stored until money is spent to buy these goods or services and use them to satisfy **wants** and needs. At that time, the value is no longer stored value, it is obtained value. Though money can be used this way, it is a poor store of value since it earns zero nominal return and a negative real return when there is **inflation**.

STRIKE

A strike occurs when the workers in an **industry** (usually members of a union) all agree to stop working. The strike's purpose is to encourage the employer to improve workers' **wages,** benefits and/or working conditions. Strikes are a powerful tool for unions in **collective bargaining**.

A worker on strike pickets outside the Mid-City Company in Chicago, Illinois.

S

STRUCTURAL ADJUSTMENT LOAN

A structural adjustment loan (SAL) is a loan given to countries by the **International Monetary Fund** and the **World Bank.** These loans are contingent on the government receiving the loan making policy changes. For example, SALs often call for privatization of government-owned **businesses,** cuts in government spending, which often includes programs for the poor, and removing barriers to foreign **investment.** There are many critics of SALs who believe that programs particularly hurt women and the poorer segments of **less developed countries.** In 1999 the World Bank lent $10.69 billion dollars in the form of poverty-focused structural adjustment loans.

STRUCTURAL DEFICIT/SURPLUS

A nation's **budget** suffers a **deficit** when it has more expenses than revenues, which means there is more **money** going out than coming in. A structural deficit is one that occurs when the **economy** is operating at **full employment.**

A nation's budget enjoys a **surplus** if it has more revenues than expenses—that is, if there is more money coming in than going out. A structural surplus occurs when the economy is operating at full employment.

STRUCTURAL UNEMPLOYMENT

Structural unemployment results when people who are available for work do not have the skills needed for the jobs that are available. Generally, this type of unemployment occurs because workers are trained in one technology, yet the economy demands **economic goods and services** using another technology. This causes a decline in certain **industries** and changes in **production** processes. Structural unemployment is most typically the result of quick technological progress. A long-term condition, it is one of four unemployment sources. The others are **cyclical unemployment**, seasonal unemployment, and **frictional unemployment**.

SUBSIDY

A subsidy is a payment the government gives to individuals or **businesses** without any corresponding **production** from these individuals or businesses provided to the government. A subsidy payment is like a **negative income tax**.

A subsidy is given at times to a business to

A group of farmers line up to collect their subsidy checks in 1934 during the Great Depression.

help reduce the price of its product to consumers, which ensures that people will continue to consume goods and services. In addition, governments give subsidies to firms or industries whose business is declining in order to help them remain in business.

Government sometimes offers subsidies to individuals such as students, unemployed workers, farmers, and the poor to help them out or to encourage a particular type of behavior. (See **transfer payments**.)

KEY POINT TODAY

Subsidies are often used by the government as a way to redistribute the wealth by reducing the **price** of products, such as bread and milk, that play an important part in the budget of lower-income **households,** or through subsidizing their **income** directly.

SUBSTITUTES

There are several types of substitutes in economics. In terms of **demand**, substitutes are goods that are economically interchangeable with one another in **consumption**. If the demand of the first good results in the **price** increase of a second good, the goods are substitutes-in-consumption. For example, if the price of Coca-Cola goes up, a consumer might buy 7-Up instead.

In terms of **supply,** these are **inputs** in **production** that can be used somewhat interchangeably. For example, if production can be done either with **labor** or **capital**, then labor and capital are substitutes. Thus, when the price of labor increases, the demand for capital also increases. (See **complements**.)

SUBSTITUTION EFFECT

The substitution effect explains why producers and consumers tend to use substitutes when **prices** for products or goods change. The substitution effect happens when a change in the price of a good makes it relatively higher or lower than the prices of other goods that might act as substitutes. As the price of a product falls, usually the **demand** increases. Conversely, if the price of a product increases, the demand will

drop. Consumers then look to another similar product to substitute for the product with the increased price.

For example, if the price of butter goes up, consumers or producers might decide to use margarine as a substitute as much as possible, because it is cheaper than butter. Thus, when the price of a good falls, more of it is consumed. There are two reasons for this. First is the substitution effect mentioned before. ,Second, there is an **income effect**. When a price falls, this is similar to getting a higher income. If the good is a **normal good**, more of it will be demanded. This is the income effect.

The substitution effect working together with the income effect explains why **demand curves** slope downward on a graph.

SUNK COST

A sunk cost is a cost that has been paid but cannot be recovered. An example would be an **investment** in a machine to manufacture goods which are then made obsolete by another good, perhaps because the new good can be made at lower cost. There is now no use for this original machine; therefore it is probably time to get rid of it, but it would not be an attractive or wise purchase to anyone else. As an alternative, it might be scrapped, in which case the sunk cost would be the difference between what was paid for the machine originally and the amount that was paid for it when it was sold for scrap. (See **opportunity cost**.)

SUPPLY

Supply and **demand** are the two sides to the **market** exchange process. Demand is the consumers' desire for a specific good or service. Supply is the amount of this good or service that is available in the marketplace.

The quantity supplied is the quantity of an item that producers are willing and able to produce in a specified time period for a particular price. In economics, the total supply of a product is illustrated graphically in the **supply curve**.

SUPPLY CURVE

The supply curve demonstrates graphically the relationship between the supply **price** of a good and the quantity supplied during a period of time. The "**supply**" is the total amount of a good or service that a company is willing to sell at a

S

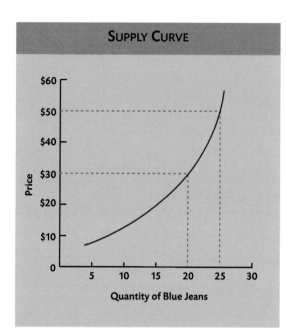

SUPPLY CURVE

Price (y-axis): $60, $50, $40, $30, $20, $10, 0

Quantity of Blue Jeans (x-axis): 5, 10, 15, 20, 25, 30

given **price**. The supply curve shows that as the price for a particular good or service increases, the quantity supplied also increases. This is the **law of supply**.

As illustrated in the graph above, when the price for blue jeans rises, so does the quantity of blue jeans being supplied by the manufacturers. In other words, companies are prepared to produce more blue jeans to sell at a higher price than they are at a low one.

SUPPLY CURVE (SHIFT IN)

A shift in a supply curve is a movement from one position to another, either to the left or the right, caused by an economic change other than a change in **price**. A supply curve is always drawn on the *ceteris paribus* assumption that all factors affecting supply remain constant. If any factors do change, particularly the cost of **production**, the change will cause a shift in the supply curve.

For example, if the costs of production drop, the supply curve will shift to the right to reflect that more of the product is supplied at each price than before.

SUPPLY ELASTICITY

See **price elasticity of supply**.

SUPPLY SCHEDULE

The supply schedule is a schedule or table that lists the prices of goods or services and the exact quantities supplied at these prices. The information found on a supply schedule is used as data to create a **supply curve** that shows the price to quantity-supplied ratio in graph form.

SUPPLY-SIDE ECONOMICS

Supply-side economics is a school of economic thought that emphasizes the producer of goods as the most important player in a healthy economy. Supply-side economists theorize that economic expansion will result from lower **tax** rates. The theory is that lowering taxes will increase supply by encouraging production. It will also provide a greater incentive to work and promote savings and **investments** that **business** needs for **economic growth.** If supply is increased, **prices** will not increase as much and **inflation** will be slowed. Tax cuts would not lower the **total revenue** of the government, because the increased prosperity would raise **incomes** and hence tax receipts. According to supply-side theory, this will offset the lower rates.

Supply-side economists generally condemn **labor unions,** because they feel that the activities of unions push the **wage** rates up past the **marginal revenue productivity** of the workers themselves, thereby restricting employment. Similar ideas have led supply-side economists to condemn some **welfare** systems and **progressive taxation,** because they feel that these programs act as a disincentive for people who are unemployed to work at low-paying jobs.

This branch of **economics** gained prominence in the 1980s under President Ronald Reagan. Its influence supplanted that of the **Keynesian** approach to economics, which had been credited with bringing the country out of the **Great Depression**. But Keynesian policies seemed to fail in the 1970s, when the United States had high **inflation rates** and high **unemployment rates**.

🌀 **KEY POINT TODAY**

Supply-side economics is associated with the economic policies of President Ronald Reagan, who served from1981 to 1989. Reagan based important econom icinitiatives on supply-side economics, which advocated a reduction in taxes and government spending in order to leave more money in the hands of citizens.

President Ronald Reagan meets with his Council of Economic Advisors.

SURPLUS

A surplus is an oversupply. It is a **market** condition in which the quantity supplied is greater than the quantity demanded at the existing **price.** Sometimes a surplus is called **excess supply.** Surplus is also used to refer to society's savings—that which remains from total **output** once **consumption** and **investment** have been met.

SUSTAINABILITY

Sustainability means meeting the needs of a population without compromising the abilities and opportunities of future generations to come. Sustainability is an important dimension of **human development** that primarily emphasizes environmental issues. Many believe that there need to be restrictions placed on **industrialization** to preserve the environment for future generations.

SWAP ARRANGEMENT

A swap arrangement is the sale of foreign **currency** with the agreement to repurchase the currency at a future date. It is also the purchase of foreign currency with the agreement to sell it at a future date. The purpose of a swap agreement is to keep a needed supply of **liquidity** in international finance.

The **Federal Reserve** and 14 foreign **central banks,** as well as the Bank for International Settlements, share short-term lines of **credit** between them. Through a swap transaction, the Federal Reserve can borrow foreign currency in order to buy dollars in the **foreign exchange market.** In doing so, the **demand** for dollars is increased and the dollar's foreign exchange value is increased. Similarly, the Federal Reserve can temporarily provide dollars to foreign central banks through swap arrangements.

T

TARIFF

A tariff is a duty (a form of **tax**) imposed on **imports** (and sometimes on **exports**). Like any other tax, a tariff generates revenue for the government.

> ⟳ **KEY POINT TODAY**
>
> An import tariff is a trade barrier that is designed to protect domestic industries by restricting **imports** into a country to protect against foreign **competition.**

TAX

A tax is a payment imposed by the government on the **incom**e of individuals and **businesses** in the form of a **direct tax**, and on **economic goods and services** in the form of an **indirect tax**. The government uses taxes for a variety of reasons—for example, to raise revenue for government, balance the distribution of income and wealth, control the distribution of spending in the **economy**, control the amount of **imports** and **exports,** and alter **consumption** habits via "sin" taxes, or taxes on things such as cigarettes and alcohol.

TAX BASE

An **economy**'s tax base is made up of all activities, **capital**, and real estate (**assets**) that are subject to **tax** within a community. The tax base consists of business activity, personal and business property, and anything else that is taxed. For example, the tax base for **income tax** is total taxable income, and the base for **corporation** tax is total taxable **profits.**

TAXATION

Taxation is the act of imposing a **tax** or being taxed. Taxes are legally imposed payments from **households** and businesses made to the government that are not made in exchange for a good or service. Government collects taxes to obtain revenue (**money**) to make government purchases, including administrative expenses and **public goods**. Taxation can have many forms. Personal and corporate **income tax**, sales tax, gift tax, inheritance tax, **social security** tax, **value-added tax,** and, on the state level, real and personal property tax. These are just some of the ways taxation takes place. Taxes are used to finance government spending and as instruments of **fiscal policy** used to regulate total spending.

TAX BURDEN

A tax burden is the amount of **money** an individual or a business is required to pay in taxes.

TAX EVASION

Tax evasion is any effort made by a tax payer to evade paying the full amount of taxes due. The means of evasion are illegal—for example, individuals may not declare all of their **income** to the **Internal Revenue Service (IRS)**, or a person may claim deductions to which he or she is not legally entitled.

TERMS OF TRADE

Terms of trade means how much, or what quantity, of one **good** is given up to get another. It is usually applied to **foreign trade**, in which case it is essentially a **price index** that compares a country's **export prices** relative to its **import** prices, but it means the same thing for any sort of exchange.

An improvement in a country's terms of trade exists if its export prices increase at a faster rate than its import prices over a period of time. Terms of trade (for foreign trade) are reflected by exchange rates and relative prices.

TERM STRUCTURE OF INTEREST RATES

The relationship between the **interest rates** on **bonds** of different terms (time of maturity) is called the term structure of interest rates. It is the relationship between yields and maturities of securities.

To find the "yield curve," interest rates of bonds are plotted against their terms. The shape of this yield curve reflects the market's future expectation for interest rates and the conditions of **monetary policy.**

TIME DEPOSITS

A time deposit is a savings account in a **bank** that is kept there for a specified fixed length of time (term). It can only be withdrawn after the fixed term or by giving advanced notice and paying a financial penalty. A **certificate of deposit** (CD) is one form of a time deposit.

TOTAL COST

Total cost refers to the **opportunity cost** for all **factors of production** used to produce a good or service. These include wages for **labor**, rent paid for land, **interest** paid to **capital** owners, and a **normal profit** paid to **entrepreneurs.** Total cost is often separated into total variable cost and total fixed cost. Total cost and total revenue are the two pieces of information a company uses to determine profit. Total cost does not include external costs (**externalities**).

In the graph, the total cost is the sum of the total fixed cost and the total variable cost. It has an "S" shape because at low levels of **output,** the total variable costs rise slowly. By contrast, at high levels of output, total variable costs rise more quickly.

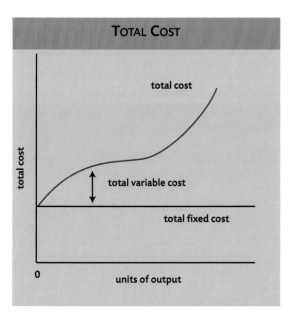

TOTAL COST

total cost

total variable cost

total fixed cost

total cost

0   units of output

TOTAL REVENUE

Total revenue is the total **money** obtained by a company from selling a specific quantity of goods. In other words, total revenue equals price times quantity.

TOTAL UTILITY

Total utility is the total sum of satisfaction (**utility**) an individual receives from the **consumption** of a certain quantity of goods or services. When a person consumes goods or satisfies **wants,** that person receives what economists call utility. The more total goods one consumes, the more total utility that person receives. The objective of most individuals is to get the most total utility out of consumption as possible—in other words, to enjoy the highest **standard of living** possible.

TOURISM

For several decades, tourism has been a major source of revenue for countries, especially for **less developed countries.** Its growth was explosive in the second half of the 20th century. In the 1950s, 25 million people traveled to a foreign country. In the 1960s this grew to 70 million. By 1997, 617 million tourists had been reported by the World Tourism Organisation (WTO) to have traveled to foreign countries. The WTO has predicted that by the 21st century, tourist travel will have generated revenues of billions of dollars annually.

Tourism is also seen as a major source of employment worldwide. According to the World Travel and Tourism Council (WTTC), tourism directly or indirectly employs more than 260 million people. In the next decade, the work force is expected to increase by 100 million more jobs, 70 percent of these in the Asia-Pacific region. The WTTC considers tourism to be the world's biggest industry. However, tourism has its costs as well as its benefits. **Globalization** and tourism have become a deadly mix for indigenous peoples and the environment. Reconciling growing tourism with its impact on natural, urban, and cultural environments is a problem facing many countries today. Total environmental **sustainability** may be an impossible goal, but there are many ways to gain more sustainable tourism.

TRADE DEFICIT/SURPLUS

A trade **deficit** occurs when a nation's **imports** are greater than its **exports**—that is, a country is

T

A trade union gathers together in a strike.

buying more **economic goods and services** from foreigners than foreigners are buying from domestic producers. To reduce a trade deficit, a country might establish trade barriers on imports or reduce the **exchange rate** so that exports are less expensive and imports are more expensive.

A trade surplus occurs when a nation's exports are greater than its imports—that is, a country is buying less goods and services from foreigners than foreigners are buying from domestic producers. (See **balance of trade.**)

TRADE-OFF

A trade-off in **economics** is much the same as a trade-off in ordinary life. It means a choice is made, which results in having less of one thing in order to get more of something else. Evaluating economic trade-offs involves comparing the costs and benefits of each of the available alternatives with each other. Producers must constantly reevaluate their trade-offs in choosing whether to produce more or somewhat

less of a particular product, whether to add a few more workers or lay some off, whether to invest in more plants and equipment, or whether to close down some of existing capacity, etc., in order to maximize **profits.** Consumers make trade-offs all the time, since they only have a limited amount of **income** and **purchasing power.** They need to consider whether to buy more of one product and less of another, depending on their subjective preferences. (See **opportunity cost.**)

TRADE UNION

A trade union is the same thing as a **labor union**—an organization of workers or employees who join together to negotiate (**collective bargaining**) with their employers over **wages**, **fringe benefits**, working conditions, and other aspects of **employment.** The main role of trade or labor unions is to protect the interests of workers. Big **businesses** do not always welcome trade or labor unions, however. In the late 1700s, trade unions struggled for the right to legally organize and negotiate with employers. It was not until the 1930s and the **Great Depression** that trade unions became powerful. Today, some prominent trade unions include the United Auto Workers, various teachers' unions, and the United Mine Workers.

TRADE WAR

A trade war is a conflict in which national governments with opposing interests try to monitor trade flows to achieve trade policy objectives other than those attained on the **market**. Typically, a trade war situation occurs when the government of one nation introduces trade obstacles in order to block **competition** in their local market by a foreign country, and the government of that country responds with its own trade barriers to the first country. Such trade policies are illegitimate when they do not abide by international trade agreements. (See **barriers to entry.**)

TRANSACTION COSTS

Transaction costs are the costs other than the **price** of the item that are necessary to make an exchange of **economic goods and services.** Some common transaction costs are time, energy, information costs, bargaining costs, policing and enforcement costs, and warranties and guarantees. Sometimes transaction costs are easy to overlook because they are not so evident. For example, if it is necessary to travel across the country to spend hours negotiating a deal with a prospective customer, a **business** owner would surely realize the travel expenses, but she could fail to realize what this extra time and energy were costing her in terms of other opportunities to sell to someone else.

TRANSFER EARNINGS

Transfer earnings are the return that a **factor of production** must earn to prevent its transfer to an alternative use. If the earnings of a factor of production are higher than its transfer earnings, then it is called **economic rent**

TRANSFER PAYMENTS

Transfer payments are monies paid out to **households** without any corresponding **production**. They are called transfers because, through **taxation,** income is transferred to the recipients. There are three main transfer payments: **social** security, **welfare**, and **unemployment** compensation. (See **national income.**)

TRANSFER PRICE

A transfer price is the **price** at which products are bought and sold between branches or subsidiaries of the same company. The transfer price is usually determined by referring to the going price for products in the outside marketplace, or it may be set according to an internal company accounting system.

TREASURY BILL (T-BILL)

A Treasury bill (T-Bill) is a short-term government security issued by the **Federal Reserve** banks for the United States Treasury to finance the federal **budget deficit**. The maturity rates (when payment is due) are 13, 26, or 52 weeks with 13 weeks, or three months, being the most common. The interest rate on T-bills is a key indicator of short-run economic activity.

Monetary authorities use T-bills to help regulate the liquid base of the banking system in order to control the nation's **money supply**. If the authorities want to expand the money supply, for example, they buy Treasury bills to increase the reserves of the banking system.

TRUST

A trust can be one of two things. The first type of trust is a legal arrangement in which an individual (the trustor) gives control of property to a person or institution (the trustee) on behalf of a person or institution (beneficiaries). A trust may be written or implied. An implied trust is also called a constructive trust.

The second type of trust is when independent firms join together to operate the firms as a single monopolistic **business,** and each gets a share of the trust's **profits.**

TWIN DEFICITS

The Twin Deficits are **budget deficits** and **trade deficits.** They are called twin deficits because they often move in the same direction. A budget deficit occurs when the government spends more money in a year than it receives in taxes and other revenue. A trade deficit occurs when more **economic goods and services** are imported than are exported. There is debate over how harmful both of these deficits may or may not be to the economy.

U–V

U.S. DEPARTMENT OF THE TREASURY

The U.S. Department of the Treasury is a cabinet-level part of the U.S. federal government responsible for certain financial matters. Among other things, it is responsible for collecting taxes and for paying the financial obligations of the U.S. Federal Government. When **tax** receipts fall short of expenditures, it issues U.S. treasury securities. It also authorizes the minting of coins. The treasury department aids in tracking counterfeiters.

U.S. Treasury securities consist of **Treasury bills,** treasury notes, or treasury **bonds**. They are issued and sold by the federal government to borrow **money**. People or companies buy them as investments, since the money is paid back with **interest** by the government.

KEY POINT TODAY

The U.S. Department of Commerce is the executive department responsible for the promotion of American economic and technological initiatives. The Department of Commerce promotes economic and technological development and manages a number of important government-held **assets.**

UNDERGROUND ECONOMY

An underground economy refers to the production, buying and selling of illegal **economic goods and services** and those goods and services that are bought and sold but not reported. Professor Edgar Feige, University of Wisconsin, estimated the size of the U.S. underground

The United States Department of the Treasury in Washington, D.C.

economy at between $500 billion and $1 trillion in 1993. However, this is an estimate because by their nature the transactions are not reported. (See **black market**.)

UNEMPLOYMENT/UNEMPLOYMENT RATE

The civilian **labor force** is the total number of non-military persons over the age of 16 who are capable of productive activity and are employed or seeking employment. The unemployment rate is the number of people in the civilian labor force who are eligible for work, but have not found jobs and are not producing **economic goods and services** divided by the total number of people in the labor force.

The unemployment rate is estimated and reported monthly by the U.S. Department of Labor's Bureau of Labor Statistics (BLS). This figure is one of the economic **indicators** that are examined to evaluate the state of the **economy**.

The ratio is multiplied by 100 to put the result in percentage form. If the number of people unemployed is 100,000, and the total labor force is 1,000,000, then the unemployment rate would be 10 percent. Think of the unemployment rate as this calculation:

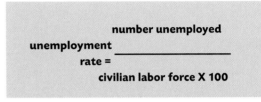

$$\text{unemployment rate} = \frac{\text{number unemployed}}{\text{civilian labor force}} \times 100$$

UNEMPLOYMENT BENEFIT

An unemployment benefit is a type of payment that is provided in the United States by the **Social Security** Act to protect unemployed workers. The program establishes unemployment **insurance** programs that are paid for by payroll taxes.

In order to be eligible, a person must have worked in what is called "covered employment" recently and must be ready, willing, and able to work. The benefits aim to provide six months' worth of **income** at approximately half of the worker's average weekly income. However, the details of the benefits vary from state to state.

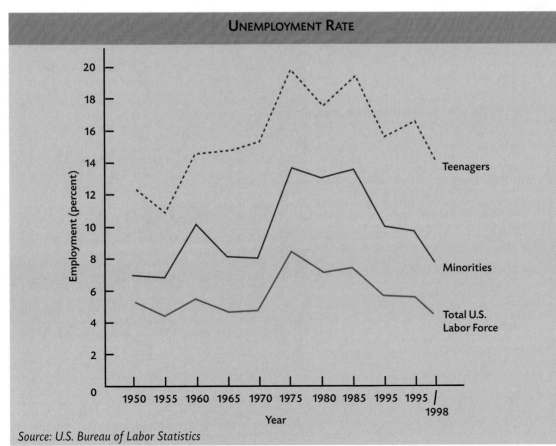

UNEMPLOYMENT RATE

Source: U.S. Bureau of Labor Statistics

UNIT OF ACCOUNT

Unit of account is one of the four basic functions of **money**. The other three are **medium of exchange, store of value,** and standard of deferred payment. Unit of account means that money is used as the measuring unit for **prices;** prices of goods are stated in terms of the monetary unit.

UNITED NATIONS

The United Nations (UN) was established on October 24, 1945 with 51 member countries. UN membership now totals 189 countries, almost all of the world's nations. Member states (countries) agree to accept the UN Charter, which contains the basic principles of international relations. The UN Charter lists four main purposes for its members: to maintain international peace and security, to develop friendly relations among nations, to cooperate in solving international problems and in promoting and protecting human rights, and to be a center for harmonizing the actions of nations.

Each country of the UN is an independent nation that retains its sovereignty. The United Nations is not a world government; it does not make or enforce laws. However, it provides a place and procedure to help resolve international conflicts. The members establish policies based on global concerns. All of the member states have a voice in making these policies.

KEY POINT TODAY

The main branches of the United Nations include the General Assembly, Security Council, Economic and Social Council, Trusteeship Council and Secretariat. There are also many subsidiary groups and affiliated organizations that work in accordance with the UN Charter, such as the **International Monetary Fund,** the Food and Agricultural Organization, the **International Labor Organization,** and the **World Bank**.

The United Nations' charter-signing ceremony in 1945.

The United Nations has its headquarters in New York City. Part of the UN, the International Court of Justice, is headquartered at The Hague in the Netherlands.

UNITED NATIONS CONFERENCE ON TRADE AND DEVELOPMENT

The United Nations Conference on Trade and Development (UNCTAD) was established in 1965 as a means to provide aid and represent the economic interests of developing countries. UNCTAD, which holds a series of conferences every four years, has focused on three main areas of primary concern:

1) **Exports** of manufactures: UNCTAD has tried to create **tariff**- and **quota**-free access to the **markets** of **less developed countries**.

2) Exports of **commodities**: UNCTAD has promoted international commodity agreements with the goal of stabilizing export **prices** as a way to also stabilize a countries' foreign exchange earnings and producers' income.

3) Financial aid: UNCTAD has attempted to secure more economic aid and transfer of technology from **developed countries** to less developed countries.

UTILITY

In **economics**, utility means satisfaction. Specifically, utility is the satisfaction of **wants** and needs obtained by consuming **economic goods and services**. The concept of utility is an important part of consumer **demand** theory and the **law of demand**. This theory assumes that people take actions to maximize their utility.

> ### KEY POINT TODAY
> The concept of utility can be traced back to the ancient Greek philosophers' attempts to determine economic **value**. In the 18th century, economists believed that utility could be measured in units, such as one, two, three, etc. This is known as cardinal utility. Later economists believed that utility could not possibly be measured on such a scale, nor was it necessary. They believed that it was more important and useful to measure rankings of preference, not amounts on a numerical scale. An abstract unit of measurement—a util—was invented to explain a degree of utility.

VALUE

Value is the economic worth of an **asset** or a product. Classical economists such as Adam Smith and David Ricardo believed that the amount of **labor** needed to produce an asset or product reflected its value. Later, economists Alfred Marshall and William Jevons stressed that the **utility** of a product to a consumer must be considered when measuring a product's value. Modern economists believe that both **supply** and **demand** are essential in determining the value of a product.

VALUE ADDED

Value added is the difference between a company's total revenue (**profits**) and the cost of the materials and services it purchased to produce its good or service.

VALUE-ADDED TAX

A value-added tax is an **indirect tax** placed on the extra value a product reaches during each stage in its **production.** Many goods in our economy go through several stages of production. In each stage something is added to the good to make it more valuable. Each producer or merchant pays a **tax** proportional to the amount by which he increases the **value** of the goods after making his own contribution. For example, if a store takes a $2 basket and adds $10 worth of fruit to it, then wraps it up and puts a bow on it, this is now sold as a $20 fruit basket. That means $8 has been "added" in value. A value-added tax would be based on this extra value.

> ### KEY POINT TODAY
> Value-added taxes are commonly imposed throughout European and many other countries across the world, but they are not in place in the United States.

VARIABLE COSTS

Variable costs include any costs that tend to change with changes in the quantity of **economic goods and services** produced. Variable costs refer to the payments that are made to use factor **inputs,** including **labor,** raw materials, etc.

Total variable cost means the combined total of all of the variable costs, while average variable cost would be the total variable cost divided by

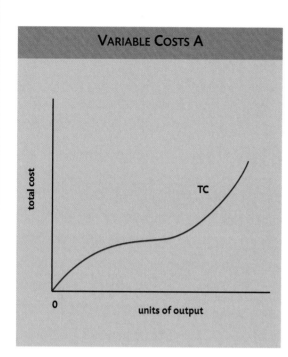

VARIABLE COSTS A

total cost

0   units of output

TC

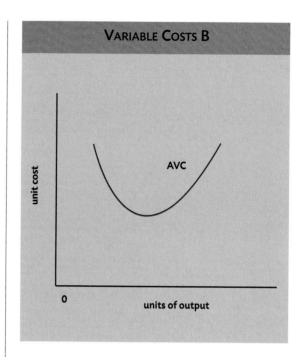

VARIABLE COSTS B

unit cost

0   units of output

AVC

the total number of items that are produced. In other words, it is the average variable cost per unit.

In the Variable Costs A graph, the short-run variable cost curve (TC) has an "S" shape. That is because at low levels of **output** (**production**), the total variable costs rise slowly. At high levels of output, however, total variable costs rise quickly, reflecting the law of diminishing returns. In the Variable Costs B graph, the average variable costs (AVC) fall at first to reflect the growing returns (**income**) due to the variable input. The AVC then rises to reflect the diminishing returns to the variable input.

> ### KEY POINT TODAY
> Variable costs depend on the quantity of goods produced. **Labor** and raw materials are costs that vary with the amount produced. A **fixed cost** would not change with the quantity of **production**. Rent on a building is an example of a fixed cost.

VARIANCE

Variance refers to the difference between the amount of money budgeted for the **production** of a good or service and the actual amount spent. In other words, variance is the difference between the planned costs/revenues and the actual costs/revenues. When the revenues fall short of the projected amount, the variance is called a negative or adverse variance. Conversely, when the revenue comes out higher than expected, it is called a positive or favorable variance.

VENTURE CAPITAL

Venture **capital** is the **money** or sources of money used to help a new **business** get started or an existing business start a new project. Venture capitalists invest in such businesses by providing the funding. In exchange, they receive **equity** in the company. This entitles them to a share of the firm's **profits**. Econmists have argued that venture capitalists have played a very important role in the "new economy" in the United States, believing that they have been behind the boom of the technology-based new economy

VISIBLE EXPORTS AND IMPORTS

Visible exports and imports include any goods such as raw materials, intermediate goods, and finished goods that are seen and recorded as they cross international boundaries between countries. The net **imports** and **exports** of these goods over the course of a given year make up the **balance of trade**. Visible exports and imports combined with invisible exports and imports (which include services like banking and **tourism**) make up the **current account** of a country's **balance of payments**.

W–Z

Wall Street on Black Tuesday, the day of the stock market crash in 1929.

WAGES

Wages are the payments made to workers for their activity on a job. Wages are typically a major source of **income** for most people and are included as a part of the **national income**. The price of **labor** is called a wage rate. In a competitive **market** the wage rate is determined by the **supply** of and **demand** for **labor**.

WALL STREET

Wall Street is an actual street in the lower part of Manhattan island in New York City. It is the center of one of the greatest financial districts in the world. Wall Street is so named because a stockade, or wall, was built in 1653 by Dutch colonists to protect the settled area south of it from attack by the English and by the Native Americans.

KEY POINT TODAY

Within the Wall Street district are the **New York Stock Exchange** and the **American Stock Exchange** as well as commodity exchanges, numerous commercial and investment banks, and financial law firms.

WALRAS'S LAW

Walras's Law was created by economist Léon Walras. It states that the **value** of all goods demanded in an **economy**, which is found by multiplying the **price** by the quantity demanded, is always equal to the value of the goods supplied, found by multiplying price times quantity supplied.

This situation can only be found in a **barter** economy or an economy that uses a form of **money** for transactions and then is immediately used again for exchange. In an economy that also uses **money** as a **store of value,** it is possible that the demand for and supply of money is not equal to the demand for and supply of goods. This is because people may either save their money or overspend.

WANTS

Wants are the desire for **economic goods and services.** The attempt to satisfy wants makes up the basis for all economic activity. Wants are not expressed by need or desire, but rather by the willingness and ability to purchase the goods and services desired.

WELFARE

Welfare refers to the economic well-being of an individual, group, or **economy.** For individuals it is defined by a **utility** function (the well-being of a consumer for all goods consumed). For groups, including individual countries and the world, it is more of a philosophical concept, since individuals live differently in different places. In trade theory, an improvement in welfare is often measured by an increase in real **national income.**

In the United States, welfare also refers to public assistance. Public assistance, or welfare, provides financial aid to people with very low **incomes.** (See **social security; welfare state.**)

WELFARE ECONOMICS

Welfare economics is the branch of **economics** that deals with overall social well-being. Welfare economics makes value judgments about what should be produced, the way **production** should be organized, and how wealth should be distributed. Because every person living in a society may have a different set of value judgements, however, it is difficult to make decisions affecting the allocation of **resources** that will satisfy everyone.

One person known for his work in this area is

ARTHUR CECIL PIGOU

Arthur Cecil Pigou, born in 1877, was one of the most prominent British economists of the 20th century. He was known for his studies in welfare economics.

Educated at King's College in Cambridge, Pigou succeeded Alfred Marshall as chair of political **economy** at Cambridge in 1908. Pigou helped make Marshall's ideas well known and provided the leading theoretical basis for what has become known as the "Cambridge School of Economics."

Pigou's most significant and influential work was *The Economics of Welfare* (1920). In this work he explored the effects of economic activity on the total welfare of society and its various groups and classes. Pigou applied his powers of **economic analysis** to a number of other problems, including **tariff** policy, **unemployment,** and public finance.

Pigou served on the Royal Commission on Income Tax from 1919 to 1920, and on two committees on the **currency** from 1918 to 1919 and from 1924 to 1925. He died in 1959.

Vilfredo Pareto, an Italian economist. He developed the notion of the "Pareto **efficiency**" or "Pareto optimum" which says that **economic goods and services** are allocated efficiently if no one person can be made better off without making someone else worse off. This means that when Pareto efficiency is achieved, one person is made better off while another must be made worse off, because something has to be taken away from one person in order to give it to another.

WELFARE STATE

A welfare state is a country whose government devotes a large part of its activities and spending to personal benefits (called **welfare** benefits) for qualifying individuals or families. In Western Europe, the welfare state emerged after World War II. Examples of such welfare programs would be old age and disability pensions, **unem-**

ployment benefits, aid to families with dependent children, **income** supplements for the poor, public housing, health care provided in state hospitals or clinics, reimbursement for the costs of privately-provided health care, government-funded drug abuse rehabilitation programs, food stamps, public education, child care, etc. Basically, benefits to qualifying individuals can take the form of services, **money**, and/or goods. Currently the welfare state in Western Europe (and other areas around the world) has been replaced by the workfare program. (See **transfer payments.**)

WORLD BANK

The World Bank was established in 1945 to promote the **economic development** of the poorer nations in the world. They pursue this goal by providing low-interest **loans** to **less developed countries** and offering technical assistance on the best ways to use these loans. The World Bank obtains funds for the loans by selling **bonds** on the world's financial **markets**. Its

long-run economic development orientation is usually coordinated with the shorter-run efforts of its sister **United Nations** agency, the **International Monetary Fund**.

The World Bank is made up of five closely related international organizations: the International Bank for Reconstruction and Development (IBRD), the International Development Association (IDA), the International Finance Corporation (IFC), the Multilateral Investment Guarantee Agency (MIGA), and the International Centre for Settlement of Investment Disputes (ICSID). The IBRD is the largest of these organizations, counting 181 member countries as of July 2000.

WORLD PRICE

World price is the **price** of a good on the world market, that is, the price outside of a particular country's borders. World price excludes any trade **taxes** or **subsidies** that might be levied on imports; but includes any that might apply to exports.

Nelson Mandela (left) leans over to speak with James Wolfensohn (right), president of the World Bank, during a conference on November 16, 2000.

Protesters opposed to the World Trade Organization disrupted a WTO meeting in Seattle, Washington, in December 1999. They carried hand-lettered signs and wore gas masks to protect themselves against tear gas used by riot police.

WORLD TRADE ORGANIZATION (WTO)

The World Trade Organization (WTO), formerly known as the **General Agreement on Tariffs and Trade (GATT),** is an international organization that deals with the rules of trade between nations. The WTO's goal is to help producers of **economic goods and services**, exporters, and importers conduct their business. With the help of WTO, consumers and producers know they can enjoy secure supplies and greater choice of the finished products, components, raw materials, and services they use. Producers and exporters know that foreign markets will remain open to them. WTO decisions are typically made by consensus among all member countries and ratified by members' governments. Trade disputes are solved through the WTO's dispute settlement process.

At the heart of the system are the WTO's agreements, which are negotiated and signed by a majority of the world's trading nations and ratified in their governments. These agreements form the legal ground rules for international commerce. Essentially, they are contracts that guarantee member countries important trade rights. They also bind governments to keep their trade policies within agreed limits to everyone's benefit. The WTO, **World Bank**, and **International Monetary Fund** have recently come under strong criticism by environmental and other protest groups for the negative impact of their policies on **less developed countries**.

ZERO-SUM GAME

A zero-sum game is a game in which the winnings of one player can only be gained by the **loss** of another player (I win, you lose). That means that all the losses and gains added together will equal zero. An example is flipping a coin and betting on the outcome. One person will transfer wealth to the other, but the total gain between the two will be zero. In contrast, many activities are not zero-sum games. For example, cooperation in an activity can increase the return to both participants.

Chronology of the Global Economy

9000–6000 B.C.E. Domestication of cattle and cultivation of crops begins, which allows goods such as cattle, grain, and plants to be traded as forms of money.

c. 3100 B.C.E. Writing is invented in Mesopotamia, most likely for the purpose of accounting.

c. 3000–c. 2000 B.C.E. Banking begins in Babylonia. Grain and later cattle, farming tools, and precious metals are held for safekeeping.

c. 1792–c. 1750 B.C.E. The Code of Hammurabi, written during this period, includes laws governing banking operations.

c. 640–c. 630 B.C.E. The earliest coins are made in Lydia, Asia Minor.

c. 600–300 B.C.E. Round metal coins are invented in China.

546 B.C.E. Athenian Owl coins are first produced in Ancient Greece.

336–323 B.C.E. AAs a result of Alexander the Great's conquest of Asia Minor, enormous quantities of Persian gold are captured and coins are minted to pay soldiers throughout his empire, thus giving an enormous stimulus to trade throughout his empire.

118 B.C.E. Leather money is issued in China.

313 Constantine confiscates the treasures amassed over the centuries in pagan temples throughout the Roman Empire.

410 Rome falls to the Visigoths. Banking is abandoned in western Europe and does not develop again until the Crusades.

806–821 Paper money is developed in China.

1086 *The Domesday Book*, a survey of the wealth of England, provides information for determining taxation and forms the basis of the new English fiscal system.

1095–1270 The need to transfer large sums of money to finance the Crusades provides a stimulus to the reemergence of banking in western Europe.

1215 The English document, the Magna Carta, restricts the right of the king to raise taxes without the consent of the Barons.

1275 Edward I of England forbids Jews to charge interest on loans, leading to a money shortage.

1275–1292 Marco Polo travels in China. From his subsequent account of his travels, Europe first learns of paper money.

1337–1453 The Hundred Years War between England and France begins as Philip VI contests English claims to Normandy, Anjou, and other French territories.

1348–1350 The Black Death, or bubonic plague, ravages Europe, causing a reduction in the size of the population and a collapse in economic growth.

1351 The Statute of Labourers sets maximum rates of pay in England at preplague levels for the main occupations and restricts mobility of labor.

1355 Nicole Oresme's *De Origine Natura Jura et Mutationibus Monetarum* is published. In it Oresme argues that the quantity of precious metal in circulation determines the value of currency.

1381 The Peasants' Revolt in England, provoked by anti-tax anger, is suppressed.

1403 Charging interest on loans is ruled legal in Florence.

c. 1450 The Portuguese begin voyages along the coast of Africa, opening a new route for sub-Saharan gold via Ghana and Mali.

c. 1455 China abandons its paper money.

1492 Columbus lands in America. However, the discovery of new routes to India and China is a more important motivation than the discovery of new lands.

1500–1540 Huge supplies of New World gold reach Spain.

1519–1521 Hernán Cortés conquers Mexico. Before the arrival of the Spaniards, the Aztecs and Mayans use gold dust (kept in transparent quills) and cocoa beans (kept for large payments in sacks of 24,000) as money.

1526 Nicolaus Copernicus writes his *Treatise on Debasement*. He argues that it is the total number of coins in circulation, rather than the weight of metal they contain, that determines the level of prices and the buying power of the currency.

1532 Francisco Pizarro lands in Peru and begins the conquest of the Inca. The Inca were unique in reaching a high degree of civilization without the use of money.

1540–1640 Europe experiences inflation, partly because of the huge influx of gold and silver from the Spanish colonies in America.

1577–1580 Francis Drake successfully circumnavigates the globe.

1599 The Dutch attempt to corner the pepper market in the Far East. This prompts the formation of the London East India Company the following year.

1601 The Poor Law is introduced in England to establish a national pattern for parishes to copy in dealing with the problems of the poor.

1602 Dutch East India Company is founded to provide the Dutch with financial backing for the ongoing competition with England for control of the pepper market.

Christopher Columbus sails from Spain to the Americas in 1492. He is the first European to arrive in the New World. This marks the beginning of European colonialism of the Americas.

Colonists in Jamestown grow and export tobacco to Europe (1610).

1619 Tobacco begins to be used as currency in Virginia.

1621 Edward Misselden's *Circle of Commerce or Balance of Trade* is published.
The Dutch West India Company is founded.

c. 1640 Reduction in silver imports causes a slump in the Chinese economy.

1642–1651 The English Civil War is fought because parliament disputes the king's right to levy taxes without its consent.

1648 In Boston, guilds for barrel makers (coopers) and shoemakers are founded. These are the earliest known unions in America.

1690 The Massachusetts Bay Colony issues official paper money.

1695 The Bank of Scotland, the first bank in Europe that is solely dependent on private capital and entirely unconnected with the state, is founded.

1796 The Navigation Act passed by Parliament prohibits England's American colonies from exporting directly to Scotland or Ireland.

1705 John Law publishes *Money and Trade Considered: With a Proposal for Supplying the Nation with Money.*

1716 John Law creates France's first public bank.

1723 The first notes by the Pennsylvania Land Bank are issued. These are secured by mortgages on the property of the bank owners.

1729 Following the publication of *A Modest Enquiry into the Nature and Necessity of a Paper Currency*, Benjamin Franklin is awarded the contract for printing the Pennsylvania Land Bank's notes.

1752 England forbids the New England colonies from issuing new bills of credit.

1759 Due to costs for the French and Indian War, the British government increases taxation in America, thus spurring the American Revolution.

1763 Economist Francois Quesnay founds the Physiocrats, who advocate laissez-faire economic policies.

1762 J. J. Rousseau publishes *The Social*

Contract arguing that government must rest on the consent of the governed.

1765 The German Royal Giro and Loan Bank is founded by Frederick the Great. This is Germany's first note-issuing bank.

1767 A boycott of imports from England begins in Boston to oppose taxes on lead, paint, paper, and tea.

1768 Russia's first two public banks are established by Catherine the Great.

1775–1783 The American Congress and individual states, finance their war effort by printing money.

1776 The Continental Congress adopts the Declaration of Independence on July 4, 1776.
Adam Smith writes *Inquiry Into the Nature and Causes of the Wealth of Nations*, launching the Classical School of economics.

1786–1787 In Shay's Rebellion, a rebel force of debtors try to secure debt relief, issues of paper money, and other reforms.

1789 Spurred by mounting resentment between the rich and the poor, the French Revolution begins..

1789 The U.S. Constitution gives Congress sole power over money creation.

1792 The U.S. Coinage Act makes the dollar the basic unit of currency in the United States.

1793 Eli Whitney invents the cotton gin.

1794 Thomas Paine writes *The Age of Reason*. The U.S. Mint starts operations.

1795 Hyperinflation in France paves the way for the rise of Napoleon.

1799 William Pitt introduces income tax to Great Britain.

1800 The Bank of France is founded. France gains a national bank over a century after England, Holland, and Sweden.

1803 The Louisiana Purchase doubles the size of the United States.
Jean-Baptiste Say writes *Treatise on Political Economy*.

1812–1814 Inflation takes off in the United States during the War of 1812.

1814 Francis Cabot Lowell raises $100,000 and founds a company to produce cotton cloth. He uses power from the Charles River to power machines. He employs farm girls to operate the machines and houses them.

1817 David Ricardo publishes *Principles of Political Economy and Taxation*.

1823 The Monroe Doctrine expresses U.S. opposition to the extension of European influence in the Western hemisphere.

1825 The first strike by carpenters for a 10-hour workday occurs in Boston.
The Erie Canal opens for shipping.

1829 New York State passes the Safety Fund Act, foreshadowing later developments in deposit insurance.
The Workingman's Party is formed in New York.

1830 The Baltimore and Ohio become the first railroad in the United States.

1837 The United States acquires legal power to issue paper money.

1837–1843 A financial panic forces all U.S. banks to suspend payment of notes. The crisis leads to a widespread depression.

1838 Factory Act in Britain limits the working day of women and children to 10 hours.

1840 The United States establishes an independent Treasury. Its powers are more firmly established by a later act in 1846.

1845–1849 Potato crop failure in Ireland causes an estimated 2.5 million to starve.

A view of Sutter's Mill, California. The discovery of gold in the mill's tailrace sparked the California gold rush (1848).

1848 John Stuart Mill publishes *Principles of Political Economy*.

1848 A series of revolutions in Europe ends in failure and repression.

1848 Karl Marx and Friedrich Engels publish *Communist Manifesto*.

1848 The discovery of gold in California leads to a massive increase in the production of gold coins by the mint and moves the U.S. toward adoption of a gold standard.

1854 Henry Bessemer revolutionizes the steel industry with a new converter process.

1854 Charles Darwin publishes *On the Origin of the Species by Means of Natural Selection*.

1854 The first oil well in the United States is drilled in Titusville, Pennsylvania.

1856 The Mercantile Bank becomes the first note-issuing bank in Singapore and Malaya.

1857 U.S. removes legal tender status from all foreign coins. By this time coins are merely the small change of commerce.

A world-wide banking crisis starts in the United States.

1859 Étienne Lenoir invents internal combustion engine in France.

1861–1865 The U.S. Civil War. A main cause of the war was the dispute over the legality of slavery. In economic terms, the Northern abolitionist campaign threatened the security of the slaveowners' property right on their greatest asset, i.e. the labor supplied by black slaves. As the possiblity of emancipation rose, so did the likelihood of substantially increased labor costs for Southern industries.

1862 The U. S. Treasury starts issuing notes that are not convertible into silver or gold but are legal tender for all purposes except payment of customs duties and interest on government securities.

1863 National Bank Act establishes a system of federally-chartered banks in the United States.

1865–1926 The Latin Monetary Union is founded. This comprises France, Italy, Belgium, Switzerland, and later Greece.

1867 Singapore makes dollars issued in Hong Kong, Mexico, Bolivia, and Peru legal tender.
Karl Marx begins writing *Das Kapital*, his ideas will form the basis for the Marxist School of economic theory.

1868 The United States Congress establishes an 8-hour workday for federal workers.

1868 Japan's isolationist policy ends. As a result, the few pre-Meiji banking organizations set up by the Zaibatsu family groups prove completely inadequate to meet the needs of liberalized trade.

1869 The Knights of Labor form.

1870 The Standard Oil Company is founded by John D. Rockefeller.

1871 Germany becomes a united country. The German states unite and adopt the mark as their common currency and base it on the gold standard.

1871 Japanese Currency Act. A national mint is established at Osaka, and the decimal system of yen and sen is introduced.

1873–1924 Denmark, Sweden, and Norway form a monetary union similar to the Latin one but with gold as the standard for their currency.

1873 Lacking a central bank or lender of last resort able and willing to supply sufficient liquidity to quell crises in their early stages, the United States proves prone to bank panics. The panic spreads across the Atlantic and causes many bank failures in Germany.

1874 Singapore makes the Japanese yen and U.S. dollar legal tender.

1875 The Greenback Party forms in the United States. It aims to secure and preferably increase greenback circulation.

1876 Alexander Graham Bell invents the telephone.

1877 Major strikes against the Baltimore and Ohio Railroad and the Pennsylvania Railroad bring the intervention of federal troops against the strikers.

1877 Thomas Alva Edison invents the phonograph and electric light bulb.

1881 The Federation of Organized Trades and Labor Unions is founded.

1882 The Bank of Japan is founded.

1883 The Civil Service (Pendleton) Act establishes the U.S. Civil Service Commission. It provides procedures for competitive examinations, and the establishment of the Merit System.

1886 The American Federation of Labor (AFL) is founded.

1890 The United Mine Workers Union is organized.
The Sherman Act obliges the U.S. Treasury to buy 4.5 million ounces of silver each month.
Alfred Marshall publishes *Principles of Economics*.

1894 American Railway Union strikes against the Pullman Company.

1894–1895 By the end of the Sino-Japanese War, Japan has acquired enough gold reserves to replace its silver standard by the gold standard. The shift to the gold standard will become official in 1897.

1895 U.S. Congress enacts the Income Tax Act, but the Supreme Court declares it unconstitutional.

1896 Henry Ford produces his first automobile. This marks the unofficial beginning of mass production.

1900 The International Ladies' Garment Workers Union is established.
The U.S. Gold Standard, or Currency, Act is passed, tying the dollar to the Gold Standard.

The Wright brothers' first flight, 1903.

1901 Guglielmo Marconi transmits messages across the Atlantic with a wireless telegraph.
A five-month strike against U.S. Steel fails; the union is weakened.
J.P. Morgan consolidates U.S. Steel.

1903 Orville and Wilbur Wright make the first heavier-than-air machine flight. Airplane transportation will revolutionize world travel and commerce.

1907 A financial panic begins with the fall of the Stock Market; many banks close.

1909 Payne-Aldrich Tariff Act raises tariffs on imports into the United States.

c. 1910 Horses are still used as money by the Kirghiz people in the Russian Empire.

1911 The Supreme Court orders the breakup of Standard Oil.
U.S. Postal Savings system is established.
Triangle Shirtwaist Company fire in New York City kills 147 workers and reveals the terrible working conditions in the garment industry.

1912 West African Currency Board (WACB) is set up to issue currency in the British colonies of Nigeria, the Gold Coast (Ghana), Gambia, Togoland, and the British Cameroons.

1912 The Lloyd-La Follette Act is adopted, recognizing the right of federal employees to organize.
China ceases minting its traditional cash coins. After having been in use for a couple of millennia, the circulation of these traditional Chinese base metal coins comes to an end.

1913 Henry Ford introduces the assembly line.
Congress establishes the Department of Labor.

1913 The Pujo Committee Report on the powers of the U.S. money trust reveals that power over money and credit is concentrated in just a few hands.
The Federal Reserve System is founded.

1914 The Panama Canal opens.
The Clayton Anti-Trust Act strengthens the position of American unions.

1914–1918 World War I. During the war, the Allied and Central powers rely heavily on the work of women to produce munitions in Europe.

1916 The Child Labor Law is passed by Congress.
The Federal Employees Compensation Law is adopted.

1917 The United States enters World War I. As a result, the national debt increases from about $1 billion in 1916 to $25 billion in 1920.

1918–1982 The United States becomes a giant creditor nation.

1919 U.S. Edge Act allows the chartering of corporations for the purpose of engaging in international or foreign banking.

1920 The 19th Amendment to the United States Constitution is passed, granting U.S. women the right to vote.
John Maynard Keynes publishes *The Economic Consequences of the Peace*. He argues against German war reparations and in favor of cancelling Allied war debts.

The Japanese economy enters a chronic depression.

1922–1923 Germany suffers from hyperinflation following the war.

1924 U.S. Federal Reserve System adopts an easy money policy to combat a decline in business activity and to encourage international capital flows.

1928 France returns to the gold standard.

1929 The New York Stock Market crashes. The Federal Reserve tightens credit, causing a slump in the U.S. economy.

1929–1930 Widespread bank failures and the surviving banks' curbs on lending cause businesses of all kinds to go bankrupt.

1930 The Hawley-Smoot Tariff Bill sets the highest duties in US history, hurting world trade.

1931 German banks cut back on lending, leading to a steep rise in unemployment. Britain abandons the gold standard. Japan abandons the gold standard.

1932 President Hoover sets up the Reconstruction Finance Corporation to provide emergency financing for U.S. financial institutions and to help agriculture, commerce, and industry.

1933 Adolf Hitler becomes Chancellor of Germany.
Roosevelt launches the New Deal. His first action is to declare a national bank holiday, closing every bank in the U.S. The U.S. Agricultural Adjustment Act gives financial institutions greater resources. Their efforts are coordinated through the Farm Credit Association. The U.S. Federal Deposit Insurance Corporation created.
National Bank of Nigeria founded. This is one of only three indigenous banks to be founded in Nigeria before 1945.

1935 National Labor Relations Act (Wagner Act) is passed. The Act guarantees the right of collective bargaining.
The Committee for Industrial Organization, (the CIO) is formed under the leadership of John L. Lewis. The organization later changes its name from "Committee" to "Congress."
Cowrie shells are still being used as money in Nigeria.

1936 France abandons the gold standard.

1937 The United Automobile Workers Union (UAW) stages successful sit-down strikes at General Motors and Chrysler plants.

1938 The Fair Labor Standards Act is passed. The Act establishes the first minimum wage. It also limits the number of working hours per week to 44 hours per week to begin and over the next couple of years reduces it to 40 hours per week.

1939 Germany invades Poland, starting World War II. The war lasts until 1945.

A World War II poster celebrates and encourages civilian women's participation in the war effort.

146

1941 Japanese bomb Pearl Harbor, and the United States enters the war against Japan, Germany, and Italy.

1941–1945 "Rosie the Riveter" becomes the national symbol for women and minorities who contribute to the war effort during World War II.

1944 "D Day" offensive by the United States, Britain, and allies. This campaign marks the begining of the end of war in Europe.

1944 The Bretton Woods agreement, negotiated at Bretton Woods, New Hampshire, creates a worldwide ecomomic system with convertible currencies, fixed exchange rates, and free trade. The agreement also establishes the International Monetary Fund and the International Bank for Reconstruction and Development.

1944–1946 Hungary suffers from the worst hyperinflation ever recorded.

1945 Germany surrenders in April.
The United States drops atomic bombs on Hiroshima and Nagasaki. The Japanese surrender.
The United Nations is formed.

1945–1948 Owing to the devastation of the war, Germany experiences hyperinflation for the second time in a generation.

1945–1948 Anti-monopoly and decentralization laws affect Japanese banks. The American occupying forces pass laws to break up the Zaibatsu by separating their banking activities from their industrial bases.

1946 The U.S. Employment Act is passed, proving the influential power of Keynesian economics.

1947 The Taft-Hartley Act makes it unlawful for government employees to participate in any strike.
The International Monetary Fund and the International Bank for Reconstruction and Development, established as a result of the Bretton Woods agreement (1944),

start functioning. The General Agreement on Tariffs and Trade, also inspired by the agreement, holds its first meeting.
The Marshall Plan proposes a huge program to assist reconstruction in war-torn Europe. The plan is implemented the following year.

1948 The Organization for European Economic Cooperation is formed. Its initial purpose is to distribute postwar reconstruction aid effectively. It also broadens the existing bilateral payments systems into wider multilateral clearings.

1948 Industrial Finance Corporation is founded in India. Its goal is to provide medium- and long-term finance to industrialists unable to get such funds from normal banking services.

1949 Communist forces seize power in China. The U.S. abandons the idea of exacting war reparations and instead supplies aid to Japan, like that given to Europe under the Marshall plan.
Economic reforms take place in Japan: rationing is abolished, runaway inflation is brought under control, the budget is balanced, and a single exchange rate for the yen, at 360 to the dollar, is established.

1949 The cold war between the United States and Russia develops as Russia builds an atomic bomb.

1950–1953 The Korean War breaks out as North Korea invades South Korea. The Korean War boosts the Japanese economy as the country benefits from being the main Asiatic base for supplies to the United Nations forces in Korea.

1950–1958 The European Payments Union is set up by the Organization for European Economic Co-operation.

1950 The European Coal and Steel Community is established. This is the first step towards the creation of the European Economic Community.

1952 Following the peace treaty in 1952, anti-trust laws are repealed in Japan and the Zaibatsu, complete with their core banks, are rapidly reconstituted.
Japan, running chronic trade deficits, joins the International Monetary Fund and International Bank for Reconstruction and Development. The assistance it gets from the Fund and the Bank in the following years help it to achieve an economic turnaround.

1954 First attempt to create a money market in West Africa. The colonial government of the Gold Coast (Ghana) issues its first tranche (a portion or series of a bond issue to be distributedina foreign country) of 90-day Treasury Bills.

1955 The AFL (1886) and CIO (1935) merge.

1956 Milton Friedman's *Restatement of the Quantity Theory* is published. This triggers the development of modern monetarism.

1957 The Treaty of Rome establishes the European Economic Community.
Congress starts investigations of corruption in American labor unions.
The first Japanese car is sold in the United States.

1958 Bank of America introduces the first credit card.

c. 1960 An increase in the world's population, especially in the less developed countries, hampers the poorest nations' attempts to escape from poverty and adds to inflationary and environmental pressures.

1961 Ray Kroc buys McDonald's.
Organization for Economic Cooperation and Development is founded.
The Lagos Stock Exchange starts operations in Nigeria.

1963 The Equal Pay Act is signed.

1965 Medicare is signed into law.

1965–1987 A rapid expansion of U.S. banks

A man sits in a bank vault calculating the store of gold.

takes place abroad.

1968 For the first time since 1893, the United States runs a deficit in its balance of trade.

1969 The International Monetary Fund creates Special Drawing Rights to help countries with balance of payments problems weather their difficulties.

1970 Xerox founds its Palo Alto Research Center.

1970s Wage stagnation begins in the U.S., initiating the beginning of stagflation.

1971 Intel invents a single-chip microprocessor. MCI is authorized to compete with AT&T.

1972 President Richard Nixon orders a 90-day wage and price freeze to curb inflation. Organized labor opposes the initiative.

1973 Federal Express begins operations.
The United States abandons the gold standard.

1974 Following the Israeli-Arab War in 1973, oil-producing countries double oil prices, which causes an energy crisis and economic hardship.

1976 John Bogle launches the First Index Investment Trust.
Maine is the first state to authorize interstate banking. This starts a widespread move to legalize interstate banking.
British government adopts monetarism.

1978–1980 OPEC doubles the price of oil. This leads to an increase in interest rates, pushes industrial countries into a deep recession, and is a contributing factor in the Third World debt crisis of the 1980s and 1990s.

1978 The U.S. Humphrey-Hawkins, or Full Employment and Balanced Growth, Act seeks to combine Keynesian concern for full employment with monetarism.

1979 European Monetary System created. Britain abolishes all foreign exchange controls.

1980 Poland's creditors agree to a rescheduling of its debt obligations, but western bankers rapidly withdraw funds from other eastern European countries.

1982 A crisis caused by the massive flight of capital from Mexico to the United States is tackled by loans from the U.S. government, the New York Federal Reserve Bank, the International Monetary Fund, and the Bank for International Settlements. However, the Mexican crisis triggers off a flight of capital from Argentina, Brazil, and Venezuela.

1984–1990 Rapid expansion of foreign banks in the United States. The value of foreign banks' assets in the United States rises from $80 billion to $209 billion.

1984 AT&T is dismantled by order of the Supreme Court.

1984 The U.S. Federal Appeals Court legalizes nationwide Automated Teller Machine (ATM) networks.

1986 Federal Savings and Loan Insurance Corporation is declared insolvent.

1987 An injection of $10.8 billion keeps the Federal Savings and Loan Insurance Corporation in existence.
A crash on Wall Street reaches record levels. The world's monetary authorities increase the money supply.
Japanese trade surplus reaches $87 billion.

1989 Communism collapses in Eastern Europe.

1991 The dissolution of the USSR.

1992 The European single market comes into effect.

1993 Kyowa Credit and Anzen Credit are rescued by the Japanese Ministry of Finance. In the United States, the Family and Medical Leave Act is passed.

1994 The North American Free Trade Agreement (NAFTA) is signed.

1995 Over 90 percent of all financial transactions in the United States are made electronically.

1999 A single European currency (the Euro) is created.
Major protests disrupt the World Trade Organization meeting in Seattle.

2000 Alan Greenspan is nominated for his fourth term as Chairman of the Federal Reserve Board.

2001 The U.S. economy slows down and heads toward a recession.

Helpful Resources

Asian Development Bank
6 ADB Avenue, Mandaluyong City
0401 Metro Manila, Philippines
Mailing Address:
P.O. Box 789
0980 Manila, Philippines
Tel: (63-2) 632-4444
E-mail: information@adb.org
Website: www.adb.org

A multilateral development finance institution, the ADB is owned by 59 members, mostly from Asia and the South Pacific. Its goals are to reduce poverty, foster economic growth, support human development, improve the status of women, and protect the environment.

Bureau of Economic Analysis
U.S. Department of Commerce
Washington DC 20230
Tel: (202) 606-9900
Website: www.bea.doc.gov

The BEA is an agency of the Department of Commerce. Its mission is to produce and disseminate accurate, timely, relevant, and cost-effective economic accounts statistics that provide government, businesses, households, and individuals with a comprehensive, up-to-date picture of economic activity.

Bureau of Labor Statistics
U.S. Department of Labor
Postal Square Building
2 Massachusetts Ave., NE
Room 4110
Washington, DC 20212
Tel: (202) 691-5900
E-mail: labstat.helpdesk@bls.gov

The Bureau of Labor Statistics is the principal fact-finding agency for the Federal government in the field of labor economics and statistics.

The Economic Commission for Africa (ECA)
P.O. Box 3001
Addis Ababa, Ethiopia
Tel: 251-1-51-72-00
Cable: ECA ADDIS ABABA
Fax: 251-1-51-44-16 (Addis Ababa)
     212-963-4957 (New York)
E-mail: ecainfo@uneca.org
Website: www.uneca.org

ECA supports the economic and social development of Africa, fosters regional integration, and promotes international cooperation for Africa's development. It is a branch of the United Nations.

Economics America
1140 Avenue of the Americas
New York, NY 10036
Website: www.economicsamerica.org

A nationwide, comprehensive program for economic education in America's schools, Economics America develops national and state content standards in economics. It is devoted to helping youngsters think, choose, and function in the global economy. A branch of the National Council on Economic Education.

Economics International
1140 Avenue of the Americas
New York, NY 10036
Website: www.economicsintl.org/

Another branch of the National Council on Economic Education dedicated to building economic education infrastructures in emerging market economies all over the world.

Economics Policy Institute
1660 L Street NW
Suite 1200
Washington, D.C. 20036
Tel: (202) 775-8810
Fax: (202) 775-0819
E-mail: epi@epinet.org
Website: epinet.org

The Economics Policy Institute (EPI) is a nonprofit, nonpartisan think tank that seeks to broaden the discussion of economic policy to include the interests of low- and middle-income workers. EPI's mission is to provide research and education to promote a fair, prosperous, and sustainable economy. It uses real-world analysis and makes its findings available to the public, media, and policy makers.

Federal Reserve System
20th St. and Constitution Ave., NW
Washington, DC 20551
Website: www.federalreserve.gov

The Federal Reserve is the central bank of the United States. Its duties include conducting the nation's monetary policy, regulating banking institutions, maintaining the stability of the financial system, and providing certain financial services to the U.S. government, the public, financial institutions, and foreign official institutions.

International Development Research Centre (IDRC)
P.O. Box 8500
Ottawa, ON K1G 3H9
Canada
Tel.: (613) 236-6163
Website: www.idrc.ca

The IDRC is a public corporation created by the Parliament of Canada to help researchers and communities in the developing world find solutions to their social, economic, and environmental problems.

International Labour Organization
Route des Morillons 4
1211 Geneva 4
Switzerland
Tel: (+41) 22-799-6111
Website: www.ilo.org

The International Labour Organization (ILO) is the agency of the United Nations that specializes in the promotion of social justice and internationally recognized human and labor rights.

International Monetary Fund (IMF)
700 19th St. NW
Washington, DC 20431
Tel: (202) 623-7000
Fax: (202) 623-4661
Website: www.imf.org

The IMF is an international organization of 183 member countries. It was established to promote international monetary cooperation, to foster economic growth and high levels of employment, and to help ease balance of payments adjustments in certain countries.

National Bureau of Economic Research (NBER)
1050 Massachusetts Avenue
Cambridge, MA 02138
Tel.: (617) 868-3900
Website: www.nber.org

The NBER is a private, nonprofit research organization dedicated to promoting a greater understanding of how the economy works.

National Council on Economic Education (NCEE)
1140 Avenue of the Americas
New York, NY 10036
Website: www.nationalcouncil.org

The NCEE is dedicated to helping youngsters learn to think, choose, and function in a changing global economy.

Office of Management and Budget (OMB)
Website: www.whitehouse.gov/omb

The OMB assists the president in the development and execution of his policies and programs. It is also involved in the development and resolution of all budget, policy, legislative, regulatory, and management issues on behalf of the president.

Organization for Economic Cooperation and Development (OECD)
2, rue André Pascal
F-75775 Paris Cedex 16
France
Tel: (+33) 1-45-24-82-00
Website: www.oced.org

The OECD, an organization made up of several countries, is dedicated to monitoring and analyzing economic issues, and assessing future economic developments.

United Nations Conference on Trade and Development (UNCTAD)
External Relations Service
Palais de Nations
1211 Geneva
Switzerland
Tel: (+41) 22-907-00-43

Fax: (+41) 22-907-12-34
Website: www.unctad.org

UNCTAD was founded in 1964 as the branch of the United Nations that deals with global trade and development. UNCTAD's main goal is to maximize the trade, investment, and development opportunities of developing countries, and to help them face challenges that arise from globalization.

United Nations Development Program (UNDP)

E-mail: webmaster@undp.org
Website: www.undp.org

The UNDP is the United Nations' principal provider of development advice, advocacy, and financial support to the countries that are home to 90 percent of the world's poor people. The UNDP helps governments of developing countries improve policies and programs that offer basic human services and reduce poverty.

U.S. Department of Commerce

14th St. and Constitution Ave., NW
Washington, DC 20230
Tel: (202) 501-0666
E-mail: webmaster@doc.gov
Website: www.osec.doc.gov/public.nsf

The Department of Commerce promotes job creation, economic growth, sustainable development, and improved living standards for all Americans by working in partnership with businesses, universities, and communities.

U.S. Department of Labor (DOL)

Office of Public Affairs
200 Constitution Ave., NW
Room S-1032
Washington, DC 20210
Tel: (202) 693-4650
Website: www.dol.gov

The DOL's purpose is to prepare the American workforce for new and better jobs and to ensure the adequacy of America's workplaces. The DOL has implemented programs to protect workers' wages, employment, and pension rights; to promote health, safety, and equal opportunity employment; and to administer job training, unemployment insurance, and workers' compensation.

U.S. Department of Treasury

1500 Pennsylvania Ave., NW

Washington, DC 20220
Tel: (202) 622-2000
Website: www.treas.gov

The Department of Treasury manages the government's finances and promotes prosperous and stable American and world economies.

U.S. International Trade Commission (USITC)

500 E Street SW
Washington, DC 20436
Website: www.usitc.gov

The USITC is an independent federal agency that provides objective trade expertise to both the legislative and executive branches of government. It also determines the impact of imports on U.S. industries and directs actions against unfair trade practices such as patent, trademark, and copyright infringement.

World Bank

1818 H. Street, NW
Washington, DC 20433
Tel: (202) 473-7660
Website: www.worldbank.org

The World Bank is dedicated to helping developing countries achieve a path of stability, sustainability, and equitable growth.

World Trade Organization

rue de Lausanne 154
CH-1211
Geneva 21, Switzerland
Website: www.wto.org

The WTO is the authority on the rules of trade between nations. Its goal is to help importers, exporters, and producers of goods and services conduct their business.

Helpful Websites:

About.com—Global Economy page
worldnews.about.com/newsissues/worldnews/cs/globaleconomy

About.com offers a list of articles and links featuring global economics. It is a good starting place for a student who needs information on a particular topic relating to world economics.

Dow Jones
www.dj.com

This site provides information on the Dow Jones Company as well as industrial averages, and links to Wall Street Journal Services.

Econolink
www.progress.org/econolink

Econolink provides links to sites for economics research and information.

EconEdlink
www.economicsamerica.org/econedlink

EconEdlink is dedicated to teaching young people about economics in new and interesting ways. The site provides lessons on various economic topics.

Economic Bulletin Board—U.S. Department of Commerce Statistics
www.stat-usa.gov

The Economic Bulletin Board provides authoritative information from the federal government for the U.S. business, economic, and trade communities.

Economic Data Link
www.usg.edu/galileo/internet/business/econdata.html

This site provides links to many economics-related sites.

Economic Development Directory
Philip O'Keefe
www.ecodevdirectory.com
E-mail: philipok@home.com

The Economic Development Directory lists websites with information for companies and organizations that are considering expansion into new geographical areas.

Economic Education Web
ecedweb.unomaha.edu

The Economic Education Web offers support for economics education in all forms and at all levels.

European Union (Europa Website)
europa.eu.int/index-en.html

This site provides news and information about the European Union, as well as links to the home pages of such institutions as the European Investment Bank and the European Investment Fund.

Internal Revenue Service
www.irs.ustreas.gov/

This site provides information on where to send tax returns.

NASDAQ-Amex
www.nasdaq.com

The NASDAQ website has information on NASDAQ history, trading, and stock market performance as well as links to other NASDAQ-related websites.

Nobel e-museum
www.nobel.se/economics/index.html

The Nobel e-museum offers profiles of recent recipients of the Nobel Prize (in all categories) and related articles of general interest.

Standard and Poor's
www.standardpoor.com

This site is dedicated to helping people make educated investment and credit decisions by providing in-depth opinions and analyses on global equities, fixed-income credit ratings, risk management, and market developments.

State of the Economy Page
www.harcourtcollege.com/econ/state.html

This site presents information and statistics on various aspects of the economy.

Time.com
www.time.com/time/daily/newsfiles/economy/

Created by *Time* magazine, this website lists links to the websites of various economic organizations as well as posting recent articles from the magazine that feature the global economy.

U.S. Imports and Exports Data
govinfo.library.orst.edu/impexp.html

The U.S. Import and Export History databases that contain the value and quantity of commodities imported or exported from 1994 to 1998 can be found here. .

Wall Street Research Net
www.wsrn.com

The Wall Street Research Net is an electronic guide to commerce which provides news and information on the stock market.

World Tables
www.lib.virginia.edu/ssdcbin/worldbin/world1c.cgi?SET=cntry&GEO=prk

This site provides information and statistics on economic and social indicators from 1950 to 1992.

Bibliography

Books:

Bannock, Graham, R. E. Baxter, and Evan Davis (editors). *The Penguin Dictionary of Economics*. New York: Penguin Putnam Publishers, 1998.

Blaug, Mark. *Great Economists Before Keynes: An Introduction to the Lives and Works of One Hundred Great Economists of the Past*. Brighton, Sussex: Wheatsheaf Books, 1986.

Blaug, Mark. *Great Economists Since Keynes: An Introduction to the Lives and Works of One Hundred Modern Economists*. Totowa, NJ: Barnes & Noble, 1985.

Blaug, Mark and Paul Sturges (editors). *Who's Who in Economics: A Biographical Dictionary of Major Economists 1700–1981*. Cambridge, MA: MIT Press, 1983.

Crane, W. Stansbury, and Slifer, Stephen D. *The Atlas of Economic Indicators*. New York: Harper Collins Publishers, 1991.

Derks, Scott. *Working Americans Volume I: The Working Class*. Lakeville, CT: Grey House Publishing, Inc., 2000.

Friedman, Milton. *Episodes in Monetary History: Money Mischief*. New York: Harcourt Brace Jovanovich, Publishers, 1992.

Goldberg, Kalman. *An Introduction to the Market System*. New York: M. E. Sharpe Inc., 2000.

Hughes, Jonathon. *American Economic History*. New York: HarperCollins Publishers, 1990.

Huq, A. M. Abdul. *The Global Economy: An Information Sourcebook*. Phoenix, AZ: Oryx Press, 1988.

Klappholz, Kurt. *The New Palgrave: The World of Economics*. edited by John Eatwell, Murray Milgate, and Peter Newman. New York: W. W. Norton and Company, Ltd., 1991.

Myers, Margaret G. *A Financial History of the United States*. New York: Columbia University Press, 1970.

Pass, C., B. Lowes, L. Davies, and S. J. Kronish (editors). *The Harper Collins Dictionary of Economics*. New York: Harper Perennial, 1991.

Schwartz, Elaine. *Econ 101 1/2*. New York: Avon Books, 1995.

Walton, Gary M., and Rockoff, Hugh. *History of the American Economy*. Fort Worth, TX: The Dryden Press, 1994.

Websites:

CanLearn—Glossary of Learning Terminology
http://laurence.canlearn.ca/English/help/glossary.html

USIA—The Language of U.S. Trade: Glossary of Terms
http://www.usinfo.state.gov/topical/econ/language/

Glossary of Terms for ARNR 201
http://agadsrv.msu.montana.edu/ARNR201/glossary.htm

REASON Magazine Online—January 1997 "Looking For Results"—An Interview with Ronald Coase by Thomas W. Hazlett
http://www.reason.com/9701/int.coase.html

GOPUBLICNOW.COM—Business Glossary
http://www.gopublicnow.com/asps/business_glossary1.asp

The Federal Reserve Bank of St. Louis—Gross Domestic Product
http://www.stls.frb.org/fred/data/gdp.html

About.com—Glossary of Economic Terms
http://economics.about.com/money/economics/library/glossary/blb.htm

The ICC GROUP—Financial Glossary
http://gfi.virtualave.net/a.html

Investorwords—Investing Glossary
http://www.investorwords.com

A Glossary of Political Economy Terms—Dr. Paul M. Johnson—Auburn University
http://www.duc.auburn.edu/~johnspm/glossind.html

Glossary of Banking and Stock Market Terms
http://info.deutsche-bank.de/global/db/navigate.nsf/Frameset/CMER

Glossary for a Course in Basic Economics
http://www.chass.utoronto.ca/~reak/glosslist.htm

AmosWeb Economic Gloss Arama
http://www.amosweb.com/gls/

Biz-Ed—Economics Glossary
http://bized.ac.uk/stafsup/options/aec/glos.htm

Glossary—Tuck School of Business at Dartmouth College
http://mba.tuck.dartmouth.edu/paradigm/spring2000/glossary/default.htm

Encarta Encyclopedia and Dictionary
http://encarta.msn.com/reference/

Famous Economists
http://www.usd.edu/econ/famous.html

LookSmart—Economics for Kids
http://www.looksmart.com/eus1/eus53671/eus87579/eus161144/eus55983/eus525812/r?l&

Timeline of Famous Economists
http://bizednet.bris.ac.uk/virtual/economy/library/economists/timeline.htm

Britannica.com
http://www.britannica.com

The Federal Reserve Board
http://www.federalreserve.gov/

The American Stock Exchange
http://www.amex.com/about/about_amex.stm

Federal Trade Commission
http://www.ftc.gov/

European Central Bank
http://www.ecb.int/

Dow Jones
http://averages.dowjones.com/home.html

FDIC—Federal Deposit Insurance Corporation
http://www.fdic.gov/

NYSE—New York Stock Exchange
http://www.nyse.com/

Welcome to the UN—It's Your World (United Nations Home Page)
http://www.un.org

The NAFTA Home Page
http://www.mac.doc.gov/nafta/nafta2.htm

WTO—World Trade Organization
http://www.wto.org/

OPEC Online
http://www.opec.org/

The NASDAQ Newsroom
http://www.nasdaqnews.com/

History of the Standard & Poor's 500
http://www.cftech.com/BrainBank/FINANCE/SandP500Hist.html

IFCI Risk Institute—Glossary
http://risk.ifci.ch/glossary.htm

John Maynard Keynes
http://www.bizednet.bris.ac.uk/virtual/economy/library/economists/keynes.htm

Index

Page numbers that appear in boldface type (**99**) indicate where main topics can be found; numbers set in light type (99) are additional references. Page numbers set in italics (*99*) indicate the presence of a photograph or drawing for a topic. Names in italics (*Greenspan*) indicate a biographical profile; numbers in light type after a name are additional references.